KHAKI PARISH

OUR WAR — OUR LOVE
1940 – 1946

KHAKI PARISH

OUR WAR – OUR LOVE
1940 – 1946

Helen and Bill Cook

HODDER AND STOUGHTON
LONDON SYDNEY AUCKLAND TORONTO

We dedicate this book to the memory of
Trooper William Penn of the Lothians and Border Horse,
Bill's constant Companion in six years of war,
and to all the other members of our war-time
Khaki Parish.

British Library Cataloguing in Publication Data

Cook, Helen, 1921–
    Khaki Parish: our war — our love 1940–1946,
    1. World War 2, Army operations by Great Britain.
    Army biographies 2. England — Social life, 1940–1949.
    Biographies. I. Title. II. Cook, Bill, 1914–
    942.54$'$81$'$41

    ISBN 0 340 51061 7

*Hodder and Stoughton Editorial Office: 47 Bedford Square, London
WC1B 3DP.*

Contents

List of Illustrations

THE LETTER

Over mine-sown, torpedo-needled deeps,
Undaunted by dive-bombers sweeping low
And all the old storm-perils of the sea,
Some ancient tub has laboured hardily,
And, winning into harbour, brought to me
In this frail envelope as white as snow
Word of your welfare and your thought of me —
Over dark wastes where danger never sleeps
And death for ever ranges day and night,
Safe in this envelope so frail and slight
Has brought your heart to me.

Wilfrid Gibson

World Record

GUINNESS BOOK
OF RECORDS

REV CANON W.G.

AND

MRS H.M. COOK

EXCHANGED 6000 LETTERS

MARCH 1942 – MAY 1946

NORRIS McWHIRTER

Foreword

Professor Jay Appleton MA, MSc, PhD.

When Bill Cook went to his first curacy in a Derbyshire mining village in 1937 he could not have known how soon he was to find himself making a fresh start in another and very different sort of parish. His new parishioners, like himself, were in uniform, and his church might take the form of almost anything within the bounds of a parish which moved about from England to Scotland, Africa, Italy and Austria. His duties were often varied and sometimes surprising, but perhaps the greatest demand on his time and energy was simply helping young men cope with the strains of this unnatural life, and not least with the pain of separation from loved ones at home.

At the very moment when he was beginning to learn how best to alleviate these strains in others he fell in love with my sister and found himself having to come to terms with the same feelings of frustration, anxiety and impatience which he was encountering in those to whom it was his duty to bring help and comfort. That this gave him a more sympathetic understanding in his work can hardly be doubted, but it brought also personal agonies and conflicts. Not surprisingly he and his fiancée set out to resolve these in close consultation with each other, but, whereas such consultations are normally conducted in private and unrecorded conversation, in the circumstances of the war they had to be committed to letters.

I suppose all of us who are old enough to have lived through the Second World War have our own personal recollections of it, many of which have by now become blurred and faded and consequently inaccurate and unreliable. What makes this story different is, first, that those letters — and there are literally thousands of them — have survived in their entirety, so that the words in which it is told recount events which took place, not forty-five years before, but often on the same day, and secondly, that the two strands which run right through the book, a love story and a chronicle of history in the making, are so intimately interwoven that each becomes a part of a single whole.

Preface

by

Bishop Robin Woods, KCVO, MA

Those of us who were enlisted as Chaplains in the Army in the middle of the Second World War found out at once what a professional job the first group of Chaplains had accomplished. One such Chaplain who saw the war through in every way was Bill Cook. His Parish was in the 6th Armoured Division, with the same driver/batman, from its inception in 1940 until its demise in 1946.

Memories of the North African Campaign are now fading, but the early Chaplains soon achieved their role in the changing fortunes of war, and in the wide open spaces of the desert. With other Chaplains he shared, under fire, the day-to-day life of his men, the care of the wounded and dying at Advanced Dressing Stations, the consequent letters to next-of-kin and loved ones at home, the rebuilding of friendship and morale when replacements came; these were all the heavy responsibilities of Bill.

After training with new weapons in an Algerian olive grove his men joined action again at the fourth and successful battle for Cassino. Here was my baptism of fire with the Fourth Indian Division. The courage of the men and the efficiency of the medical staff and chaplains was beyond dispute. This was part of a worthy campaign in Italy that will never be forgotten.

During the summer of 1944 he and I enjoyed the first visit of a Bishop from home to the troops for many months. There were crowds of men who were ready for Confirmation; their faith had been hammered out on the anvil of hard warfare. There were several hundred Chaplains who had received little spiritual guidance or refreshment and who needed the renewing care of a senior man. The Bishop chosen was my father, then Bishop of Lichfield. He toured the Divisions, and Bill Cook or myself were commissioned to look after his constant Services, Confirmations and meetings with the men. Senior officers and the rank and file were all very responsive. It was a memorable visit, my father confirming over two thousand candidates and meeting with Chaplains of every denomination.

The partnership that we enjoyed in establishing Refresher Courses for Chaplains, first in Rome itself and later in Assisi was a real pleasure. Bill was on the first Course at the Waldensian Seminary. Our final meeting was when I went to Padua to bid him farewell on the eve of his demobilisation in May 1946. As we dined in the Mess we talked of our family joys.

The mutual support that Chaplains from all the Churches gave each other was, in many ways, a remarkable foundation laid for the Ecumenical Movement that has developed in the last three decades. The Churches, when together, can and will rise to meeting every new situation.

+ Robin Woods

October 1987

Acknowledgements

We would like to thank many friends for their help:

Mrs. Sheila Hardy of Tattingstone in Suffolk who, after an Eastertide Service, as the fortieth anniversary of European victory came up, suggested that we might have the makings of a book in our letters.

Miss Beatrice Osborne of Diss, a war-time interpreter of aerial photographs, who gave us help and encouragement.

Miss Janet Calver, granddaughter of Mr. and Mrs. Burlingham, for her secretarial skills, and her parents who helped to interpret our handwriting.

We thank Sir Peter Walker-Okeover for permission to quote from his father's *Derbyshire Yeomanry Scrap Book 1939–1946*, and the Ministry of Defence for permission to copy some photographs from *The Royal Engineers, 6th British Armoured Division, War Book, 1939–1946*, and Mr. Peter Faiers and Mr. Geoffrey Ward for further help with illustrations.

Finally, we are most grateful to our Editor, the Reverend Keith Freestone, who has had the uneviable task of drastically reducing our manuscript. This has, we believe, made a more coherent story.

If, inadvertently, the authors or publishers have omitted acknowledging the use of copyright material, either photographic or textual, they apologise and will rectify the matter in any future editions.

Introduction to the New Edition

As Chaplain, Bill worked out his ministry according to his whereabouts and circumstances, with men available — at hand, or in reach. This kept him and his driver, William Penn, busy together for six years, in a variety of cultural and historic surroundings, through experiences from the horrific and traumatic to the sublime, amusing and joyful.

Love claimed Helen and Bill in England, in 1941, and this book owes its being to the 6,000 letters — airmail, airgraph and seamail — written compulsively during four and a half years of separation. This correspondence enabled love and faith to grow in the context of all-involving war.

Mercifully we both came through and, after marrying on leave and enduring the final pre-demobilisation stint, gratefully settled to further adventures of on-going ministry for over forty years in English parishes. With us we took, from rectory to rectory, our letters in a gently rusting six-pounder anti-tank ammunition box.

In the early spring of 1985, when we were beginning to think about the fortieth anniversary of the defeat of the Axis Powers we opened the box . . . and met again our treasured correspondence, a unique collection, since acknowledged as a world record in the 1989 *Guinness Book of Records* (page 88!) and a time capsule that many national archives are eager to house. Our letters were all written with fountain pens — before the invention of biros and plastic, Bill took his ink bottle with him everywhere in a bakelite case, even into battle!

The story which we were able to unfold tells of our experiences, overseas and on the home front, imparting, from contemporary evidence, the atmosphere of those sometimes daunting but stirring and gallant times.

Since the launch of *Khaki Parish* in the Imperial War Museum five months ago we have received letters of appreciation from all over the world, from a wide variety of people of all ages, showing that every aspect of the book has spoken specifically to someone: 'I could not put it down' . . . 'it made compelling reading' . . . 'I finished it at 3.30 a.m.'.

This made us feel glad we had dared to share the thoughts and hopes of our young hearts. We have been relinked with friends from childhood onwards. Old comrades were glad to have vivid memories recalled and half-forgotten events evoked. We have had moving letters from widows who felt they could 'share' with us, never having had anyone with whom they could communicate. It has been good to hear from the next generation whose parents have never talked about the war; some are encouraging their children to explore it as a lesson of living history. Priests have quoted it in wedding addresses and on Remembrance Day.

A university friend of Bill's, a priest and critic, wrote 'I have often tried to imagine what it was like actually fighting . . . as I read on I was conquered by your eagerness. I cried, I laughed, occasionally I protested. I knew the end, but HOW I wanted you to have your leave and to meet each other again. I could not give a reasoned assessment because I became too subjective. One cannot analyse what one loves. I am most grateful for reading it. I shall love it – and read it – and from it – again and again until I die.'

We have experienced many blessings through contacts this book has brought, and we hope that this second edition may generate further friendship.

Helen and Bill Cook
St. Valentine's Day, 1989
Diss, Norfolk

EDITOR'S NOTE

This book consists almost entirely of a series of letters between Helen and Bill Cook. In order to distinguish them more clearly for you, the reader, Bill's letters have been set in **Baskerville Bold**, while Helen's appear in *Theme Italic*.

The general text of the book, together with any linking words between the letters, has been set in a third typeface: Baskerville Medium.

Where explanatory matter has been added to the letters at a later date, these words have been enclosed in square brackets. By noting the different typefaces the reader will, I am sure, have no difficulty in identifying the provenance of each section of the book.

The style and punctuation have been kept largely in their original form, and the letters should be read bearing in mind that they were written in the emotional stress of difficult wartime conditions.

H. Keith Freestone
Publisher's Editor

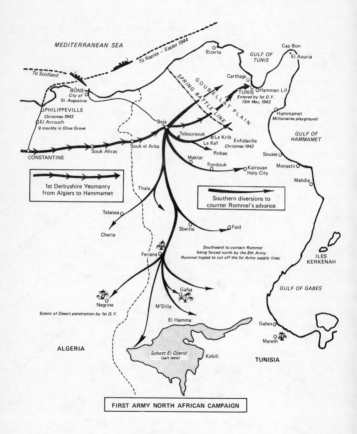

MEDITERRANEAN SEA

To Naples – Easter 1944

To Scotland

GULF OF TUNIS

Bizerta

Cap Bon

El Aouria

Carthage

BÔNE
City of
St. Augustine

TUNIS
Entered by 1st D.Y.
13th May, 1943

Hamman Lif

PHILIPPEVILLE
Christmas 1943
El Arrouch
9 months in Olive Grove

GOUBELLAT PLAIN

SPRING BATTLE LINE

Hammamet
Millionaires playground

Beja

GULF OF
HAMMAMET

Teboursouk

CONSTANTINE

Souk Ahras

Souk el Arba

Le Krib
Le Kef

Enfidaville
Christmas 1942

Robaa

Sousse

Maktar

Monastir

Fondouk

Kairouan
Holy City

Mahdia

1st Derbyshire Yeomanry
from Algiers to Hammamet

Southern diversions to
counter Rommel's advance

Thala

Tebessa

Cheria

Sbeitla

Faid

Southward to contain Rommel
being forced north by the 8th Army.
Rommel hoped to cut off the 1st Army supply lines.

ILES
KERKENAH

Feriana

Gafsa

GULF OF GABES

Negrine

M'Dilla

Extent of Desert penetration by 1st D.Y.

El Hamma

Gabes

ALGERIA

Schott El Djerid
(salt lake)

Kebili

Mareth

TUNISIA

FIRST ARMY NORTH AFRICAN CAMPAIGN

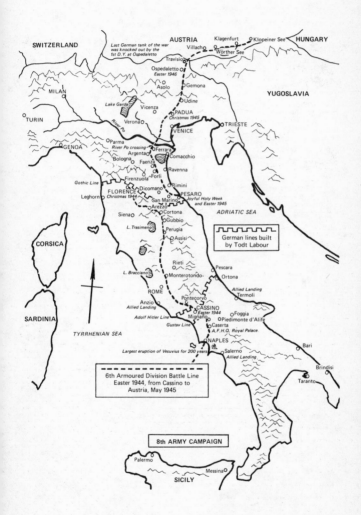

SWITZERLAND

AUSTRIA

Klagenfurt O Klopeiner See

HUNGARY

Last German tank of the war was knocked out by the 1st D.Y. at Ospedaletto Villacho
Travisio Wörther See

Ospedaletto *Easter 1946*

MILAN O
Asolo O Gemona
O Udine

Lake Garda *Vicenza* PADUA *Christmas 1945*

Verona O *River Po* VENICE

TURIN O

YUGOSLAVIA

O TRIESTE

GENOA O
O Parma
River Po crossing Argenta O Ferrara Comacchio
Bologna O Faenza
O Forli
O Ravenna

Gothic Line Firenzuola O
Dicomano O Rimini
Leghorn FLORENCE *Christmas 1944* San Marino PESARO *Joyful Holy Week and Easter 1945*
O Arezzo
Siena O Cortona
L. Trasimeno O Gubbio
O Perugia
O Assisi

ADRIATIC SEA

CORSICA

Rieti O
L. Bracciano O Monterotondo O
Pescara
O Ortona

Allied Landing Termoli

╔══════════════════════╗
║ German lines built   ║
║ by Todt Labour   ║
╚══════════════════════╝

ROME O
Anzio O *Allied Landing*
Pontecorvo O
Adolf Hitler Line CASSINO *Easter 1944*
Mignano O
Gustav Line Caserta
O Piedimonte d'Alife
O Foggia

SARDINIA

TYRRHENIAN SEA

A.F.H.Q. Royal Palace
O NAPLES

Largest eruption of Vesuvius for 200 years Salerno
Allied Landing

O Bari

O Brindisi

╔═══════════════════════════════╗
║ 6th Armoured Division Battle Line ║
║ Easter 1944, from Cassino to   ║
║ Austria, May 1945   ║
╚═══════════════════════════════╝

O Taranto

┌─────────────────────────┐
│   8th ARMY CAMPAIGN   │
└─────────────────────────┘

Palermo O
O Messina

SICILY

1

War — September 1939

After conducting mattins on September 3rd, 1939, in St.
Mary Magdalene's, Creswell, I came out of Church at 11.30
to find that we were at war. Apart from a feeling that the
inevitable had happened I recall nothing else of the day.

Not so my Helen! She has the whole picture in a page of
her diary.

Sept. 3, 1939. Sunday.

*Last Friday at 5.30 a.m. German Troops opened fire on the
Poles on the west of the Corridor. German aeroplanes carried
out aerial attacks on 8 towns.*

*Hitler said this was not war (so the world waited). H.M.
Government asked Hitler whether he had declared war on
Poland.*

No reply all Saturday.

*News many times daily on the wireless programmes. The
suspense is like wondering whether you are going to be sick.
Doesn't bear thinking about. If you do think, you can't
realise where it will lead. Evacuated children etc. will
probably arrive tomorrow.*

10.00 a.m. Message from Downing Street . . .

*If Hitler does not reply before 11.00 a.m. there will be war
between England and France against Germany.*

*11.00 a.m. A service in All Saints Church, Stibbard,
Norfolk, consisting of Hymns and prayers.*

Dad had brought a wireless set into Church to hear Chamberlain speaking.
It was WAR. The tension was relieved.
5.00 p.m. France at war. 6.00 p.m. H.M. King speaking.
6.30 p.m. Evensong. 9.00 p.m. Bed.

BILL'S STORY

During the phoney peace after Chamberlain's return from Munich a neighbouring Curate and I had often discussed the possibility of volunteering as Padres. My friend said that it was not for him, and he was soon to be doing an important job in a large Parish. I myself wrestled not so much about whether I should get involved in the Armed Forces, but as to whether I would ever make an effective Chaplain. So I wrote diffidently to John, my Bishop of Derby, in these terms. He had ordained me Deacon in Derby Cathedral under three years before. I placed myself in his hands, and told him that I was prepared to be used in any war service for which I might be considered suitable. He thanked me, and said he would keep me in mind.

Creswell was a modern and successful pit of about forty years of age. Its main feature was a Model Village consisting of two concentric rings of houses, facing outwards and inwards. Between the two circles were the washhouses, lavatories, and, most important of all, the coal houses. Two pavements enclosed the road, down which ran a railway. Each month this railway was used to put a ton of coal into each coalhouse. There was a well laid out recreation and sports ground. A large Miners' Institute stood in the middle of the village. These were the heady days of the Creswell Colliery Band, which practised regularly in the Institute under Harold Moss. Rightly did it carry the title of 'Prize Band'. The ability to play an instrument was a sure way to a job in the Colliery.

Creswell stands at the edge of the Dukeries, and Welbeck Abbey was very near. At the outbreak of war the Dukeries became the depot of a Cavalry Division that was to sail with horses to Egypt, and eventually to become the nucleus of the

8th Army. The Colliery Institute became a military Hospital, and a number of doctors found billets in the village.

After about a year I received a telegram to have a medical examination by one of the army doctors. Having already got to know them I had a chat with one of them, and after two minutes I got my certificate. The next move was an interview by the Assistant Chaplain General of Northern Command at York. My only recollection of the interview were questions as to which school I had attended, and which games I played! There seemed to be an assumption that I had been accepted as an Army Chaplain. A few days later a letter came to say that as I was only 25 I would not be needed for a long time, if at all.

Having been effectively rejected for military service it was time to find a second Curacy. So I went to the large and busy Parish of St. Giles in Derby. There was a daughter Church at Sinfin, with its own Priest-in-charge.

Nightingale Road in Derby was the home of Rolls-Royce. The factory worked night and day to turn out the stream of Merlin engines so desperately needed to power the Hurricanes and Spitfires. These engines were run in and tested, night and day, on the test-beds at Sinfin. It seems difficult to understand why Hitler did not flatten Derby and bring our Air defences to an end. There were very few raids. But there were two important defences. One was the building of a ghost town in the next bend of the river. Twenty years later I was to be the Rector of those two Parishes of Aston and Weston-on-Trent. The other defence was the creation of artificial smog whenever the moon was up. The pavements of one whole side of Derby were filled with a continuous line of dustbins, each having a chimney built into the lid. At dusk, members of the Pioneer Regiment would come along and throw burning rags into the thick oil in each bin. People would close all doors and windows, but by the morning everyone woke up with smarting eyes and funny throats.

After five weeks the War Office changed its mind. I had not yet even been officially listed or licensed by the Bishop to the new Parish, when a telegram ordered me to report to the Royal Army Chaplain's Department in Chester in the next few days. Elliotts, the tailors in Derby, managed to provide me with a Service Dress, other clothing, and let me have a greatcoat that had just been made for another officer.

The Depot was in the Chester Church Teacher Training College. Here for a fortnight we had lectures on the working of the Army, a little physical training, and some good devotional addresses by Ronnie Sinclair. We were a group of about thirty. Walking out into Chester on the first evening, with one or two new Chaplains, in our newly-donned uniforms, it took quite a bit of getting used to returning the salutes of so many other ranks in this Garrison town. We did wonder whether many of them might not be as newly in the Army as we were!

My posting was to the H.Q. of the 6th British Armoured Division, being newly formed at Chippenham in Wiltshire. Here I was met, and bedded for the night, by the Senior Chaplain, Victor Shearburn, of the Community of the Resurrection. Later he was to become Bishop of Rangoon. The next day he took me to Hungerford, to be attached to the 1st Derbyshire Yeomanry, who were the Divisional Reconnaissance.

The country Vicarage in which I grew up stood twelve hundred feet above sea level in one of the largest parishes in England. Five steep miles out of Buxton, Earl Sterndale's 33,000 acres stretched over twelve miles, containing four stations of the old High Peak Railway. This was the only church in Derbyshire to be destroyed by enemy action.

My boyhood and working life were spent among the dairy farmers, miners and quarrymen in the varied geography of the Peak District. It could have been this Derbyshire background that resulted in my attachment to the 1st Derbyshire Yeomanry as their Padre. I was part of their roots and background. By the time of my demobilisation, six years later, Regimental personnel had changed completely.

THE REGIMENT

The Derbyshire Yeomanry had its H.Q. at Denford House, just outside Hungerford. It had its own Chapel, also toilet furniture such as I was to encounter in other large houses at later camps. But this was the first large throne room, with a very wide seat of polished mahogany and the toilet bowl covered with beautiful blue floral decoration, while the flush was operated by an upward pull from the seat itself. The bath had a hood, and a very complicated control box, whereby one could choose a bath or a shower with sprays which came from all directions! As soon as possible I went to Bath to purchase a camp bed, valise, camp bath and washstand, a mattress and sundry other necessities.

Perhaps this is the place to register my 'culture shock'! Half of my Parish was the Divisional Engineers. Being composed of men with trades and professions they were without exception friendly, and so easy to get on with. The Derbyshire Yeomany were of another world! The officers were mostly county types and country squires – many with titles; never before had I encountered such attitudes and expectations. The second-in-command, Sir Ian Walker, was so kind and thoughtful. Later on, in Italy, he was to take over command of the Regiment, and to prove himself a distinguished Colonel with a well deserved D.S.O. It was typical that he brought his butler, cook, valet, agent and secretary with him! After Sir Ian's demobilisation, his agent, Eddie Clarke, was to take over Regimental command.

One of the Squadrons was commanded by one of our Derbyshire squires. His men were tradesmen and quarry workers and gamekeepers. He was most punctilious of all the Squadron leaders in arranging Church parades. In the Mess, however, custom demanded that he should ignore me, until I had proved my social acceptability! At the end of the war he offered me the Incumbency of his home Parish.

The Mess was still ornamented with Regimental silver and a silver mounted elephant's foot formed our letter box. For transport I was given an Austin utility truck and a driver/batman, who was a Londoner, from the Lothians and Border Horse, one of the three tank regiments in the 26th Armoured Brigade. William Penn came to me because, like me, he had been attached to Divisional Headquarters. We were to be together for six years, and we were still in touch until he died in Autumn 1986. He and Julie, his wife, came to live in the depths of Cambridgeshire at Christchurch.

Each month I had to send in a return of services to the Senior Chaplain. I still have this register from 1st December, 1940, until we finally sailed away from the British Isles at the end of 1942. The first parade service was by 'A' Squadron, Derbyshire Yeomanry, at Standen Manor near Hungerford with 80 men on parade. My last, before going overseas was attended by 100 Engineers at the Gun Site at Irvine Explosives Factory in Scotland on 22nd November, 1942.

November 1940 to February 1941 was a time of settling in for everybody – certainly for me. Many specialists, in things mechanical and wireless, made up the complement of the Derbyshire Yeomanry – also its Chaplain who was to remain with them until well after the end of the war. It was a time of learning to become the eyes and ears of a new Armoured Division – the Sixth. A divisional emblem of a white mailed fist on a black ground became the sign proudly worn on each shoulder and on each vehicle.

The Division was to have to wait for a long time to receive its full equipment of vehicles and armoury, so settling-in was the order of the day. At breakfast one morning, Sir Ian Walker asked me if I had heard of the bombing of my father's church at Earl Sterndale. This was a great shock and I was given leave to go home. I have a picture of the ruined burnt out church, and a press photograph taken two days later, of a wedding in the ruins with a card table as an altar. After that the church was formally closed and services were held in the little stone school next door, until the church was rebuilt a few years after the end of the war. The stout thick limestone walls of the old church had stood unmoved. Perhaps the present church is more attractive than the earlier one, and contains a memorial window to my parents.

The last wedding taken by Bill's father in the bombed church of Earl Sterndale in Derbyshire during the winter of 1940. This was also the last service until the church was re-built fifteen years later.

2

Summer 1941

The Division moved into the Cambridge area at the end of February 1941 and D.Y. H.Q. was a few miles south, at Newton Hall. Here training gathered momentum. My Register lists Services at Newton, Harston and Hauxton. Little groups of the faithful made their Communions with the local people, and a Squadron Parade usually produced sixty men. Easter Day was well observed. There were forty men at the 7.30 a.m. Holy Communion at Newton. At Wimpole the 9.30 a.m. parade totalled 120 men. H.Q. Squadron produced 75 at Newton church at 10.50 a.m. and C Squadron came to Hauxton at 11.45 a.m. to the number of 90. Our organist, Trpr. Henson Maw, from the Regal cinema in Derby, gave an organ recital after this parade. Perhaps the most notable gathering of this period was the National Day of Prayer held on Sunday, March 23rd. A scout round the countryside showed that Haslingfield had the largest church. 315 Derbyshire Yeomen packed the building to enjoy an address by our Colonel Harrison. Later on I was asked why my sermons were not up to our worthy Colonel's standard! In fact his address was mine verbatim!

May brought us to Dalham Park, the delightful estate belonging to Lord and Lady Milford, shipping magnates. The Officers' mess was in part of the Hall, and tents were under avenues of trees. It was good to have the whole Regiment together. By the Hall was a beautiful medieval church, with

trouble in the roof. It had a splendid monument to Sir
Francis Stuteville who sailed round the world with Drake.
There was a tiny organ — the black notes were white and
vice versa.

At the beginning of the war R.S.M. Robinson had tempted
Henson Maw to leave his rising organ console in the Regal
cinema, Derby, by painting rosy dreams of how useful he
would be in entertaining the men. But all too soon poor
Henson was square bashing like everyone else! Occasionally
he had access to a piano, but by far and away I was to be the
greatest user of his musical talents. Many were the services at
which he played, and very often he would throw in an organ
recital as well. Being a gentle and diplomatic man, he never
really exploded when in the summer of 1941 his main musical
outlet was a tiny single keyboard.

When we came away to Diss we had a testimonial from
Lady Milford and about thirty-eight parishioners of this tiny
and charming village, to thank us for the way in which the
Regiment had integrated into the life of the village and the
Church.

MILITARY UNIFORM

In 1940 I bought an Army Chaplain's black scarf of heavy
silk, beautifully embroidered with two large Chaplain's
badges in gold and many colours. The cost was £5. After 47
years it is fraying a little at the edges, like its owner! A
replacement today would cost £150.

At Dalham, in the summer of 1941 Mr. Davies' tailor came
up from London to measure for any new Service Dress uniforms. The cut and the quality were excellent, and the jacket
had a few extra refinements such as buttons on the sleeves.
Never did a seam come undone or a button need to be sewn
on again. On August 1st I paid the bill of £13.13.0 plus 16/-
for collars and rank badges. Purchase tax was £1.10.4. It was
respectfully intimated to me that if I paid in cash there would
be a discount of £1.16.6. I still have the beautiful bill, written
in a copperplate hand, from Davies & Son of 19-20 Hanover
Square, London. The heading shines with the crests of satisfied customers — By appointment to the late King George V
and Prince of Wales, 1920–1936. Also to H.M. The King of

Norway, H.M. the King of the Helenes, H.R.H. The Duke of Connaught, and H.M. the King of Spain. Some company! It is now in the care of the Military section of Derby City Museum.

This was the time when our professional and dynamic new Colonel appeared, Eroll Prior-Palmer. The Regiment really was shaken up in every possible way. A new Squadron was formed, also a motorcycle cadre, where I learned to ride a motor bike. There were groups of blitz boys trained to tackle any emergency. The regimental assault course was surely the most fiendish thing ever designed by man. Every day the latest Armoured and Scout cars arrived, as well as Jeeps. Many were the regimental and divisional exercises, and in every way the Regiment was becoming a formidable fighting force. I virtually took over the Church, and the Vestry became my study. I even had time to spare to work on my first ambitious scale model of the St. George 1701, a 100 gun ship, made to a scale of ⅛ inch to a foot. I had worked on it for a year or two before the war, but it was to take another 25 years before completion.

The Derbyshire Yeomanry parties were proverbial. Each new Camp produced the best ever! By summer the organisation was in top gear. Food was scrumptious, and dancing went on all through the night. About 2.30 a.m. breakfast was served, kippers, bacon and eggs and everything else. Towards 6.30 a.m. one of the Subalterns was found sprawled on a seat at the bottom of the delightful walled garden below the house, sleeping quietly, with a seraphic look on his face. Gently his Batman aroused him, and he was properly shaved and accoutred to be the Duty Officer at 7.0 a.m.!

ENCOUNTER

During the summer we were told that we were going to live in winter quarters at Diss in Norfolk. So in the middle of the summer Charles Woodford, the Intelligence Officer, and I set out to prospect. He needed to know many things, and I went to see what facilities the little market town of 3,000 inhabitants might have for 1,000 troops. After lunch at the *King's Head* in Mere Street, he went his way and I found my way up Mount Street to the Rectory. I was shown into the drawing room to meet the Rector, Canon J. A. Appleton, who had just finished lunch, a tea cup by his side. In the bay window at a table sat his daughter. She looked over the sewing machine, our eyes met and that was it. I was 27 and she was a beautiful, tiny, brown-eyed redhead, not quite 21. I had always hoped and dreamed that there might be such a one, and as she offered me a cup of tea I knew that I had found her.

Bill as a young Chaplain in 1939.   *Helen in 1940.*

Diss Rectory as it was in 1940.

HELEN RECALLS

I, too, remember the moment that began the reorientation of our lives. This time after lunch was special in any such day; Dad resting in his armchair across the fireplace from Mother's matching chair – empty – since she died at Easter – my sewing was 'make do and mend' – making a 'new' skirt out of a dress with tatty sleeves; Mother's Singer hand machine my helper.

Hollow-sounding, gentle knock on the door, 'a Padre to see you, Rector'.

A light coloured army mac – a black and purple Forage cap in hand – a tall man . . . dark hair . . . a springy front tuft over a handsome face and . . . what deep eyes . . . my heart did a little skip and dared to warm a little to this manly, military figure. 'Would you like a cup of tea?' . . . I heard my Father say . . . I slid out to fetch another from Mrs. Burlingham's generous teapot. The Burlingham family lived, by day, mostly in our kitchen where 'Mrs. B' did the cooking for us all. They had their own part in the half-timbered end of the house – the ground floor and, up twisty stairs, past our Big Room, their attic bedrooms.

The teapot obliged, and back I came into this new presence, which was making our time extra special.

Sometimes we catch the significance of a very special moment, wishing its potential could be realised . . . if fulfilment comes. Our memories return to savour the magic of that haunting time.

HELEN'S STORY

When my Father was offered the Living of Diss we had to consult the map, although we had lived in Norfolk for eighteen years. We found Diss on the southern border, where the river Waveney marks the county boundary with Suffolk. Hence the saying 'when you cross the border the first town in Norfolk Diss appears'.' With a population of only three thousand in 1939, Diss was important as the market town and centre for a wide area in both counties.

My Mother was in hospital with terminal cancer when we

moved in April 1940, in a snowstorm. So with us came the Burlingham Family: Charlie a cowman, now to work in many gardens; Bessie his wife who, through capable housekeeping, taken in her cheerful stride, was to hold together our household; their elder daughter Phyllis, who helped in the house before going to war work, was sad to leave a boy-friend, but her sister Kathleen, then ten years old, was thrilled to find a Woolworths!

My brother was 'at' Christ Church Oxford and I was 'at' Froebel College evacuated to Hertfordshire.

Not only for us, moving from country to market town, from the home of our childhood to the base of our young adult years, did this new beginning signal the end of an era, but for Britain and much of the world this was the moment after which nothing would be the same again.

We soon settled to life in Diss. Mother was with us and able to get about until the Autumn, but, in the Spring of 1941, two days before her sixty-first birthday, she slipped Home. We were sad that she never met Bill; they would have been good friends. So, when he called at Diss Rectory, in July 1941, he found my Father, and me, and the Burlinghams with their generous teapot.

Mr. and Mrs. Burlingham – Uncle Charlie and Mrs. B.

3

Winter in Diss — 1941

I have little record (other than Church Services) of life in Diss.

After having fallen in love at our first and short encounter I 'laid low' whilst the Regiment arranged billeting for the forthcoming winter. The Regiment never quite knew what to do with its Parson. On the eve of our moving into winter quarters at the end of September the Rector invited me and William to live in the Rectory. I messed at the Uplands and slept at the Rectory. The little town was a delightful place, and the whole Regiment was quickly made to feel at home. I used to cycle everywhere, and soon got to know everybody.

I slept in Helen's room. Being an Elizabethan wood-framed house the door frame was not very square, and the door was cut to match. By the front window on to Mount Street there was an ancient chimney breast in a little passage, where hung Helen's coats, and her shoes sat in neat rows.

Winter 1941 was one of the coldest winters on record. Only once since then has the Mere been sufficiently frozen for a proper period of safe skating. My longest journeys were to Cambridge and to Mildenhall. This latter journey always seemed particularly cold.

I tried not to obtrude too much on the Rector's hospitality, but as I let myself in by the front door he usually heard me, and invited me in for a chat. Sometimes I like to think that in some way my company helped a little to fill in the void caused in the household by his wife's death at Easter.

Never have I met a greater and more effective Parish Priest. In his way he was a scholar, though at Shrewsbury School it was his athletic prowess that I think has never been equalled. He represented his school at Fives, Rowing and Soccer all on the same day. For several seasons he stroked the Shrewsbury Eight to victory at Henley. Between leaving school and going up to Keble College, Oxford, he broke his wrist. This impaired his rowing, so he kept goal for Oxford for all the three years he was up there. For several years afterwards he was goalkeeper for the Corinthians. Sunderland F.C. tried to sign him on professionally.

He was a gentle Christian leader, using his education, and teeming insights, in making the Gospel come alive in all kinds of ways. He wrote a Pageant called *The Lightbearers* in his tiny Norfolk village, and it has been performed all over the world. It tells the story of Christianity and its growth to a world faith by means of simply dressed characters progressively lighting hundreds of candles until the church glows with their transforming light.

There were to come waves of evacuees from London's blitz. Some of these Londoners, including my Batman's family, found refuge in the Rectory. Airmen from surrounding airfields, and men from searchlights in the vicinity came into Diss. Many found their way to the Rectory for baths and cups of tea. A thousand Derbyshire Yeomanry were stationed in this small town for the winter of 1941, and later on a large contingent of a Guards Brigade. Padres and Batmen of both Regiments were billeted in the Rectory, some with their families. I was the first of all these, and only one among crowds of people who found the Rector their welcoming host. This Rectory's hospitality became legendary as, down the years, warm welcome was given at its 'Mind the Blackout!' open door.

With the coming of Christmas 1941 great plans were made for festivities of all kinds. I found myself dreaming of ways of inveigling Helen to join in some of the Regimental Dances and Dinners when she came back from college. She stayed in London with her brother, and was late in coming home. On the night of her return I tried to let myself in more quietly, by coming through the back door, and the Burlingham's kitchen. But my entry was heard and I was invited into the drawing room. There was the Rector. There was his daughter. We chatted for a while, and then I made my way upstairs, with a little flutter in my heart, (to her room). Helen had been given a bed in the large bedroom, and later on they came upstairs with peals of joyful laughter. It was good to hear them. Soon I was seeking to invite her to Christmas events in the Regiment.

ENGAGEMENT

Sadly she developed measles and mumps. Perhaps it was a blessing in disguise for me, because her return to college was delayed until the end of February. So began my sick room visits, bringing in a bit of contact with the outside world. We drank to the New Year, Helen with a glass of medicine and I with a glass of sherry. The more I saw of her the more my love grew. So it was that in the Drawing Room on February 18th, while her father was out firewatching, I asked her to be my wife. 'Do you really mean it?' was all she said. 'More than anything else in life', I replied. She was in my arms, and henceforth life would be completely transformed.

The Regiment left for Scotland, and foreign parts, soon after Easter. A couple of weeks before Easter I was ordered up to Scotland with the Divisional Advance Party. My billets were in the old explosives factory at Irvine in Ayrshire. From here I went all over Ayrshire seeking out facilities for the arrival of the Sixth Armoured Division.

Looking back, my life had become tantalising. I had found my life's partner. In our cruel separation of 3½ years we became compulsive letter writers.

TO SCOTLAND

But Rectories always have a great pull on me, and by Easter I was billeted with the Samuels at Troon Rectory, until the Regiment was established. Helen came to join me here for a blissful few days at Easter. William and I picked her up at Kilmarnock Station, and we brought her to the Rectory in the back of our pick-up truck, wrapped in my great coat, pretending to be a soldier! On a trip to Edinburgh, in one of the famous silversmiths in Princes Street, we found a Chaplain's Badge: the most jewelled military badge I have ever seen! Later at Allans, the jewellers, at Ayr, I found an engagement ring with a sapphire set in a cluster of diamonds. It turned out to be too large, and I had to send Helen a ring gauge to find the best size for her finger, so that the ring could be made to fit.

OUR COLONEL'S THANK YOU LETTER

Billeting was new to the people of Diss in October 1941. Being a small market town, and well integrated, the people really took the Derbyshire Yeomanry to their hearts. Many were the wives and sweethearts who were given shelter, and I think it was with real regret when the Regiment went north to Scotland before embarkation. Many a Yeoman left his heart behind.

Here is a letter from Lt. Col. Erroll Prior-Palmer, the Commanding Officer, written to my father-in-law, the Rector of Diss:

'22.4.42.
Dear Appleton,

It is for ME to write and thank YOU for all you and your good folk have done for us. On every hand I hear tales of kindness and generosity. Our men have loved being in Diss and are very sad to go.

You were more than kind in helping us with our Parade Services, and I know very well how much your excellent sermons (if I may say so) were appreciated.

We'll all be very sorry to leave and I know the men would wish me to "thank you" for all your help and kindness.

Yours sincerely,

Erroll Prior-Palmer. Lt. Col.'

(Note: Erroll was to die before his daughter Lucinda became so well-known in the Show Jumping and Eventing world.)

HELEN'S FINAL COLLEGE TERM

After the whirl of measles, mumps, budding romance, engagement and . . . parting . . . I might have returned to college feeling somewhat deflated, but such joy was generated when the news broke on my fellow students that I was quite bouyed up. When I reported to our Principal, however, and gave her my proud tidings, she sat down plonk! on her hard study chair. Perhaps she thought this signalled the end of any teaching career I might have planned. None of us knew how long it would be to my marriage nor how long the war would go on. It may have been as well that we did not know.

Because I was the smallest (5 ft.) the largest bed had been saved for me – a huge four-poster – now on view (at a charge) with knights in armour, and all the other treasures of Knebworth House. When Bill sent a jeweller's gauge for me to find the best fitting for my ring, I took it to the smallest stately room, the 'Throne Room', on the top floor; the loo seat was set in a wickerwork frame, and round the walls hung photographs of royalty, given to Lord and Lady Lytton by generations of members of the Royal Family. Surely this was a worthy place in which to discover that my finger fitted the 'K' hole – for king – perhaps. I told Bill 'k' for kisses!

Letter-writing became an important part of every day, a few moments when I could hope to lose myself in trying to express the inexpressible condition of my heart, and the soaring of my soul. English seemed a factual, tame language; how could it express the feeling in a deep, loving look, let alone the assurance of belonging imparted by a kiss!

Lectures and essays kept me busy enough, while I also attempted to catch up on work missed. We braved the rigours of Teaching Practice in 'local' schools. At Pirton Rural our psychology Lecturer called to cast an eye on my efforts. In the play-ground a small boy pointed to an aeroplane overhead, 'Wha's that?' he asked, 'That is an aeroplane, little boy' she said. He looked astonished at her, then snarled 'Gaarn tha's a Spitfoyer'.

The full round of our college course included productions of drama, the most memorable of which was The Tempest *in black and white. Costumes were made of blackout material (what else?). The need for flashing lighting, and storm noises* challenged our 'Froebelian' aptitude. From Froebel's teaching about learning through experience we had evolved the idea that 'making what was needed out of materials available' was 'Froebelian'. This was an essential ability for practical living in wartime Britain, and stood me in good stead as the wife of a 'poor' parson in years to come.

Nancy was my great College friend and she promised to help me choose wedding clothes, and to support me on the great Day. When would that Day be . . .?

Knebworth House,
Knebworth, Herts.

2.4.42.

My Dear Bill,

The gardens here are so beautiful. I've just been for a brisk evening trot to 'The Winderness' to see and smell and feel the loveliness of Spring. My dear, life is so full and flowing with the wonder of being, and in it all is your wonderful love that fills me with an elevating desire to be what God intended me to be, and humbles me at being so incomplete. These frail flowers, blooming all round, have the germ of life that no negative force, like hate in war, can stifle. Their stock goes on after all the war-mongers are gone from this earth. Wouldn't it be a joy if God created generations from us to glory in the life of the successors of all the flowers and trees we enjoy in these special days of Spring.

I love you very much. Your Helen.

OF SCHEMES AND TEWTS AND EXERCISES

At the commencement of the war the Derbyshire Yeomanry were preparing to go to France. The fall of France and the threatened invasion turned the Regiment into an anti-invasion force. It really was a 'Dad's Army' situation. They had to defend most of the Lincolnshire coast with improvised weapons. Some of the armoured cars were said to have dated from before the First World War. Rolls Royce and large American cars were mounted with makeshift gun mountings, and the Regiment did its best to become a fighting force.

After the threat of invasion abated the Regiment became the Reconnaissance of the newly forming 6th British Armoured Division. Slowly equipment began to arrive. A great improvement in radio communication was the arrival of the number nine wireless set.

Soon troops and squadrons, regiments, brigades, divisions and armies began to learn to work and to fight together. In Wiltshire began the two years that welded the Division into a fighting force. Schemes and exercises were constantly taking place, each designed to test out, or to learn, something. A TEWT meant a Tactical Exercise Without Troops. Leaders of all grades would get into huddles with maps suitably prepared to play war games.

In September 1942 was a huge exercise called Bumper. It took place all over the south of England. The D.Y. scrapbook tells us of a brilliant summary of the exercises by the German General Staff! This was quite a help in assessment by our own General Staff!

A four day exercise called Bulldog took us into Lincolnshire. On a very hot Sunday evening it was announced that Hitler had invaded Russia.

Exercise Madcap lived up to its name. It involved a night drive without lights. The exercise was littered with casualties, and my first military funeral service at Woking Cramatorium was that of a very promising Subaltern.

Our Colonel was driving the Regiment very hard. One phenomenon was to turn day into night and vice versa for a week. Fortunately I had parishioners other than the D.Y. so it was difficult for me to take this very seriously!

In Scotland there was a vast exercise called Dryshod. The first part of the exercise was in glorious sunshine and the Pentland Hills were lovely. It was a splendid chance to write even more letters to my beloved. I give a vivid description of a bed on the heather under a tarpaulin sheet tied at two corners to the car and with the other two anchored in the ground. Morning ablutions were very convenient as the burn bubbled a few feet away. The second week it rained continuously.

Sometime in July in an exercise named Fist a home-made commando bomb was tossed at a dispatch rider. This stick of gelignite with fuse attached landed between the rider and his petrol tank. It was a mercy that he was blown off his machine before the tank exploded. I certainly had to visit him in hospital several times. In the same exercise a cunning attempt was made to exploit the Padre! It was decided that if a recce had to be made as to whether a certain bridge was strongly held, that I should divest myself of any D.Y. connection and cycle up to the bridge to assess the situation! The armoured car to which my bicycle was tied backed, bike first, into a wall and one wheel emerged a figure of eight!

Carnell House.

27.4.42.

Dearest lovely Helen,

Thanks for this evening's sweet letter. I live for my Hellenic epistles. Thoughts seem to come to me most easily in my bath — I'm probably a decendant of Archimedes! While soaking tonight I pondered about life and how lucky I am, and came to the conclusion that mine is for me the most satisfying, worthwhile job in the world. There really is nothing I would rather be doing. And now, right in the middle of all my plans and hopes there's YOU . . . you're sweet and lovely and there isn't anyone else in the whole world whom I would want to be my partner. Our love gives strength and purpose at the core of everything.

You will marry me won't you? Thanks very much. Keep happy and full of joy. Lots and lots of love, Pip.

4

Eight Scottish Months

COMBINED OPERATIONS I

We had come to Scotland at the beginning of the formation of Combined Operations. It was seen that no longer would the various armed forces be able to work on their own anymore. Combined Operations H.Q. was in Ayrshire on the south-west coast of Scotland. In summer 1943 Colonel Errol Prior-Palmer dreamed up a Regimental exercise called 'Sick'. The beginning was a sea journey with all our vehicles on 8 Tank Landing Craft. I believe that they were the first ever built. We embarked at Troon and Irvine and sailed round Arran, lying-to for an hour just off Ailsa Craig. What splendid views we had of the island, especially of the northern part where Goat Fell falls sheer down into the sea for about 2800 feet. I took lots of photographs which I sent to Helen who gave me a real 'rocket' for my disregard for security.

We undid our tins of commando rations: a tin of bully, sardines, cigarettes, matches and cheese in tins, a packet of raisins, a couple of bars of chocolate, cocoa and sugar ready mixed and a packet of Army biscuits. This was for 24 hours.

It was an exciting trip as we looked over to the Mull of Galloway, and the Irish coast merging in the background. It made me wonder what it would have been like if it had been the 'real thing' for which our boats were designed.

At 11.00 p.m. all the Tank Landing Craft turned and streaked for Ballantrae Bay, and nosed up the beach as far as their impetus drove them. The Home Guard were waiting for us, and bullets whistled overhead and mines were exploded on the beach. Commandos jumped out and went to gain a foothold. The Engineers were next, and they laid the beach roadway for the vehicles. So up the beach and into the night.

There had been a conference before. The beach and countryside had been carefully studied. Each Squadron and Troop knew where they were going to make for and the radio was going all the time, each car keeping correct distance, wondering whether the enemy would be waiting round the corner. It was difficult to read a map in the twilight, and to work the wireless and the car all at the same time. One of the sergeants who is an old hand at these things rushed up the wrong road. He was just in front of me, but I saw his mistake and kept along the right road. How I had begun to admire these men. They have so much responsibility and so many things to do, bless them. We fought all night and got back about 8.30 a.m.

COMBINED OPERATIONS II

Whatever may have been in store for us at the end of our training it looked as though there would be some 'watery element' in it. The plain truth was that at least 300 men of the Regiment could not swim at all. So I was made O/C swimming! This was largely organising lessons at the swimming baths at Ayr and Kilmarnock. Kilmarnock had a super pool with the only wave-making machine in the land. My job was to see that it was not just an enjoyable splash but a time of learning to swim. Progress was being made. So far, so good! The bit that wasn't good, I fear, was our own local reservoir. It was grim and square and very deep, and oh so cold, and swimmers were required to swim in it. To begin with it was in bathing costumes, then came the time to swim in full kit. To show that I took my own medicine I quote from a letter to Helen: 'This afternoon I went up to the reservoir again. I swam from one end to the other, at least 100 yards, with a pair of old Army boots on, one or two sizes too large and in a very billowy battledress. First the battledress gets full of air and tries to turn you upside down. Then it fills with water and feels like lead!'

The finale of these water sports was made into a Regimental Competition.

The grounds of Carnell House were beautiful, and full of daffodils when we arrived. When we departed overseas the trees were gloriously golden. I was given a large marquee which I was able to furnish as a Church Tent, and it was well used. Sometimes in high sunshine the tent got so hot that the altar candles melted and bent over into a '∩' shape!

A foretaste of Africa was flies. Summer in that part of Scotland produced clouds of flies. As soon as anyone appeared in the open air he collected a huge convoy which refused to go away.

Knebworth House,
Knebworth.

14.5.42.

My Dear Bill,

Thank you for lovely letters. It is magic — I slit an envelope (to use again), pull out and unfold a bit of paper; eyes bury themselves in pages of writing which in no time melt into your thoughts, and wonderful visions, set down in great clarity, come to life again in my mind . . .

When I wake in the morning life seems to be dealt out again and entrusted for a new day, I accept afresh, from the Great Power that gives, the great joy of your love. Birds pipe outside and sing as if in gladness for a new day — sparrows twitter and chatter and seem to be commenting on your merits, trying to get a hearing above the racket of competing birdsong. In those early moments there is the sheer joy of love and living — then the call for doing as well as being — emphasised by the harsh clanging of the calling-bell growing louder as it passes the door and dying away down the long passage.

It is so easy to enjoy the love of people round and to feel the power of your love in me.

Ach weel, it's farewell to ye, a haggis o'hugs and a wee wurrld o'kisses, your Helen.

THE IRISH BRIGADE – RULE BREAKING!

'I've been given some of our Irishmen to look after temporarily. They are very well drilled, they turn up for Church Parades like clockwork and sing their heads off. The trouble is that they live quite a distance from here.

Harry Graydon, the Baptist Chaplain and I are going to break all Army rules next Sunday by holding a joint service. If this works well we will be able to be much more effective in pooling our resources. Certainly this will help to bridge over our present Chaplain shortage.'

LOVE SEPARATED

Having been parted for three months, I wanted to give Helen a chance to review her engagement to marry me. It was what I wanted most in life, but there was a war on, and standards and customs of former years no longer seemed to apply. Helen was young. Was she just impressionable? Had she accepted my uniform, or what I was seeking to do, rather than me for myself?

It was a rather muddled but honest attempt, after three months of separation, to give her a chance to say whether she really wanted to have me as her husband some day.

15.5.42.   Kilmarnock.

Beloved, it is 11.15 p.m. and I've just come in to find your letters. It is three months since you said you would be my wife. Now all my life is changed. It has a discernible purpose. There is someone to grow with, and to belong to at the end of this war, however long it may be. You are sweet and lovely, and you fill my soul with the continuous joy of your presence. You are all I need, and far more than I ever dreamed or deserved. But I have been wondering whether in a world as it is, it was right to ask you to be my Wife while you were so young. Into your home comes an Officer in a smart uniform. He is lonely. At the back of his mind there is a longing for a Partner. His soul cries out for a loving response, and he finds it in You.

But is it fair for you? Even more than my love for you I

believe that I would wish you to do the right thing for yourself, for your own fulfilment. Am I really the one you need?
Can I really help you with all your future?

I'm not doubting your response to my love in any way,
but is it the right thing for you?

It's late and I'm so muddled. Dearest Heart I love you so
much. Instead of saying I need you so much, I should be
saying 'what do you need?' Do you need me? Sweet Lovely
Woman, please be yourself and don't feel that in some way
I have trapped you.

In a day or two came Helen's reply — a loving and gracious
letter. Yes, she too had fallen in love. Yes, her life had a new
meaning. Yes, she would marry me however far away that
time might be.

So I lived again, and in our thoughts and prayers, and in
countless letters our love grew and deepened and blossomed.

FROM MY LETTERS TO HELEN

16.6.42.

I went to Ballochmyle hospital this morning where we have
20 men. Between 45 and 50 are in one hospital or another.
After Ballochmyle I went to another in Ayr, and on to the
Educational Centre, returning 2 boxes of gramophone records
and collecting more.

In Ayr I visited Commando H.Q. to finalise their Swimming Exhibition, in full kit, in our reservoir tomorrow.

My last call was to County Library. Here I collected 50
more books for our library.

This evening's choir practice was a flop. It should have
been last night, but there was a film show in the Naafi.
Tonight was a Regimental football match which I'd forgotten
about.

So ends a typical day of rushing about in good causes!

17.6.42

I went on to the Isolation Hospital to see William who has
Scarlet Fever, and to leave mail and cigarettes. I thought it

would mean a distant peep but Matron said 'Come right in'. So I donned a white coat and was bundled into the ward. Perhaps the infection has left him.

Last night I went out with H.Q. Squadron as the Gunner in an Armoured car. We got into a wood in Capington Castle, the other side of Kilmarnock and waited for the Rifle Brigade to attack us. I was to give warning of the enemy approach by tootling on my Recorder. Imagine my dismay when before starting out, and before the whole Parade, the Squadron Leader said 'Well I think the Padre ought to show us what he will play'. I wanted to play 'Road to the Isles' or a bit of the Choral Symphony, but in the end it was 'Daisy Daisy'!

We got there about 11.30 p.m., and soon after an enemy Scout car came blundering into the middle of our pitch. I gave the warning, and we shot it up with Torch Flashes. We got home about 4.00 a.m.

SUMMER – TROON, ON MANOEUVRES

The 'battle' seems to be progressing according to plan. I had quite an exciting morning searching for two umpires with urgent mail. But now I've nothing better to do than write a letter!

Yesterday I went round Turnberry Hospital for the second afternoon running. There are so many men there. Then I went down the road to Girvan which is likely to be our Regimental winter Headquarters.. Its a seaside town of about 3-4000. Population is now double. There are lots of shops and cinemas. I visited the Episcopal Church there, with a nice young spikey Mirfield priest. He was genuinely glad to see a fellow Episcopalian. I think he leads such a lonely life. He took it for granted that we would have everything in common. He was such an obvious Dear, but he made me chilly round the heart when he began to talk about the Presbyterian Churches. He said he was on excellent terms with the ministers. 'One of them plays a very good round of golf, another shares my musical tastes, but religiously we haven't a single thing in common'.

Honestly, Darling, he said this. In a world war with Christian civilisation in peril he admitted that he had absolutely nothing in common at all with other Christian Bodies.

Darling, am I mad or batty or what? I didn't feel inclined to challenge his outlook. Whatever our Churchmanship we've all got our common loyalty to Christ. We all accept the same creeds. Surely we've practically everything in common, even though an Episcopalian is in a minority in a Presbyterian land.

Goodness, Darling, if I thought that my own particular bit of the Church was the only bit with all the truth I think I couldn't go on.

GUINESS BOOK OF RECORDS?

HOSPITAL VISITING IN A HUMBER ARMOURED CAR!

Lt. Kenneth Oglethorpe had just taken delivery of a new car, which of course needed running in! So when I suggested that he took me hospital visiting he readily agreed. These hospitals are all very widely scattered, and we had time only to go to one, at Drymen, the one on Loch Lomond. It was fun careering right through Glasgow in a great clanking armoured car! It would have been nice to have got out of the car with a smug countenance, and no suspicion of a smile, in front of all the people who always crowd hospital entrances, as though I always went visiting in an armoured car! Kenneth came in to visit a pal. Most of the men had gone away and I only saw three. It had taken us 18 gallons of petrol, but Kenneth assured me that it was a very good way of running an engine in!

Coming back, we met one of our sergeants who was at a convalescent home. He was at a crossroads, waiting for a bus. So we gave him a lift.

(During six years of Army life I covered thousands of miles keeping in touch with our men in hospital, both in the British Isles and overseas, but do not think I ever had such an unusual form of transport! Is this a record?)

SCOTTISH HOSPITALITY

The Darvel area of the W.V.S. were always very helpful and friendly. One of the plans which evolved was a sock-darning service! Weekly the men brought in their socks which I collected and took to the good ladies. Next week when I took the next lot the last ones were all ready, neat as new and so well darned. Sometimes they even refooted a sock.

MORE HOSPITAL VISITING

Summer 1942.

I've been hospital hunting, and I've done 99 miles today. This is nothing to what I used to do, and in view of the present petrol economy drive it's quite a lot. But I am the only link, and I believe that Regimental morale and continuity depends on keeping this link alive. If you are away from the Regiment too long you cease to be a member, and have to go back to base and start being reposted all over again.

It was fun to be at the beginning of the Highlands. All in front Loch Lomond was laid out. The sun was bright, the sky blue and white and very clear. The distant mountains had that blue haze. I just told William to stop the car, and there we sat. How I wish you could have been there.

And so we came to Drymen Military Hospital, a great enormous place in the grounds of Buchanan Castle, belonging to the Duke of Montrose. The castle itself is fairly new and rather small, but the hospital has overflowed into numerous little huts and wards. There were soldiers and sailors and airmen, Free French, all sorts in fact, including Italian and Vichy prisoners who are sick.

There they were in this paradise, on a lovely day, with Loch Lomond in the backyard, and those glorious eternal hills beyond. Darling I was awestruck.

Back we came to Kilmarnock. And as if to offer some consolation as we came home good old Arran reared her head as we were on top of the moors. There she was with a narrow strip of glinting sea in the front. I think that those hill and colours, those trees and the sky seemed so extra wonderful because my eyes have been opened to behold much more beauty since you came along. One sees the loveliness of men and women and trees and mountains in a new light because ones eyes have been set in a new and better focus by drinking in the loveliness of the greatest and sweetest source of loveliness in the world, my Beloved Brown Eyes.

Carnell.

21.6.42.

My Darling,

I've just been over to Divisional H.Q. at Troon. It made me rather homesick and full of longings for lots of things, to see Arran and Ailsa Craig, and to pass the Samuel's rectory where we spent our Easter.

My present book is by Rosalind Murray called *The Good Pagans Failure*. Surely I'm becoming a realist these days. We're all set for the coming battle with the Dictators, and for their utter destruction. It's my job to help build up our morale and faith in the undoubted rightness of our cause. Our morale is very high I think, but sadly I don't see many signs of a real change of heart in humanity. Our faith may well continue for a long time as the witness of the few. Often my role is prophetic: sometimes the solitary voice in the wilderness, often misunderstood by the multitudes.

We need a reason for the faith that is in us. Pagan culture, the humanist outlook of man's ability to save himself by science and education, is bankrupt. We need a Saviour and a change of heart. We need to be utterly and joyfully dedicated to hope in a Loving Lord. An advantage of a priest being an officer is that no one can push him around as he seeks to follow his profession. But he must be seen by all, and known by all, as utterly approachable, and belonging to no class or stratum. For a long time I've been trying to work out the idea of thinking 'classlessly'. In the Army one is an officer and a gentleman, and this doesn't help. Our culture is changing though it is hard to sense this in a Yeomanry Regiment. I try to think of everybody in a completely friendly way, of everybody as an individual and as a precious human being, as a person with unlimited talents.

Behind all our present deadly struggle in which I'm completely involved I've been trying to think of the new way, and the reconciliation that must follow. Dearest I need you so much to help to bring our vision of love to fruition. For love in this bitter world is ultimately the only invincible asset that humanity has.

OUR ALLIES

8.7.42.

Dearest,

We have two charming Polish doctors from the Polish Corps staying with us for a few weeks. This evening I've been sitting in the Mess for a long time after dinner talking with one of them. Goodness, he's had an exciting time. Poland, France, Belgium, Germany, China, Manchuria, the World! He's seen lots of bitterness and hatred. His family and friends are being decimated by the Germans, and still he's able to keep his faith and cheerfulness.

The other night William found them both in Kilmarnock trying to get their car back to camp. They were roaring drunk. So he went up to them and said 'move over, you'll kill yourselves and everybody else!'. So he drove them back to camp, to be met by R.S.M. Robbo. He looked a bit surprised, gave the Doctors a salute, and then wired into William – 'What have you been up to?'. 'They were a danger to themselves and to all on the public highway, so I drove them home.' R.S.M. seemed mollified and thoughtful. Finally he gave William a kindly look, and said 'Well done lad'. Anyway these are great men. I wouldn't wish that I could have loved you in any other less eventful days. These are days of greatness and unbounded opportunity – days for forming great and strong character.

England is putting many of her best sons into this force up here. She's certainly giving us her latest equipment. New weapons materialise all the time. In a way that is perhaps unique in history she is pinning great hopes on the things that are going on up here. [This rather remote and peaceful part of Scotland with its wide open spaces, rivers, mountains and sea, was the beginning of 'Combined Operations'.

So many have used my Church Tent these last seven months. The Q.M. refused to let me have one, although he had four in stock, so I had to go to Div. H.Q. to Major Messenger (Div.

Ordnance) who let me have one right away. I think this has been the only Unit in the Division to refuse a Church Tent. It will be interesting to see whether the Regiment (or Frank!) value me any more when we go to war!

Today there was excitement and sadness at teatime by the announcement that our Colonel, Errol Prior-Palmer is going to be in charge of the Sandhurst Officer Training Establishment. It is a heavy responsibility. We shall miss his drive and his electric presence. He has done great things for the Regiment. [Soon we were to get a Squadron Leader of the 11th Hussars, Colonel Peter Payne-Galwey. He was a peace-time champion amateur jockey, tiny and quiet, with a fire in his being, and he had done great things already in the desert. He inspired the Regiment to do great things, gaining a further D.S.O., and the American Silver Star. This latter award for leadership was given to few who were not American.]

WASHED OUT!

LOUDOUN MANSE, NEW MILNS, AYRSHIRE

November, 1942.

Beloved,

Lots of exciting things have happened today – you will have guessed this by the address. The Camp finally got washed away yesterday, and its even worse today! My poor old Church Tent is flattened, and the borrowed tiny harmonium is a little damp in the bellows. So now we are scrambling for new homes. They all have to be within a radius of 15 miles. I came to the Manse at New Milns, which I liked so much when I called here several months ago. The Colonel said that accommodation was rather limited, and would I like to try to find a billet for myself? 'Not half', I says, so I came here. I've a bedroom and shared meals and house with Mr. and Mrs. Hewitt, awfully nice young people, with two sweet and pretty young girls of about two and four. So please send any letters here. Leave 1st Derbyshire Yeomanry out.

William and I spent hours this morning looking for somewhere for him to stay. At last I went to one home and knew that it was the place – a middle aged man and woman, both good church folk with a boy of ten and a married daughter.

The wife is motherly and the man was in the last war, Peggy and Johnie Smith. You should have seen William's face as he walked into the warm, bright, kindly house, with his pack and rifle and damp overcoat and blankets! He'll have the time of his life, and the house is only just round the corner from the Manse.

By the way this is the place if you should decide that it is possible to come here at your half term. They've both met your picture and would love to meet you very much. It's over two hours since I put my phone call through to you. It will probably be too late. At any rate my beloved we'll be one at our 10.30 p.m. tryst.

Wednesday morning. It is cold and frosty again, although the sun is coming through. We had a tweedly day in Glasgow yesterday. Eddy and Mrs. Hewitt and I went by bus. We got to Glasgow by about 12.30 to find a pea soup fog! Towards the end of lunch one of Eddy's parishioners who is very wealthy, and owns lots of lace mills, came over from another table to pay for the meal! We had coffee together in a comfy lounge and talked for hours. He's a kind of fairy godfather to ministers, and of course, when I told him about you he promised to give us the curtains and furnishings which he makes in his factories! Then we went shopping. Mrs. Hewitt nosed out some powder etc. Coty which is very rare, and said you ought to have some, so here it is! I'm sorry if it's wrong. If so, please say, and I won't be so daring in the future!

Then we had a lovely tea in a jolly shop with antique chairs with price labels on them, and dinner wagons full of all sorts of buns and pastries.

After tea a cinema was on the programme. The trouble was that the cinema was so full of fog that we couldn't see the screen! This made us return to Kilmarnock where we saw the Spitfire film *First of the Few* – a very good film. Now I'm off on my bike to do some visiting.

WHERE ARE WE GOING TO?

We had only two clues:

(1) Officers were ordered to purchase tropical kit.

(2) All cars, trucks and lorries were fitted with a two-gallon petrol tin clamped above the front bumper, and in front of the radiator grill. A pipe connected the tin with the radiator overflow. Hence if we went to a hot country, the water lost from the cooling system would collect in the tin.

15.11.42.

Dearest Heart,

I think we'll be away soon, probably within this week. When I am allowed to say anything I'll give you details. I was to have had five services for Remembrance Sunday, last Sunday, but all had to be cancelled.

The Officers and men continue to get married and engaged, right and left! My Darling, I think we have done the right thing to wait, though my whole being yearns for you. All .these marriages and engagements do give us a stability, an aim and hope for the future, in a very uncertain world. I do really believe that our lives lie together in the future. Wherever we go, and whatever we do, you will always be my inspiration and sweet delight, Beloved Redhead. One day soon my address will no longer be Loudoun Manse, but some Army Post Office Number. Then you will know we've set off on our adventure, and that every day will bring you closer to my arms.

[On October 15th, H.M. The King came up to Irvine to inspect the Division. This was followed by visits from the Corps and Army Commanders. On October 31st, B Squadron went down secretly to Liverpool to be the spearhead of a small mixed group called 'Blade Force'. It was to land at Algiers, to test the reactions of the French, and to see whether it was possible to secure the French North African coast against the Germans. By the middle of November these landings had taken place, and we realised that we were bound for North Africa.]

HELEN'S FIRST JOB

My first teaching post was with the Kindergarten of Ipswich High School from September 1942–July 1944.

Ipswich, being 10 miles from the North Sea, up the navigable Orwell river, was a 'restricted' town; a visitor needed a pass. School provided me with a list of potential landladies which I took to the Police, but they were not allowed to show me their map. Ultimately I found Mrs. Read, whose husband was away in the RAF, and Tony aged two, and they shared their home with me for three terms.

165 Brunswick Road
11.11.42.   *Ipswich*

My Darling,

What a specially lovely letter you wrote me on Monday night. It's all so wonderful that you can feel your life's purpose being worked out through whatever comes along. Of course you can do it, because you have grown into a strong faith in God's Love, and a great trust in the Eternal Powers.

Sometimes when your love, or something else brings home the Magnitude of God's Love, it makes me feel so happily, utterly helpless and I know that these are the strongest assets of all, when selfish influence gives way to the Wisdom of God. Do you sometimes want to cry when you think how much God loves? Perhaps you can get to a different conception of the Being Who is Righteousness and Love. But there is something which reaches down to link us up with the pain and agony of God. It is something more purifying than sheer happiness and joy, in beauty and loveliness. I think physical longings are a kind of miniature of the pain of love, which is always there, giving depth and selflessness to all real love.

Music, with it's stirring minor passages, and great poems which use exactly the right phrases, and pick out eternal essentials, or bold paintings which are embodiments of truth – a vase of flowers arranged in just the right way that you feel 'all the plants these flowers have descended from went on growing inevitably, so that these flowers should be here now, just like this'. In all these things there is that element of the Right which comes from Eternity, and which seems to be expressive of thoughts too great for our minds to think, or our spirits to grasp.

We are like beings groping in a strange world where we are blind until we cease striving to look, and are content to receive sight bit by bit, as it is given to us. Gradually, if we are not pig-headed, or too lazy, we learn how to see, but there are times when it seems too dark to see; not because we cease to look properly but because there is a mystery, and things are too bright or darker and deeper than our eyes can fathom.

Then instead of our trust being in the strength of the light to illuminate everything along our way, we grow to trust in an even Higher Guide, confident that we are going the right way — just because we know it to be so.

Please don't try to think what all this means! I can't tell you — silly child. It all comes of your outpouring of great thrusts of faith and love, which seem to encircle me like your strong arms, and then I long for you so much that my spirit must overflow. It's so badly trained in working via my brain and my pen that it is apt to dictate things which aren't sense.

But it is odd (no it isn't really, but it would be if the Spirit Life were not the most important) that when you are far away physically you seem to be very near.

My Darling Billy I love you utterly. Don't take my scatty remarks too seriously! I just can't explain, but I love you, love you, LOVE you. See? Good old Bill. Your loving Helen.

5

To War — November 1942

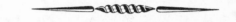

The year was rushing by, and at the end of November it was time for us to go abroad to do whatever destiny had to make out of our three years training in England.

It was almost with relief that I wrote in my last letter to Helen from Scotland, for we sailed on November 29th, a sort of profession of what I believed we were called to do:

Loudoun Manse.

Monday Evening.

Dearest Wee Appleblossom,

It will soon be time for your Bill to take part in this rending of the nations. I'm quite ready, in fact even pleased, to go. I want to be part of the body of people who are making history. I want to help tear down the great monstrous growths that have been trying to poison the world, so that when the time comes to rebuild I'll be better equipped to help.

The present task is to take love and comfort and courage and inspiration to those who need it most — to help to show that God cares desperately for all the things that spoil His World. At the end of it I'm going to have a faith that will never shrink, and has come triumphantly through the Valley of the Shadows. I know I can do this. My instincts tell me. And on the top of it all there's a great and a devouring love which was kindled when I first saw my own lovely Redhead.

And so, My Darling, don't get worried or anxious in the long silences. We're one. We belong to each other, and are still linked by God's Good Spirit.

And when its all over (perhaps much sooner than we dare to think now) I'm coming back to ask if you can marry me. It won't be a matter of sharing parts of each others life. It will be one big common life — with love and pain and pleasure, with physical and mental and spiritual things all shared, perhaps with children, all linking the whole thing up in Life. Goodness, I want to be with you, and pray with you and hold you very closely to me — but the time is not yet. This will be when the clouds have departed, and the sun is shining through once more. I would never have believed that I could have got such a 'Kick' (sorry!) out of being in love. It's great and immense and ever growing. It's with me every waking moment, and when night comes you're the centre of all my dreams.

And so, My Darling, be very happy — using each day and each experience as a step towards the time when we can build our own community of fellowship and service. Good night and God bless you my Darling. Your very much in love Bill.

P.S. I'll always keep on writing! Maybe even a Diary, here and there. XX

165 Brunswick Road
Ipswich

13.12.42   Sunday 8 p.m.

My Darling Bill,

I want you to realise what a tremendous difference you make to my life. Days are all so much happier because of the wonder of You and your love. Somehow I have felt it . . . inadequate . . . to take out a pad and write to you. What is there new to say? Each day the same wonder of love and joy is renewed when I wake to realise that this is the world that has you in it! Tony is in bed, and Mrs. Read is knitting and enjoying short stories; we are in the front room as it is

Sunday. The fire is blazing in a Christmassy way. It reminds me of a night when we put out the light and sat by the fire . . . you played your recorder and we put the world straight. Suddenly you got out of your chair and sat beside me on the hearthrug . . . it was painful to be so close to you in those days . . . but then it was so wonderful to discover that we felt the same about each other! I didn't really love you in those days, like I do now . . . I was still a kid and didn't know what it was to love so much that it didn't tear one's inside out to see the door shutting on one's dream man, or to see him whizz off in a car for the day. It was not long before you taught me to love, and I am still learning (although I feel I couldn't love you more), not only love for you, but utter givingness to others. Somehow it goes from you all the time. Wherever you go it radiates to others and helps them to love too, and that makes it good that you are able to contact so many lives.

It looks as though I found it a tough job falling in love! It was so difficult not to that I soon gave up trying! I suppose women folk don't usually blather like this to their men folk, but I can't bear the thought of your not knowing that you mean more to me than anything or anyone . . . more even than bananas! Rough seas and stormy skies, miles of land and water cannot cut us off from each other. One day the bells will ring again . . . they'll ring for us and it will be my happiest day. I belong to you. Tony is two; he calls me 'Aplun' and I pick him up, race down the garden and hold him to see over the fence when a train runs past in the cutting. I haven't found a holiday job . . . helping Mother B. will be a good plan. All my love, Helen.

IN THE LONG SILENCE

TORCH – AFRICAN JOURNEY
THE THIRD FRONT – A SUMMARY

These seemed to be the darkest days of the war. With the Japanese assault on Pearl Harbour, America had been brought fully into the war. Hitler's bid to conquer Russia nearly succeeded. U-boats were sinking millions of tons of shipping, and Stalin was impatient for an Allied invasion of the continent in 1942 or 1943. It was not until Summer 1944 that this was possible.

Operation 'Torch' was launched to relieve pressure on Russia, to free the Mediterranean and to deny Africa to the Axis Powers. In October, General Montgomery began the Battle of El Alamein, and 'Torch' was timed to fit in with the British offensive. The greatest Armada of history, 850 ships, set off from the Clyde, Liverpool and American ports. Shipping and naval protection were highly stretched. Allied security was so tight that the Germans could not guess our destination. Forty German and Italian U-boats were waiting off the Azores. They sank thirteen homeward bound ships off Sierra Leone. But 'Torch' sailed on and into the Mediterranean. Churchill called this enterprise the Third Front. Some Americans landed at Oran and Casablanca and most of the rest of the convoy landed in Algiers. I was in one of the two ships which, suitably protected, went further east to land at Bône, the port nearest to Tunis, our final objective.

Part of the convoy taking Allied Troops to North Africa.

FIRST DIARY

Here are bits from a diary, written on small pieces of pink paper, to record our journey from Scotland to Africa. The pages where kept inside the front cover of my zip-fastened Bible.

JOURNEY FROM SCOTLAND TO BÔNE, ALGERIA
November 1942

Nov. 27 Friday, 12.15 p.m.

S.S. Orbita anchored off Gouroch

We left Troon at 8.35 a.m. on the Wednesday before, and came to Greenoch where we spent the night in a Transit Camp. On Thursday we went down to the pier at the railway station at 1.30 p.m. I rushed back to fetch my communion set which I had left behind. After much waiting and making dumps of equipment, we did not get to the *Orbita* until 6.00 p.m. There was another wait until 8.30 p.m. in the cold and blackout, amidst the greatest shambles. The officers were alright, but the men – goodness it was like the slave galley in *Ben Hur.*

I'm sharing a First Class Stateroom with Father Dommersen R.C. Chaplain, Captain Crawford the R.E.M.E. wireless man, and Colonel Jock Moore. The cabin should take two but there are bunks for six. Fortunately only four are full.

Boat drill this afternoon. We sail sometime tonight. This part of the world is full of ships of all sizes, and all preparing to move. There are eight Parsons aboard! Really! Four Anglicans – three R.Cs. – one Presbyterian. Andrew Stewart (my Presbyterian friend) told me about Helen ringing up on Sunday night, bless her. He said her Father rang up too.

This ship is about 15,000 tons, and holds nearly 3,000 men – just how, I don't quite know. She was built before the last war, serving as an armed merchant cruiser 1914–18, and now a transport. All the notices are in English and Spanish, and sometimes in French. I'm hungry as we don't have tea. Breakfast 8.30 a.m., lunch 12.30 p.m. and dinner at 6.30 p.m.

10.00 p.m. Alone in the cabin. I've just bought 2 tins of 50 Capstan cigarettes at 3/8d a tin – one for Andrew Stewart, four 5 oz. packets of Canadian sweets, two coupon-free tablets of saltwater soap, and one packet of matches, from the Canteen. The chappie gave me a dozen boxes and seemed quite grieved when I took only one! [I was a non-smoker!]

Nov. 28. Saturday. Just before lunch. We're on the move. 20 or 30 ships. We left last night about 10.15 p.m. The ships lights were off, the moon was lovely and the sea very calm. One felt that it was a great moment. Earlier on the Chaplains had had a Conference and fixed up lots of services — morning and evening prayer, Sunday services, etc. We seem to be rounding the top of Ireland. During boat drill, when we all had to be up on deck, the various ships were testing their guns. The ship was pitching a bit this morning at breakfast and I thought I caught a glint in the Steward's eye as he asked whether we wanted the meat course after the fish one!

ADVENT SUNDAY. Nov. 29. 9.15 p.m. After a day of finding it difficult to take an interest in people, yesterday, I've eaten well at every meal, and I'm hoping I'm finding my sea legs. I've groped my way up on deck. It's very dark and takes a few minutes to be able to see clearly. We must be doing about 12 knots. There's a phosphorescent wake, and in the distance are the dark shapes of the other ships. There is something grim and determined in the way these ships keep plodding on. At midday the destroyers were careering around with black flags flying — a sign of hunting. Rumour is that they claim a U-boat.

H.C. this morning in the Sgts. smoke room. About 30 were there. This afternoon after lots of vain previous attempts, I managed to get into the forward baggage hold for prayer books, etc. Then after lunch, to the after hold to see the Ship's Q.M. with Andrew Stewart. We got the use of blackboards, gramophones and records. Before dinner, I had a bath in hot salt water, a curious experience. Even the sea soap wouldn't lather very well — still it was good fun. This evening we went round with a gramophone and hymn books. The trouble is that there just isn't an open space in the whole ship, except for the Officers and Sgts. dining quarters. The rest is just hammocks slung from everywhere.

10.0 p.m. I've just been out to deck L2 with Col. Moore to

see the chaps tucked up in bed. Lights out, fans going – an occasional blue bulb. There you sleep, a tiny cog in a vast system of humanity – tightly packed like sardines – row upon row, deck upon deck, heat upon heat.

ST. ANDREW. Nov. 30. Monday. From an Intelligence Summary I gather that the Derbyshire Yeomanry, B Squadron, have been in action – bless them. I wish I could be with them. Had a colossal breakfast this morning. Porridge, fresh white rolls (always white bread), kipper, liver and bacon, coffee. Our money is being changed into this new currency today. I'm curious to know what it looks like. I spent about an hour doing a map of the Mediterranean in coloured chalks for the lectures which are to take place. There were a few drops of rain up on deck this morning. This is the first we've had. It is very warm considering we're in the Atlantic. We must be about 700 miles out, heading south-west.

This new money is very exciting – printed in £1, 10/-, 5/-, 2/6 and 1/-. The colours are lovely. The paper is watermarked, and just as well done as our own English currency. They're headed 'Issued by the British Military Authority' and have the Crown surmounted by a lion and Britannia's head in the watermark.

Dec. 1. Tuesday 9.45 a.m. last night we had logged 850 miles – we've probably done 1,000 now. Its quite a mild morning. Boat drill without greatcoats. P.T. at 10.45 a.m. which I think I'll attend. P.T. is rather a problem. There are only the port and starboard promenade decks available for 3,000 men, so the times have to be staggered. Reading Hildebrande's *Life of Magellan* from the ship's library – very interesting. Had a long talk with Victor Pike, the Deputy Assistant Chaplain General 5 Corps, last night during Boat Drill. He's a great but simple-hearted chappie. His father is an Irish Episcopal Vicar. He was asked to come into the Army because the Army was keen to get hold of some rugby players. He's a very outgoing Leader.

Afternoon. I've just been to L2 to help inspect the men's feet. They weren't as clean as they might have been. Some had broken toe nails. Very few men ever seem to make an effort to darn their socks. The wind is rising and the sea is getting up a bit now. Poor old Dommy is not liking it very much. We had quite an enjoyable P.T. this morning in a confined space.

Dec. 2. Wednesday 11 a.m. Poorly! The wind got up last night and the sea was rough. It was bad enough in the middle of the boat — I can't imagine what it must have been like fore and aft. Anyway I was sick! I came away from food after the soup, which is an awful pity as there was chicken to follow. The great snag is that we're heading east and the waves are on the beam. This gives a nasty roll. P.T. is on at present but I'm staying right here.

6.0 p.m. It's been a lovely day today, but I haven't ventured out for a meal since breakfast. The sea has been blue and there's been a good sun. Rumour is that we captured a German supply vessel last night. At any rate there's a new vessel in the convoy today, and three destroyers raced after a strange vessel coming in the opposite direction about 4.0 yesterday.

Dec. 3. Thursday 10.45 p.m. Just a few lines in my bunk. Jock Moore and I have been up on deck. The stars are simply terrific. One star in particular was reflected in the water like the moon. Tomorrow night we should go thro' the Straits of Gib. So here's hoping there's no torpedo waiting for us. Lord if it be Thy Will grant us a safe journey.

I took the Officers' and Sergeants' Service in the Officers' mess this evening at 8.0 p.m. for 20 minutes. About 100 were there. We sang 'Thy Kingdom come' and 'When I survey' to the accompaniment of Sgt. Ruffles on the accordion. I tried to show the connection between the personal and corporate sides of our Faith.

Dec. 4. Friday. This afternoon there was a lecture on tropical hygiene. Tomorrow I give a lecture on Tunisia. I saw five seagulls wheeling over the sea. Harbingers of land. Must be Gib. Whoopee!

7.15 p.m. — lights ahead. The lighthouse before Tangier on the starboard and lights of Spain on the port. We lose an hour tonight. Pooh! Bône and Algiers are being bombed night and day. Ah well! We'll hope for the best.

10.40. Such a thrill. Spain all twinkling on the left – Algeciras etc., – lighthouses flashing, towns lit up, how queer. What a complete contrast to blacked-out Britain! And just away on the port bow are the searchlights of Gib. There doesn't seem to be any blackout there – but of course there's not much point of a blackout with Spain brightly twinkling all round! In the channel there are light buoys – we have quite a lot of navigation lights showing. We've passed one or two neutral ships. On the starboard is Spanish Morocco with towns brightly lit up – all twinkly promenades – one town showed up especially well – probably Tangier.

11.30 p.m. Bedtime. Still sleeping in full clothes. Lots of exciting noises and happenings. Flashes like gunfire away to sea – coloured lights coming on, and sirens sounding to do a zig-zag. Light and darkness. Like a new world. We've been at sea for a week now. Seems like three months. O Lord give us faith and strength and courage to wait upon Thee, and ever to seek after Thy Will.

Dec. 5. Saturday. 10.35 a.m. Such an exciting morning. Here we are in the centre of the Ancient World – ploughing the waters ploughed by the ancient Roman galleys. On the port side the mountains of Granada covered with snow, glistening in the sun. To the starboard is the African coast, further away. The latest is that we put into Algiers instead of going on to Bone.

7.35 p.m. We are due in Algiers tomorrow morning. There was a lovely sunset. Most of the day has been spent in packing – (i) The kit to be collected by Transport (ii) The kit to be carried. We're probably in for a 10 mile walk [This is what actually happened to those who landed at Algiers, and had to march to Maison le Carré]. We have a small pack with food etc., a blanket, tin hat, water bottle and respirator. The men have their weapons as well, poor things. Time for evening service now.

Dec. 6. Sunday. ADVENT II. 9.40 a.m. It's just like a picture book outside. I was up on deck and saw the sunrise in all its colour and glory, with the crescent moon overhead. Then H.C. in the Officers' Mess. Then breakfast and on deck again, this time for the full sunrise. It was terrific. Then half speed.

Algiers ahead. Built at the bottom of the hills and up the sides — old and new houses — wharves and skyscrapers. Lovely mosques. With a calm sea, cruisers, destroyers and transports, all nosing into harbour or lying to. Will I ever be able to make other people realise how lovely it all is? There's a possibility now that we may go on further.

11.30 a.m. So we're off to Bône after all. At present we're at anchor. What a sight. Small craft buzzing about like flies — with an occasional plane overhead. We can see the vehicles moving along the waterfront — there are oil storage tanks on the seafront, the wireless station at the top of the hill.

Our baggage is loaded on the decks. As we're going into some nasty stuff, we're going to remove what we value from the deck.

1.15 p.m. Part of the convoy is slipping out of Algiers. The anchor was weighed about an hour ago. Harbour, mosques, Cathedral of Our Lady of Africa (a wonderful mosque-like building), slave-stained waterfront, wireless station — all passing by. The colour of the sea is like the green of the dress length I gave Helen. I've seen jellyfish and strange creatures of the sea, and one or two people on the waterfront, though the place seems almost deserted. Well here's hoping for a safe journey, during the next 24 hours especially.

8.40 p.m. Evening service just over. Taken by Philips (Rifle Brigade). We were packed out. We're now only four ships protected by about six or more sloops and destroyers. Two ships put into Philippeville, and our two into Bône. One ship was torpedoed at this stage of the last convoy and disappeared in 3 minutes! Still, I've a feeling we'll all get through.

10.15 p.m. Really the last entry today! Just been up on deck with Dommy. One or two depth charges sounded quite near an hour ago.

Love. Joy. Peace. Thank God for it all.

BONE – HOME OF ST. AUGUSTINE

Dec. 7. Monday 10.50 a.m. We got here about 8.30 a.m. with the other Transport which went into dock first. There were about 6 sloops and a Light Cruiser, as protection. To our relief we had a sky full of Spitfires, 6 or 8 at any rate. At last we're alongside – but there is no sign of disembarkation yet. Bône has certainly had a plastering from Jerry. There is a destroyer down by the stern in the harbour and quite a lot of houses are blitzed. I can see palms, and the Tricolour flying. There are hills all round, with more green than I've noticed before. There is a little rain now. All the buildings seem large and modern – white with red roofs.

6.15 p.m. Bône. In a room with Dommy at the Co-operative Ouvrerie. I feel I can't begin to start to describe things. The town is quite a big one, with a large attractive modern French quarter, and a filthy Arab one. The trouble of course is the Jerry bombing. The town in parts is little more than a shell. Frenchmen with cycles and berets, the women smart and sophisticated – Arabs unbelievably filthy in rags and tatters, bargaining for old clothes with oranges. The lovely R.C. Basilica of St. Augustine is on a hill outside the town. If we're here very long my French should improve quite a bit. There's a rumour we may be going up to the front tomorrow. The front isn't very far away.

Dec. 8. Tuesday. Rain all day. We've fed on the compo rations, which are extremely good. We were allowed to send one airletter for Christmas, today. I got an advance of pay booklet this afternoon and 1500 francs, i.e. £5. Later on I stopped to shelter from a particularly vicious shower and got talking to a French 'ancient combattant'. We talked for hours, or rather he talked chiefly and I listened. I could understand nearly everything he said, but found it rather difficult to express myself. I must take this opportunity of brushing up my French. French (or is it an Algerian speciality?) lavatories are funny things. The tops are very simple and sensible! This afternoon I bought a kilo of oranges for 10 francs. There were seven oranges. The rest of D.Y. H.Q. Squadron, with Jack Harris, are due to arrive tomorrow, and the transport on Friday. We may move up to the front sometime after that.

Dec. 9. Wednesday. 7.00 p.m. Quite an interesting day and warm. To change the Squadron money this morning I got to the Bank at 10.15 to find a queue of hundreds. At 11.30 I was only about 5 away from the office when it was closing time! In the afternoon I had another long walk with the Methodist CCS Padre up the hill to the Basilique of St. Augustine — built at a cost of 5,000,000 francs (pre-war rate). There is supposed to be a bone of St. Augustine. Just below is the Roman water cistern which was restored in 1880 and is still in use. Nearby is the theatre, where I tried to get the atmosphere of the old Roman days. Coming down the hill I met Dommy and Hayes (the other RC) and we went to see the town of Hippo. About 100 yards square has been excavated including the entrance of the forum. Tea and then to our room. We have a room with a blacked out light here, and are lucky, as most of the other men are living in the blackout.

Dec. 10. Thursday. 7.45 p.m. Very nice day. Went to Bank of Algeria to change men's money, I got the money changed into 1,000 franc notes, and went over to the queue for smaller change when the alert went and the bank was closed! So I went round the corner and managed to get half of it changed into smaller money. Went shopping. Bought aspirins in metal tubes, Coty powder for Helen (2/- a tin instead of about 5/-) and two books to brush up my French. Afternoon went to beach with Agg-Manning of the 16/5 Lancers, and his troop. There were lots of other men there. We bathed naked. Swam out about ¾ mile and back. We walked back across the railway bridge, on the sleepers alone with the water down below. After 100 yards we jumped on a train and continued to the docks. Bought the usual 2 kilos of oranges. Goodness, old Jerry has impoverished these people. They are almost starving. They never see meat at all. Long argument with Dommy this evening. We have quite a lot of these nowadays!

Dec. 11. Friday. 6.15 p.m. This morning I went for a walk around the town and shops. This afternoon went with Agg-Manning and a Sub. from the Lothians and Border Horse up the hills behind the town. We got to the top of one ridge to find that the range was just beyond. The hills were full of Arabs who had fled from the town. It has been a lovely day.

Dec. 12. Saturday. 7.00 p.m. This afternoon I pottered around the ruins of Hippo. Goodness it is exciting. Only a little bit

has been explored so far. A chappie from the Catering Corps
gave me 10 coins that he had found in an urn earlier on. Most
are French and Italian coins of the last century. But two are
old and irregular in shape. I'm hoping they're going to be
Roman ones! Tomorrow H.C. is in the Commandant's room,
and if fine a service in the Amphitheatre at 10 a.m. Should be
great fun and certainly an experience.

Dec. 13. Sunday. ADVENT III. 2.30 p.m. There were 30 at
H.C. and about 500 at the voluntary service, which Andrew
Stuart (C of S) and I took in this amphitheatre. The singing
went well, and it was a good place for talking in. 200 more
men collected at the other ruins by mistake. What a privilege
it was to have officiated in the Amphitheatre which St.
Augustine must have known so well, and to try to picture the
scene as he lay dying, in 430 A.D., with the Vandals hammering at the City gates. Andrew and I talked about St. Augustine's 'The City of God'. Rome the Eternal had been sacked
twenty years before, and Augustine set out to contrast the
permanence of the City of God with the rise and fall of
worldly Empires.
      There were several troublesome raids last night. The first at
11.15 and the last one this morning after dawn. The night
fighters did well, and got quite a bag.

Dec. 14. Monday. 7.20 p.m. All alone tonight. Dommy and
Harry Simon have gone up to the front. Last night I went with
Jack Harris and the Squadron to spend the night on the
beach. We lugged our blankets for about 2½ miles. We were
in bed by 8 p.m. A few planes went over the town, and we
had a good view of the fireworks. The dew was heavy and
things got rather wet. We had a splendid sunrise. Today has
been lazy.

Dec. 15. Tuesday. 8.10 p.m. Ten days to Christmas. How
funny and far away it seems! I expect the siren will be going
soon. We usually have an early raid and a dawn raid, plus an
odd raid or so in between. I expect the raids will continue
whilst the harbour is full. The sounds of a divebomb attack
are just as we were told. I think the Beaufighters are doing a

good job of interception out at sea. Very few planes get through, considering that this is the forward base.

Dec. 16. Wednesday. 7 p.m. Town and docks this a.m. Ruins with William, this afternoon. We got some more coins and a few odds and ends. The ship with the car is supposed to come in on Friday. I do hope it will come, but it has been put off so many times. I most want to try and get up to the Derbyshire Yeomanry. This morning I saw Darlan (French Admiral). He came into the town and laid a wreath on the war memorial. The few French people who saw him gave him a clap.

Dec. 17. Thursday. 7.50 p.m. Made a tour of the town and docks this a.m. There's a lot of stuff coming out of the ships. Called at the ruins on my way back to lunch. My Arab excavator gave me 10 small coins. This afternoon to the shops. Bought powder and perfume for Helen. Very good perfume I was led to understand. Collected some more trophies at the ruins on the way back. With luck the ship with my car may be in tomorrow. William bought some aluminium today. There's a shop full of things, plates, pots of all kinds. Even the aspirin and shaving cream pots are in aluminium. At present I'm cleaning my coins in vinegar. It works very slowly, but is already having a good effect.

Dec. 18. Friday. A week to Christmas! How funny in these parts! My car has been unloaded today. I hope to go up to the front on Sunday a.m. Met Ralph Watts (D.Y. H.Q. Squadron) in Bône at the bank this a.m. I showed him round. L/Cp. Swan and driver were there too. It was good to see the D.Y. again. I showed them the aluminium shop. I bought a kettle and coffee pot to send home.

Dec. 19. Saturday. 9.50 p.m. All teed up to go off tomorrow. Packing done, rations prepared (box of compo rations). Sent wires off for Christmas home and to Helen. Went for maps to Itie Embassy. Rain last night very heavy.

Dec. 20. Sunday. Sunday before Christmas. H.C. with Philips, Rifle Brigade, in the large Co-operative Tobacco factory (full of great bales of tobacco which made excellent mattresses). Then packed up to come away. The car seemed full to overflowing. We got away at 10.30 and when almost at Morris, about 19 kms. away, I realised I'd forgotten my mac and my greatcoat — so back we came to collect them, and to have lunch. We opened a tin of bully beef, a huge tin of Scotch broth (2 or 3 lbs.) and a large tin of beans, a huge meal! We set off again about 1 p.m. and came the coast way by Le Calle, then across the mountains on a corkscrew mountain road, with a slippery surface and sheer drops — very exciting. At Souk-El-Arba we reported to the Town Major, and set off for Le Kef. At about 5.30 we stopped for the night in a sort of depression (geographical!) and parked between two prickly bushes. Then we got busy with the car cover for a bivvy. Then supper of tea and biscuits — very good. Now with a bright light in the car we are reading and writing before bedtime — it's 8.45 and soon will be bedtime. Here we are in the wilds of Tunisia, happy and snug.

Dec. 21. Monday. 7.15 p.m. A large French farm (La Ferme Cassard) just behind Teboursouk. We came away at 9.30., through Teboursouk to this farm which is D.Y. Regimental Headquarters. How good it is to have caught up again.

Here my diary finishes!

CHRISTMAS HOLIDAYS

Diss Rectory.

18.12.42.   Friday.

Hello from home. School broke up yesterday and I was going to pack and then come home next day, but at dinner time I decided to come, and leave the packing until next week. You see I go back on Monday to fire watch, and stay for Tuesday night as well. It is good to be home again although I do enjoy Ipswich immensely. Christmas is taking possession of thoughts and jobs at present. Charlie B. has kept some yellow chrysanthemums going for Christmas, great, tall, spidery ones, and they look gay in the drawing room against the dark clock.

Mr. & Mrs. Robson (Evacuees) are going away for Christmas, so Mrs. B. won't have quite so many to 'do for'. Mrs. Penstone (Evacuee) is still in hospital so Mrs. B. has the kiddies to look after. Phyllis (Burlingham) joined the Naafi three weeks ago and much prefers it to the nursing job she left, because she was not passed as strong enough. Mrs. B. said that she would like to write to you and William but she is 'rather busy'! Most days she has continuous work from 7 a.m. – 10 p.m. but she appears to enjoy it, and seems to keep fit.

Going from School the other day, I caught a glimpse of bare trees, in the Park, looking grey and rather lonely in the twilight mists. I thought of all the holidays that I would probably spend without seeing the one person who matters most to me, but still I didn't feel lonely; and then I KNEW that never again would I feel that little empty hollowness I used to feel before you came along.

Now it is time for Dad to go to the Wardens' Post – do you remember those two (magic!) nights when he was on duty earlier in this wonderful year? Home just rings with the spirit of you now. Christmas is going to be such a happy one. You may be far away, but I love you, and vice versa and that is what will always matter most. God bless you my Darling.

Your very own L.M.P.

LETTER-LINKED AGAIN

Diss Rectory,
England.

Christmas Day 9 p.m.

My Darling Bill,

It's Christmas Day and Dad and I are here by the fire, with the light out. This is a wonderful Christmas. You are right here with us in a way. Your love lights up all my days, and you are just everything I need and long for and ever dreamed of in my visions of the beauties and joys of life.

We had a 'blackout' 7.30 a.m. Service with ninety there. Dad had a very busy day, with a wedding this afternoon. Bertie Harrison mustered seven bell ringers so we had a peal before Morning Service.

Yesterday I woke to find Mrs. B. beside my bed with the best present this Christmas . . . yes two letters in one, from *you. They can't have taken long to come, as you write of passing coasts, and being hot. Each letter had a bit cut out, at the bottom of the last page . . . did they cut out the juiciest bits or was it the mystic, Latin abbreviation i.e. T.C.T.C.A.? Douglas and Barrie (Penstone) discovered their stockings at about 6.30 a.m., so we had children's happy voices beginning the day. Charlie B. cut a tree from a yew hedge for them. It is a real Christmas! How is William? Bless you. All my love. Helen.*

> A.P.O 4330. H.Q. Squadron
> 6th Armoured Division.

Christmas Eve 1942

My Sweetheart,

It does seem so warm and un-Christmas-like. I have caught up with Regiment in time for Christmas, thank goodness. William and I are on our own, and seeking out our men. We plan to keep Christmas with as many as we can reach.

It seems funny to think that we were so happy together for OUR Christmas just a year ago. You have changed my whole life. How much I love you. Sometimes I dare to picture the day when we have a Christmas Tree and little children opening their stockings.

So Happy Christmas, My Darling. May the real inner Peace of the Babe be in your heart and in your home this Christmas. I expect all our mail will catch up, and our link will be forged again. I certainly have sent you plenty of letters! Your loving Bill.

A WARRING CHRISTMAS

Christmas Day 1942.

Merry Christmas Darling,

Please I love you simply terrifically much. It is rather a damp rainy sort of day and I'm sitting in the car camouflaged in a wee wood of evergreens and ladslove. I've had four very jolly services this morning. The job is infinitely worthwhile here. The men are so welcoming and responsive. If only it were like this at home! Jerry isn't very far away, and it's silly to rush about the roads too much in day time. You know Darling, I think we got very near to the real meaning of Christmas this morning. It had to be stripped of all the rather shallow fripperies that seem so necessary to peacetime Christmases, and we really understood that Christian Peace, born on Christmas Day was won through the Cross. M. Le Patron of our last farm showed me some Roman coins which he had dug up and which he had identified. Some of them were like mine. I've got a large coin about the size of half-a-crown which is of Titus, Emperor from about 60–80 A.D. Remember, he destroyed Jerusalem? I've had quite a lot of practice with my schoolboy French! I can read and understand other people, but am still slow in expressing myself. We've discussed the war, religion and all kinds of deep topics in my travels.

[45 years later a trooper recalls:

'I remember so vividly the Service you took at R.H.Q. Farm at Tally Ho Corner on Christmas Day, 1942, when your prayers brought much hope and consolation to a very young and homesick lad. I also remember your calm and understanding approach when things things became unpleasant.'

Brian Rolph, 25.5.88]

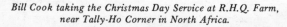

Bill Cook taking the Christmas Day Service at R.H.Q. Farm, near Tally-Ho Corner in North Africa.

1st Derbyshire Yeomanry,
British North African Force.

26.12.42.   St. Stephen's Day

My Dear Dear Heart,

Please note our new address.

William and I have just had our tea — biscuits and hard boiled eggs (bartered from the Arabs for 2½ francs each). We're sitting in the car which is carefully blacked out with blankets and ground sheets, with an inspection lamp burning brightly. We're in a kind of gully with small scrub and prickly bushes round about. The engine cover is fastened to one side of the car with my bed underneath it — a kind of bivouac, and William will sleep in the car. We had to be rather careful about the camouflage tonight as jerry's planes are very inquisitive. So half the car is covered by a camouflage net and the other half by a blanket and a pile of prickly.

Today has been a lovely contrast with the wet days we've been having. It was good to be able to dry blankets and to remove the mud from our boots and to clean them. Last night, Christmas evening, we set out for a distant Squadron in the hopes of holding an Evening Service, but some of the roads were frightful. It was now too late to make our objective, and with the moon rising we reached part of Divisional H.Q. — who were making merry. After wishing them a Merry Christmas and finding out that there is mail for the Division on the way, we set out for a harbour.

This morning the sun was shining and we were in no hurry to be away. We cleaned the car out and repacked it and washed ourselves until we were as clean as new pins. The last part of the operations, including our shaving, was watched by a couple of very friendly Arabs, who stared in amazement at the sight of soap and folding beds, and more than one pair of boots or trousers!

Tomorrow I've got three services in the morning, and I hope to make my way back probably by Monday morning. We shall do the last bit of road as dusk falls. I've said my Office and prepared for the morrow, so I think it is bedtime. Dearest Heart, you are very precious and I love you so much. Be very happy. All is silent, save for an occasional passing

vehicle and the barking of dogs in a distant Arab village.
These huts are made of straw and sticks, and look like hay
stacks, except that they usually smoke in the middle.

COMPO RATIONS

You may like to know a little about our food. It is awfully
good and is called Compo rations. It is packed up in a wooden
box – a 14-man pack. This lasts fourteen men one day or
two men a week! So William and I have the same rations daily
for a week until we pick up another type of box. We have
box X at present. It contains a tin of 6½ lbs. of army biscuits.
This is a huge amount. The biscuits are large and square and
flat and very hard – a mixture between ship and dog biscuits!
We have fourteen 2 oz. bars of chocolate, 12 tins of bully,
2 large tins of Scotch broth, 3 tins of salmon, 3 tins of prem.,
2 tins of carrots, 3 tins of beans, 3 tins of apricots, 1 tin of
apricot jam, a tin of margarine, 3 tins of tea, sugar and milk
powder mixed, 2 tins (60) cigarettes and 2 tins of boiled
sweets, salt, matches and toilet paper. So you see we get a lot
to eat. The other types of pack have different contents.

Sunday after Christmas.

Darling Red Head,

Such news! There is 9½ tons of mail on the way for the
Division. It should arrive by Wednesday or Thursday. I hope
I have 90 with about 70 from you – first mail! I fetched up
with Harry Simmons, the Divisional Postal Officer, this afternoon. We were great friends on the boat and at the transit
camp. He invited me to spend the night with him, rather than
in a field, in a room he's got in a farmhouse. It has got electric
light and a civilised lavatory! I've borrowed his camp bath and
had a good tub. By the way if you should ever see a folding
bath, do buy it for me. [a bit later Helen was to send me the
bath her Father had had at Alamein in the First World War!]

Today has been another unusual one. A Service at a Squadron at 10.00 and then to one a few miles away for 11.30.
I got there at 11.00 just as someone accidentally fired a Verey
pistol into a farmer's large and sole remaining hay stack,
which promptly caught fire. I helped to put it out and about

11.30 when it was all over, with smoke in my eyes and straw all over me, I shouted from the top of the stack 'Now it is your turn to come to my Service!' Great fun! Good old Sgt. Bales – you remember him – the Ordinand and stalwart Anglican – had fixed up a garage for a Celebration, and 21 came which was quite good.

This afternoon I collected another 14-man pack to last William and me a week. This time it is type A and contains 14 tins of steak and kidney pudding and tinned sausages or bacon. Type A is quite a favourite. And so life goes on. It is good to be a Chaplain out here – really it is. And all the time I'm thinking about and getting inspiration from the sweetest girl in all the world. My eyes have been opened since I took to censoring letters. Goodness how much we think of you people at home. The further away the more you mean to us. On second thoughts that may not seem to be too complimentary! Still you know what I mean Dearest!

Tomorrow I've to get up at 6.30 a.m. in order to be at a Squadron a few miles away for a Celebration at 7.30 a.m. Sleep well, Beloved, Your Bill.

WARTIME RELIGION

An Army Chaplain wears an officer's uniform. He has the relative rank of Captain, but his title is The Reverend Joe Bloggs, C.F. It took me a long time to persuade the Derbyshire Yeomanry to cease to address me as Captain. I like to think that my rank did not get in the way of my relationships with the men. It did have the value, however, that the authorities had to take me seriously in my efforts to be a Priestly presence in a military formation.

For most Chaplains the great bogey was the Church Parade, as it was to the men! To march to Church the men had to be spick and span, but to link it up with kit inspection and much parading meant that most men came to church in the wrong frame of mind, and I didn't blame them. A Chaplain really comes into his own during warfare. There were many secret comings and goings among the senior officers. Time and again I would return to Divisional H.Q., on whose strength I really was, and there I would learn a great deal of what was afoot! This was necessary for me in order to make my own plans, especially when warfare was highly mobile. In war the Sunday Church Parade disappears. A Chaplain is always welcome when a battle is on, and he needs to be able to know enough so as to be at the right place at the right time. Therefore I kept an account of my movements and of the services which I had taken. These details had to be sent in monthly to the Senior Chaplain. It will be seen that all days provided opportunities for worship and those opportunities seized were usually the result of being in the picture! Two practical observations may be made:

(i) It was rarely possible or prudent to wear clerical robes.

(ii) A Humber armoured car, a Daimler scout car and a Sherman tank, all had ammunition boxes fastened to the rear of each vehicle. These were just the right size and height to form a simple altar. Among my most treasured possessions are a very heavy pair of brass candlesticks and a large brass crucifix, which were made for me at Christmas by my Sappers during the Tunisian Campaign. The Chaplain has a portable communion set. I still use mine regularly 40 years on for home communions. Not only does it carry the sacred vessels and flagons for water and wine but it has space for books, stole and surplice.

END OF JOURNEY TO AFRICA – A SUMMARY

A few days before Christmas we caught up with the Derby-shire Yeomanry.

Early in November a convoy had assembled with a view to taking control of North Africa. Americans and British were to land at Oran, Casablanca and Algiers. The sixth Armoured Division was to go on further and to land at Bône, the port nearest to Tunis.

With the destruction by the British of much of the French Fleet, and the co-operation with the Germans of the Vichy Government, it was not known how French North Africa would view these landings. Therefore it was felt that the

Americans might be more welcome than the British. So all vehicles were painted with the American white star.

A fortnight before the main landings took place a small mobile force, called Blade Force, landed at Algiers with orders to press on to Tunis, and to seek to deny the whole of the North African coast to the enemy. Italy was full of German supplies, men and airfields, and it was essential that speed and surprise should make it possible for this small force to succeed. It consisted of the 1st Parachute Battalion, B Squadron Derbyshire Yeomanry with armoured cars, a group of 17/21 Lancers Tanks, an Infantry Company of the Rifle Brigade and a Battery of the Royal Horse Artillery. The Derbyshire Yeomanry motored 500 miles to Medjez el Bab, not very far from Tunis, and the rest of Blade Force proceeded to catch up. The enemy had reacted quickly and were soon pouring men and materials the short distances from Sicily and Italy. There was quite a bloody encounter, and a number of Germans were taken prisoner. It is a matter of conjecture whether if British supplies could have been maintained that this little company could have finished the last lap of the journey to Tunis to hold the country.

By the time the new convoys of the First Army had arrived a battle line had been fixed between Medjez el Bab and El Arussa. There were many skirmishes, and an attempt by Rommel, defeated at the battle of the Kasserine Pass, to cut the First Army by driving to Le Kef and on to the coastal bases. The Derbyshire Yeomanry were not to enter Tunis until the beginning of May, though a push to Tunis had been planned for Christmas Day. It was held up by heavy rains, which made roads and the tracks impassable. Historically the cause of the Allies was probably best served by the way in which the matter turned out. Victory in Africa was the first Allied victory of the war, and it meant a loss to the enemy of a quarter of a million troops, together with all their equipment. So, a few days before Christmas, William and I were with the Derbyshire Yeomanry, and more importantly were able to minister among a constantly changing group of fighting units that were rapidly becoming the First Army. By January 13 we had become suffiently established for regulations to have caught up with us. Amongst these I had to send in regular returns to the Senior Chaplain. Accordingly I include a somewhat scrappy diary of my movements between January 13 to March, 1943. For the time being my parish was not the Derbyshire Yeomanry or the Divisional Sappers. It shows that anybody in my vicinity became my spiritual responsibility. It also shows that Sunday had disappeared as a regular day of worship. Instead every day became a Sunday. I no longer wore a cassock and surplice. Services were taken for groups of men, large or small, in the open air, in olive and cactus groves, and very occasionally under a roof.

After the war we were to hold our Thanksgiving services for Victory. For the first time abroad I was able to wear full clerical garb — cassock surplice, chaplain's scarf and my furry hood! It took a long time to get used to wearing such hot and restricting clothing again!

ARNAUD'S FARM

D.Y. Regimental H.Q. was soon established conveniently behind the Front, at La Ferme Cassard, Cassard's Farm. It was a large and prosperous farm with plenty of good standing for vehicles. The Cassards were good Roman Catholics, but they always made me very welcome to take Services and

Bill Cook and his Utility van in Tunisia which clocked-up over 20,000 miles but rarely on a road.

to celebrate the Sacrament in their long large drawing room. They produced spotless linen and joined in the Service.

I cannot remember how William and I discovered a much smaller Farm, La Ferme Arnaud. We may have been on an egg hunt. Monsieur and Madame Octave Arnaud were Protestants, and they always called me Monsieur le Pasteur. The farm lay at the end of a long track that wound between wheat and vines and lentils. Whenever we had time to spare we would return to our retreat. Soon we were to be offered the comforts of a real bed and a bathroom, and a chance to have our laundry well washed. This, I think, was our best war-time friendship. We learned all about their family, part of which was in Tunis, and cut off by the war. As soon as Tunis was freed we were able to reunite the family. After the war we continued to exchange cards and greetings at the Festivals for about eleven years.

There had been a discovery of our farm a little later on by a small unit, but the Arnauds politely said that the farm was reserved for M. le Pasteur!

2nd DIARY – JANUARY TO MARCH 1943 – TUNISIA

It is quite an accident that this bit of diary remains, on small bits of paper in the end sheets of my zipped bible. We had to send in regular reports to our Senior Chaplain of what we had been doing, and where we had been. It does at least give an account of daily movements, and of our extreme mobility. This is a selection of entries.

WED. JAN. 13. Left Derbyshire Yeomanry Regimental H.Q., and visited Bud Porter's Troop, D. Squadron in Divisional Reserve. Arranged a Service, followed by Holy Communion for tomorrow at 4 p.m. to be combined with the Gun Survey men (Corps Troops). Crossed to the farm of an Advanced Dressing Station of the 1st Field Ambulance to find that Chaplain Harry Graydon already was there.

Visited the Corps of Military Police. Next I called on three Troops of 5 Field Squadron, Royal Engineers. One Troop had three men killed, and several others seriously injured, by a

mine exploding yesterday at Medjez el Bab. Then on to
Divisional Artillery A Echelon, Military Police in Testour, and
finally the Mobile Bath Unit.

THURS. JAN. 14. Spent the morning on the Tally Ho corner
to Medjez el Bab. Most unhealthy road! I visited the Ayrshire
Yeomanry, 1st Field Ambulance, A Squadron Derbyshire
Yeomanry, 72 Anti Tank HQ, calling at Lothians and Border
Horse on the way back. Met Andrew Stewart, their Chaplain.
Arranged Holy Communion for Saturday morning. Service
with Porter's Troop, and Gun Survey people, under a hay-
stack. About 50 present – some real harmonists among the
Gunners. Good service.

SAT. JAN. 16. H.C. at 7.30 a.m. Set out, but car got bogged
down. Not freed till 9.0 a.m. Went to 1 Corps Delivery Squadron in Le Kef in the afternoon. Had a good chat about the
world after the war, and the need for a new spirit, as well as
for social planning, with Captain Keith Leslie, D.Y. Commanding. [Hints of the Beveridge Report?!]

SUN. JAN. 17. Most unusually, a large spit and polish parade
for the whole of 1 Corps Delivery Squadron, followed by
Holy Communion. It held men and machines for D.Y., and
for the 26th Armoured Brigade – 16/5 Lancers, 17/21
Lancers, and Lothians and Border Horse.

MON. JAN. 18. Bloody battle at Bou Arada. Six funerals at
sundown at a cemetery I opened at the top of a little wadi.
Lt. John Donne was killed in an armoured car.

TUES. JAN. 19. Recovered John Donne from Djelida railway
station, and Lt. Ted Phillips took him back to a central cemetery at Teboursouk. I spent the day being useful at the 1st
Field Ambulance Advanced Dressing Station. Such a busy
time. 97 casualties came in. [This was the Battle of Longstop
Hill.]

WED. JAN. 20. Buried Cpl. Alton, D.Y. A Squadron, beyond
Bou Arada. He was blown up on mines. Returned to Advanced
Dressing Station. There was little doing. Visited A, C and
R.H.Q. Squadrons on Bou Arada–El Arussa road. Returned
to our farm.

THURS. JAN. 21. Spent morning doing Burial Forms, and writing to the next of kin. Met the Senior Chaplain at the Advanced Dressing Station outside Bou Arada.

SAT. JAN. 23. Quiet day at M.D.S., organised a Chaplain's Rest centre, but Chaplains won't play! Arranged services at Main Dressing Station, D.Y., H.Q. Squadron, Rear Division, and A Squadron D.Y. Pottered about M.D.S. quite a lot.

SUN. JAN. 24. Services at H.Q. Squadron D.Y., and A Echelon Farm D.Y. at 9.15 a.m., 11.00 a.m. at A Squadron D.Y., 11.30 a.m. H.C. Spent afternoon and evening at hospital.

MON. JAN. 25. H.C. D.Y. Farm at 7.30 a.m. 4 present. Breakfast afterwards. Got eggs, butter and flowers for Main Dressing Station. Two funerals at 2 p.m. and 5 p.m. A fellow chaplain turned up in the evening. He had had enough, and was very jittery. I bedded him down.

TUES. JAN. 26. He went to find the Senior Chaplain, who sent him back at lunchtime till things got sorted out. Two funerals at 2.0 p.m.

WED. JAN. 27. Visited R.E.M.E. sections on the El Arussa Road in the morning. Called on D.Y. D. Squadron, and H.Q. Royal Artillery, and arranged service for 3.0 p.m. Arrived at R.H.Q. at teatime.

THURS. JAN. 28. Well attended service at D.Y. R.H.Q. at 9.30. Lunch at D. Squadron. 3.0 service well attended by D.Y., but no Gunners came, though it had been advertised in R.A. Orders the previous night.

FRI. JAN. 29. Visited D.Y. C Squadron doing an anti-parachutist role on the El Arussa – Bou Arada road. Service at Divisional H.Q. at 11.0 a.m. Bad feeling to begin with as some of the men had been press-ganged, and made to stay up after guard duty all night. We all enjoyed ourselves in the end! Afternoon service with D.Y. C Squadron, Glover's Troop, and a Troop of Light Ack. Ack. Gunners at the same farm at 3.0 p.m. Called on C. Squadron H.Q. to arrange service at 12.30 tomorrow. Bought organges in El Arussa for R.H.Q. where I spent the night.

SAT. JAN. 30. Morning with C Squadron. Good service at 12.0 noon. came to A Echelon in the afternoon.

SUN. JAN. 31. Best service ever with D.Y., B Echelon. We even had our Jewish Equipment Repairer! A Echelon at 11.0 good turn up. My talk was a bit flat. H.C. with 12 communicants at 11.30.

MON. FEB. 1. With A Echelon in the morning. Took the rest of the day off — writing letters and sleeping in the sun. Sent my returns to the Senior Chaplain.

TUES. FEB. 2. Visited D.Y., A Echelon in the morning. Went to El Arussa, and up the Mejez road to visit 8 Field Squadron R.E. Two Troops were moving in so I went on to Spitfire Farm with 2 Troops of D.Y. D. Squadron. Also there was B Echelon of the Northants. At teatime we were all forcibly ejected by 78th Div. Recce Regiment, who claimed it as their area. So we moved off, and spent the night by the road side, on the way back to El Arussa.

WED. FEB. 3. Unsuccessfully sought for R.Es who seem to have disappeared. Went to D.Y. R.H.Q. to find that R.H.Q. plus 2 Squadrons were going deep south to American 2 Corps, south west of Tebessa. It seemed that my Sappers had done the same! Decided to follow them, but had to get permission of S.C.F. first. I found him at Gafour, but he would not let me go yet as everything is so fluid.

THURS. FEB. 4. Teboursouk. Spent the day going round. Fixed up service at 1 Field Ambulance A.D.S. for 7.0 this evening. Also service at 16/5 Lancers and 17/21 Lancers, 2 Lothians and Border Horse tomorrow, also H.Q. Squadron Divisional Headquarters.

FRI. FEB. 5. Morning of services. Rather flat one at H.Q. Squadron at 9.0 a.m. Excellent one with 16/5 and 17/21 B Echelon at 10.0 a.m. and Lothians and Border Horse at 11.0.

SAT. FEB. 6. Went to Le Kef for a new battery, as the old one leaked. Had lunch at 1 Corps Delivery Squadron.

SUN. FEB. 7. Very large service for part of C. Squadron, and B Echelon, D.Y. at 10.00 a.m. followed by H.C. in houses.

WED. FEB. 10. H.C. at 7.15 a.m. with R.E's. 3 attended. Too early! Pioneers were unable to find the place. Morning service at 8.30 a.m. Good one. Met Deputy Chaplain General, and Deputy Assistant Chaplain General, at H.Q. Royal Artillery at 10.00 a.m. Came back to farm, having fixed up services with C Squadron and Gun Battery.

THURS. FEB. 11. Snowed and rained. Services cancelled.

SUN. FEB. 14. Went round observation posts for Djebel Mansour, a fearsome wooded hill held by Jerry Parachute men, with Major Wesley Watson. [He was later on to be the first Squadron Leader to be killed.] Evening services arranged for 8.00 p.m.

MON. FEB. 15. At Main Dressing Station. I was allowed to witness a few routine operations by the Field Surgical Unit. Earlier on I had stood up fairly well to helping with wounded men, but to see a red streak open up when a nice white tummy was cut by a scalpel for an appendix operation nearly made me have to go outside!

TUES. FEB. 16. Returns sent into the Senior Chaplain. I saw him today at the M.D.S. We are about to go south to the Battle of the Kasserine Pass.

WED. FEB. 17. Went with Bob Martin (Padre 17/21 Lancers) from Gafour down to Maktar, where we had lunch. Continued across the mountains to the Main Dressing Station at Ebba Ksour, and spent the night there.

[This was the time when Rommel and his men were withdrawing north and tried to cut the 1st Army off by a thrust to the North African coast. The 26th Armoured Brigade Regiments were all in Algiers taking over their new Sherman tanks, equipped with 75 mm. guns. When the Germans struck on Feb. 17 they captured Gafsa, threw the Americans back in confusion from the Kasserine Pass, and it was too late to take the tanks, so they rushed back and went into battle with their old Valentine tanks with tiny two pounder guns. There were many casualties and much bravery. A newly arrived battery of secret 6 pounder anti-tank guns had arrived, and they helped save the day, by shooting at the soft bellies of enemy tanks as they came up and over the final slope at point-blank range.]

THURS. FEB. 18. Battle of Kasserine Pass. We came along a valley strewn with thousands of tins of American Field Rations, litter, and abandoned tanks and half tracks.

SAT. FEB. 20. Battle hotting up. Main Dressing Station became fully operative. In the morning I visited the Americans and Military Police who were trying to sort out as much movement of transport – 9th Tank Transporters who had made long journeys to get their tanks into action – 26th Armoured Brigade H.Q. where I got put in the picture. Visited Brigade, saw Bob Martin and arranged services for tomorrow.

SUN. FEB. 21. Busy day at Main Dressing Station. Battle at its height. Services cancelled. Two funerals in the morning.

MON. FEB. 22. Busy day and night at M.D.S. at Thala. It was bombed, although marked by red crosses on the roof, and in the playground of the school we were using. One man died in my arms. Many were hurt, 5 casualties evacuated further behind. My car had its windows blown out, and shrapnel through the door, which William had just vacated. I pointed out that the blast had moved the large blocks of concrete of which the building was made, and so we moved out into the fields.

TUES. FEB. 23. Had a good night's rest and an easy morning.

THURS. FEB. 25. Bath in the morning. Visited the battlefield in the afternoon with the grave party.

FRI. FEB. 26. We are still camping out in the fields. During the night Arabs stole some of our kit – woollies, shaving kit, hairbrush, my Roman coins and my Saxone red shoes from Kilmarnock. William was sleeping in the car, and had his battle dress top taken off his toes while he slept. After lunch we came north, as Jerry had been contained, and returned to our own sphere of action. We spent the night at the Arnauds farm.

SUN. FEB. 28. Burial at Gafour at 10.00 a.m. Service at 11.00 a.m.

MON. MARCH 1 – FRI. MARCH 6. Visited A and C Squadrons D.Y. Had car patched up, doors glazed and holes welded

up at 38th workshops R.A.S.C. and 144 Field Park Squadron
R.E. who finished the job off. They made the handle work!
On Friday afternoon William and I buried a German we found
sprawled out of a burned out half-tracked Armoured car,
near Steamroller farm on the El Arussa—Medjez el Bab road.
It was hard work as the ground was so hard and rocky.
Along the road I found a Troop of A Squadron D.Y. and
asked for some help in this particular bit of grave-digging in
the very hard ground. The young Troop Officer who was
later to play a gallant role in the fall of Tunis, flatly refused
on the grounds that it would be bad for his men's morale.
I let this pass, sadly, and William and I completed the task.

SUN. MARCH 7. Very good service for the Squadron at
8.45 a.m. 10 stayed on afterwards for Communion at 9.15.

So ends my diary from Jan. 13 to March 7.

The following is taken from a scrap of paper which contained instructions on how to find a group of Sappers:

> 'Last house on the left. Turn sharp left. Follow the track
> for about two miles, cross wadi with water. Follow
> straight on to three burned out vehicles on the track.
> After the third come to a well defined cross track. Go
> straight over, follow four miles on to the main road.
> (N.B. There is a track before, which is not well defined,
> go over it!) Turn right, across water. Down to the farm
> in the almond bushes on the right!'

I cannot remember the sequel.

Diss Rectory.

23.1.43.

My Dear Bill,

*Your Christmastime letters are here and are a very great
joy, also we had great fun looking at the Roman pottery, we
were able to have a dissertation on the five foolish virgins and
their lamps. I have read a lot of your Christmas letters to Dad
and the Burlinghams (the descriptive parts!). You give us a
very good idea of the way you live. It must be difficult to*

pass on a picture of your life without saying dangerous things. You manage marvellously.

This town is now known to the Daily Mail *readers as 'The Tom Thumb town with an outsize heart'. At the canteen we had a reporter and the next day a long article appeared about 'Little Mrs. N. and Buxom Mrs. S. Etc!' The hospitality the folk have given to Tommys seems to be outstanding.*

If we can't get you anything to tub in we will see about Dad's old one — It cruised the Middle East during the last war and found its way to Egypt, El Alamein and other places, so it can't be as good as new but might provide a puddle for you to sit in.

I expect you have read Dorothy Sayers Greatest Drama . . . but I'll send it in the bath in case it might prove useful at Eastertime. Don't bother to cart round and keep books if I find any to send you. Diss people miss your 'Are you happy?' greeting.

The High School,
Ipswich

30.1.43.

10.30 p.m.   Fire watching.

Hello my Love, just a good night line to say I love you and a big 'thank you' for NINE letters I had this morning, the last of which was dated Jan. 8th. You had arrived back after your trip to Base camp. These French on the farms must be a great comfort to you. I am sad you have only had two letters from me, I wonder if you will get the bath we sent last weekend. Letters take three weeks from you to us and parcels probably take much longer. We went to see Mrs. Miniver *this afternoon. There was a long queue; we got in after half an hour and saw the main film. It was very good.*

Sunday. How very encouraging it is to know how responsive the folk seem to be to your work — you live your work so much, it is part of you, isn't it. The Burlinghams have given me a lovely casserole for my birthday — we'll 'ave 'ot pot, and you can eat the onions, but you will have to grow them first.

People are talking about post-war homes. No new furniture is being made except Utility, and you need a permit to get

*that. If you see Madame again please thank her for the violets
which travelled very well and kept their colour. It was a sweet
idea. We think those French folk very brave to carry on working on their farms near the front and keeping life going with
Jerry just over the way. God bless them. Please thank them
from us for showing you such kindness, we love them for it.
All my love, Your Helen.*

A.R.P. Shelter, School.

3.3.43.   9.30 p.m.

*My Dearest, this week has brought letters from you Jan. 25—
Feb. 7th. News of mimosa, Services, house and YOU. Thank
you for all the details — they may seem dull to write, but
they add the necessary colour to the picture we are building
up of your lives out in the line.*

*The Home Front is wide awake tonight. Our Bombers have
been over German territory non-stop for four days and nights.
Last night Berlin had the biggest raid it has ever had. Tonight
Jerry is evidently trying to make an impression on us.*

*10.30. The all-clear went some time ago, and we have had
our sandwich supper. Before the siren went we roasted
apples . . . delicious. Funny life, this — you tell me when you
have a proper meal and I tell you when I have a picnic! Two
more letters from you today.*

Good night my great joy.

*Thursday 5.30. They didn't do much damage last night —
dropped a few bombs in a field, trying to do something to tell
about at home!*

London.

16.4.43.   Friday.

My dear Bill,

*I have spent the afternoon with William's wife and Brian,
in their home in Tottenham. Brian is the image of his Dad,
and is a very cheery little lad. He had been quite poorly but
is better now, and I hope William has had good news of him.
Both he and Mrs. look very well. She gave me a marvellous
tea! I did enjoy my visit . . .*

A CHANGE?

20.3.43.

Darling Brown Eyes,

Its a lovely African day and spring time everywhere. I've been over to see the Boss who asked me if I'd like a change. Our Divisional Guards Brigade will be needing another chaplain shortly but though I do get fed up with the D.Y. sometimes I expect I'd get fed up with other people too! I fear that a chaplain usually faces the dilemma of living permanently as a Priest. Often things work out well enough, especially when we are all united in battle, but sometimes we do seem to be like fishes out of water. Could it not be that if a Priest is sensitive, and not always a conformist, he must always live in a tension. Anyway we've been together for three years, and I know so many men so intimately that it would be wrong to change now.

I enclose a picture of the Fig Market in Kairouan. After Mecca I suppose Kairouan is the second holiest city. The parents of Mahomed are buried here. Some of us climbed up to the top of the minaret of the Great Mosque for a view. One of our Ambulance Doctors produced a pencil to write his name 'Os Williams' on the parapet. I gave him a rather sad look and said, 'Oh Ossy', and he desisted! I would love to have bought you a small carpet or a prayer mat, but they are far too costly. Love and kisses, Bill.

PREPARING FOR THE END OF
NAZIDOM AND FASCISM IN AFRICA

In the middle of April, the Division disappeared from the scene. We had in fact gone up into the hills and away from the flies and gnats. The Division was preparing for a break out through the Infantry to capture Tunis, and to deal a final blow to the enemy.

Once my bedding soaked in the sun all day, laid over a clump of cactus bushes. In the evening when I made my bed up I had the hottest night of my life! There was a real air of anticipation that this was a moment of history, and I found all my men in good spirits.

20.4.43.

We went into khaki shorts last night. They were too long and shapeless so I chopped off bits of the legs. In fact I've two pairs of marvellous Jerry shorts. They seem to be properly tailored and full of straps and little pockets. One is a bit dark – olive green rather than khaki. The other is much lighter. It's moonlight and I'm writing this in a blacked-out car. Outside the air is alive with the croaking of crickets, and lots of non-entomological sounds as well! William was thrilled to get lots of pictures of his little son. He's gone off to display them.

WEDNESDAY IN HOLY WEEK – LUNCHTIME

21.4.43.

I got in a service this morning, and I've been round the men and fixed up another for this afternoon. Nobody worries about the rain because we dry out so quickly. Things are brewing up in these parts. I mustn't say more except that the 8th Army started their new offensive yesterday morning. You probably heard it on the wireless.

Derbyshire Yeomanry Armour in North Africa.
In front a Daimler Scout Car and behind a Humber Armoured Car
with 2-pounder gun.

21.4.43.

We are on the move again. We had to collect 3 days rations and pack up our tent and belongings to move to the Main Dressing Station, Light Field Ambulance. It was dark and the moon was obscured by a cloudy sky, so we had to grope about to find a pitch for the car and tent on a rocky hillside. And all the time there were two letters from my Sweetie burning my pocket, waiting to be read – yours of March 17 and 21. Goodness, how lovely it is to have paper that has actually been in your hands.

How about the business of getting married? If we should come home as soon as the North African Campaign is over, which seems unlikely, I'll probably say 'Will you marry me now please?' And you'll say 'No'. And it will be the right answer again. Of course it was right not to get spliced before I came away. Perhaps my mad impulse was just a new way of saying I love you utterly. You see all my life and hopes – all the things I hold dear and strive for are bound up in your loveliness. And so to belong together completely, or as completely as possible in war time is just a way of being more completely bound up with one's Love and Inspiration. No! I'll probably say, 'Will you marry me?' – long before it's really time. Men arn't very logical creatures. Then it will need your farsightedness to say 'Not just yet'. And in the meantime I'll have my memories and inspirations to keep me going. I always remember how you looked that time I landed in St. Pancras in a half-boiled state, and you looked sweet and cool, as fresh as a daisy. Oh, about time. Time out here is the same as English Summer time. At present you are on double summer time, so the 9 p.m. news comes to us at 8 p.m. – comprenez? The old 10.30 time is at 9.30 with us. Is it still the best time for our Tryst?

Maundy Thursday.

Good morning my Sweet. William seemed rather sleepy last night, so I went to bed with this letter unfinished. Darling you'd love to be here for this spring weather. We had a thunderstorm in the night. Quite a lot of the noise was thunder [Some was the guns starting up for the Battle of the Goubellat Plain] but it is warm and fresh again now. The fields are simply ablaze with colour. Some fields are red with poppies, and some are all colours. Two days ago we went into tropical kit – very cool and sensible. A Field Surgical Team has come to the Hospital. They do a great work, these surgeons. Everything that they need is packed up into army lorries and in an hour or two they can set up and do the most intricate operations.

Here's to the Great Day, my Darling. We'll vow our Vows and I'll put a ring on your finger and then you'll be my Mrs. What fun to say 'Meet the Mrs.'. Darling Dearest child always I love you.

24.4.43.   Holy Saturday.

We did have a Good Friday Service after all. About 7.0 p.m. quite a number of the Ambulance laddies gathered in the corn and we had a very moving service. All these things seem to be happening in cornfields and poppies, and I'm sure that the message of the Love of God on the first Good Friday just fitted in with this present tragedy. But I'm deeply happy, my Dearest, because I hold on to the love of God with both hands, and because I've got you to love.

29.4.43.   Easter Day.

Happy Easter, My Darling. May the strength and hope and joy of the Son of God rise anew in your heart. Perhaps next Easter I'll be able to buy you a chocolate Easter egg. Its half past nine and a lovely morning. With a bit of luck I'll be able to get an Easter Service with the Ambulance, but it depends on how busy they are. Yes, my Darling, there are countless heroisms here again, and slowly Jerry is being compressed into one tiny corner of Tunisia.

Easter Tuesday, 1943.

Dearest Woman,

Sometimes it's a jolly good thing to live in a world of dreams. There are hatched the noble things that make this world become more noble. Anyway somewhere in that world, where we all are at our best, menfolk dream of THE GIRL. Yes, I dreamed, dreamed often. She was wonderful and sweet and marvellous. I tried to read her into the girls I knew, or came across, but never was it any use. Came the Great Day and I met her. Goodness it was a wonderful thing, that first meeting. There was no fitting or comparing – the two were just one. But I had dreamed so highly and wonderfully, as one is able in dreamland, that my longings seemed as though they would never be satisfied. The great wonder and thrill of my life has been that she has become mine. And every day I'm full of wonder and love. Wherever I go she goes with me – soon we're hoping to be together always, and then life will be complete. By the way, she's wee and brown-eyed, she's got red hair and dimples. Dearest Beloved I didn't really have to write this did I? You do know it already, don't you?

Perhaps I'd better give you the news that you will get later on in the sea mail. It is lovely warm weather. Cool nights and wonderful days. The heat is quite pleasant 'cos we're suitably clad. For the last few days, William and I have been part of a Field Ambulance. There are many excitements and sadnesses, and many great heroisms. We had tea with the Arnauds (at our farm at Le Krib) about a week ago, and they were cutting the hay. Their vines had been frosted and I'm afraid most of them were spoiled, also one of the mimosa trees had been blown down in a gale – otherwise all was well. Here we are in a cornfield with ambulance and dressing rooms all around. Two laddies are bathing themselves in the corn by their vehicles, but as there aren't any ladies about, not even Arab ones, nobody's propriety is outraged.

I've been wondering whether you understand what I mean when I talk about this Ambulance. An ambulance is one vehicle marked all over with Red Crosses – but the Field Ambulance is a larger affair with a large Main Dressing Station, with several Doctors, a Dentist, and lots of day and night staff. Then it has quite a few A.D.S. (Advanced Dressing Stations) each with staff and Doctor. So there are lots of Doctors, orderlies, drivers and ambulances in the whole concern. The circle is gradually narrowing down round Jerry out here. We get the short wave wireless news. William found a tortoise about 4 inches long under the car and he's playing with him. I don't know whether he intends to adopt him or not! There are quite a few in these parts. Dearest Helen, I love you terribly. You make me so happy. God bless you always. Your very own Bill.

28.4.43.   Easter Wednesday.

We are in rest and I've gone over to the D.Y. to see how they are. When we got back we were covered with dust from head to foot. Anyway we cleaned the car out, and then had a bath in a basin of water in the sunshine. The Regiment has been extremely bold and busy. There was a great pile of mail waiting for us. I've only had time to read mine through 1½ times, so there's bliss in store. At home they're having a 'Wings for Victory' week and I'm sending a cheque for £70 to buy certificates. I've saved it all out here, maybe more.

29.4.42.   Easter Thursday.

William and I are taking the day off, writing letters, darning socks and being lazy. I've just put you in a new frame – the Sun Dial and the Ipswich picture, back to back, bound in a

Leatherbound Inspiration.
One of the pairs of leatherbound pictures of Helen that Bill carried in his pocket during his six years of service.

bit of leather which William picked up on a mountain top near Kairouan. I've wallowed in your latest letters. So you have a Guards Chaplain and his batman at the Rectory. I'm glad the new one has a Missis!

Lunchtime. Someone produced some lettuce, but the medical people are so careful about disease that it tasted too strongly of Chlorine to eat! However they rinsed it again and I think it's alright.

The Ambulance is having an open air concert between tea and dusk tonight. The star will be one of our Doctors. He is a concert in himself. Really he is at home with Handel, Purcell and Bach, and is a pupil of Sir Henry Wood. He has a habit of singing a lovely song and then switching to the filthiest songs and tales I've ever met, to the accompaniment of his mandolin. He's such a contrast. Still we've got the saint and sinner inside us and its the grace of God that keeps us from living in the cellar.

1.5.43. (A week after Easter).

We are out of things for a day or two, and I'm getting some Easter Services in. We are overlooking the Goubellat Plain. I've a feeling that history will be made here. There are lots of tortoises, a great big one on this slope, bugs, beetles and giant aphids. But give me an English meadow! Doc. found a tarantula in the mess the other day, rather like a crab with a sting in his tail. They put him to sleep with an overdose of morphia, and he shrivelled up, poor chap.

Evening. We're sitting in the car in the blackout. Last night we held an Easter Service with a Squadron that was still in action. It's gone cold tonight and we are pleased to be cooking in the car. There's a tin of bully, a tin of American hash and a large tin of whole carrots, all warmed up. This morning we had an Easter Service and Communion in a cactus grove, and this evening in a cornfield. Easter hymns have seemed very appropriate this year. We've had services in all sorts of places. Fortunately its not so wet and showery as in England, so my men haven't often had their spirits damped!

Tomorrow we're hoping to do a spot of washing. I want to boil some altar linen and purificators. I miss Mme. Arnaud for the altar linen. Many of the front line troops dip their clothes in petrol, with quite good results, when they haven't time for anything else. The Quartermaster gave me two toothbrushes today — one English, the other American. Easter Day was a very warring day and very few chances for me to mark it.

3.5.43.

For breakfast powdery egg and very good bacon and marmalade. Then we had a session of censoring a huge pile of letters which inspired me to write to my Beloved. We're at the Main Dressing Station and still resting. [I think this was a happy way of saying 'waiting for things to happen!']

5.5.43.

Yet another of those waiting expectantly days. I've already scribbled you a couple of very short letters and practically finished a book called *Young Ames*. Its a good exercise to write letters when you can't give any news. Instead one can describe the scenery, or, most of all, one can attempt to write of love of the Beloved. Poor folk in the old days when they had a hundred years war, or a thirty years war. I pity your poor father being away from home for 3 or 4 years in the last war. Come to think of it I suppose this could be our fate too! I changed pants, shirt, socks and a hanky and washed the old ones which are almost dry. I don't think we'll have chance for any more washing for a few days.

165 Brunswick Road,
Ipswich.

5.5.43.   Wednesday.

My Dear Billy,

Thank you for your Palm Sunday letter. Darling, a dog-collar sounds very hot — couldn't you devise some system of tying it on to your person somewhere to avoid having to have it round your neck? The lamp is wonderful and the vase also arrived in a complete condition thanks to the bandaging and dressings! I'm fire watching now at the High School. I get

*time to write 'on duty'! It has been a busy evening, because
we decided to go on a thorough tour of the premises – up
ladders and through trap doors and along the roof. This
afternoon we took a lot of junk up into the loft in readiness
to clean out the shed where we do clay later in the term.
Then we had stirrup pump practice, and we had to be careful
to spot the 'fires' in places where the cabbages needed
watering! When we went for fire-fighting practice in an old
school in the town, we had to don navy boiler suits. They
were all enormous – I climbed into one, rolling up the
trousers, and spent a long time floundering about inside trying
to find my hands up the sleeves! We took it in turns – one
manned the tap whence a long hose snaked across a yard
where an iron bedstead was piled with dry bracken and
gorse; the other waited for the pile to be lit then shouted
'water on' . . . 'water off', as applicable. It was quite a feat
to avoid getting soaked plodding about feeling like the
sorcerer's apprentice! Our caretaker is in hospital with
appendicitis, so we won't get any help in the odd job line for
some time.*

*It is interesting to know what a difference a dog-collar
makes – the tragedy is that in parts of the country it has the
opposite effect . . . of course it depends who wears it. I think
the music in the stubble field sounds lovely; which reminds
me I've promised Mrs. Weigal, wife of the Guards Chaplain,
that she shall learn my recorder so we can have duets. Both
recorders are in good condition but I don't seem to tootle
much – just enough to keep them aired.*

*I've been living too much in the past and future – something
happened to make me feel the joyfulness of the present
lately – perhaps the Spring making me realise all the more
fully how terrific it is to be in love with YOU. Anyway
darling, life can never be purposeless. Of course we'd be
pretty hard kinds of folk if we didn't feel a bit achey inside
sometimes when we think of our other half far away, but we
know it's all for the best really and God's everlasting arms
are underneath. Life wouldn't be possible without knowing
that, and it would be impossible to go on living if we hadn't
this love. Good night, I love you always with everything,
darling.*

Thursday. 8.30 p.m.

Darling, I've been reading umpteen letters April 8 – 13 sort of time. You are wonderful the way you write so much and such lovely long letters. Dear Heart, I can't tell you how terribly much I love you and need you. Darling, I am so tremendously thankful that you are just as you are. I wouldn't have you one whisker different except perhaps to have you in another part of the world. Goodness how we long for you to be back, not so much out of the struggle as for this mess to be over. It's all so mad and babyish – this business of bashing our brothers. But you don't know what great things you are doing. I expect you won't ever know. Sometimes, my dear, I wonder if it would help you more now if we had gone the whole way and married. I suppose it's no use at all wondering now and of course there is always the possibility that, had your dreams materialised, you might be very disappointed!!! God bless you my Precious. Dearest Love. Your Helen.

NEWS BLACKOUT DAYS

6.5.43.

Good morning my sweet. Its a quarter to nine, and it seems like teatime. We were up at 4.0 a.m. We're waiting in convoy, and I'm shelling and eating ears of wheat and barley. We're very fit and well. The news I'd like to send you will probably be coming to you via the wireless.

7.5.43.

Excuse this Jerry Field card. I don't know what our postal authorities will think of it. We're much too busy catching tadpoles and other small fry to be able to write long letters. But I love you always.

8.5.43.

Progress with the mail today! We happened to run into the D.Y. bit of the convoy that had the postman, so William climbed up into the lorry and helped to sort the letters while I followed in the car!

6

African Victory — May 1943

9.5.43.   *Diss Rectory.*

Beloved Man,

At last we know where you are! How splendid to be in Tunis. It was like the father when his son came home — 'lost and found again'. You weren't lost, but now we find you in Tunis, and this is a sign of success — a triumph — after so much slogging. No wonder we feel so Whoopee inside. Goodness knows there have been set-backs to suffer but we British have a way of making triumphal successes out of defeats — like Dunkirk. What a tremendous achievement it was when all the little river craft crowded the waterways and bobbed out to sea to rescue battered, waiting men from bombarded beaches. I had a child in my 'School Practice' class who announced, round-tummied with pride, 'My Dad was at Dunkirk'.

But this is a straight Victory, and we must not be so British that we miss out on celebrating worthily . . . oh yes the bells are ringing. Well done the Lads! Your 'Central Mediterranean Force' address led us to believe you were probably in the North African mêlée before you wrote about the sand.

With all my love, your proud, walking tall (!) little Helen.

A VICTORY AIRMAIL

10.5.43.

Hello My Darling,

I've scribbled lots of victory tweedles for the ordinary post but here is a fleeter messenger to say — please my darling, I'm very well and I love you utterly. Yes, we've collared all the Jerries now. They're crammed in prison camps hastily prepared. They've left guns, vehicles and equipment galore all over the place. I expect you will have a better idea of the whole picture than we have out here 'cos we don't get the wireless very often. William and I went into Tunis on the following morning and it was a great sight to behold. All the French were beginning to realise that they were free again. And so they were cramming the streets, shouting, and throwing flowers. We found the abode of the Arnaud's family and I gave them reassuring messages from home. They were very relieved.

After Tunis our people had to keep driving on 'cos Jerry insisted on fighting to the end. So now we're down by a wonderful bit of blue Mediterranean with millionaires' houses everywhere at Hammamet on the Cap Bon Peninsula. It is perfect for swimming. I wish you could be here.

Yesterday we went back on a flying visit to the Arnauds. It was a long journey, and it was very late when we got back.

Some of the 20,000 prisoners at the Grombalia P.O.W. cage.

On the way there we went to collect the children (in Tunis) but found they had been taken the day before. The husband, in the Free French Air Force, had called and we found them all at the farm. It was great fun. Coming home we brought four evacuees back to Tunis. It was an awful journey. The car was crowded with our own kit plus perambulators and cases galore — as well as an elderly mother with one married daughter and her two months' old baby and another daughter of about twelve. And, of course, you know that daughters of twelve are always sick on such journeys!

Then we lost the way, and finally arrived in Tunis long after dark. As we came down the street some of the houses were mere shells, and there was great trepidation as to the fate of their own flat. Fortunately it was standing, though the next door ones were not. At any rate all ended well, and we did our good turn. Always you are in my heart. I dream of you eternally. Be happy, my Sweet, you're such an inspiration. My love to everyone. Your Bill.

FALL OF TUNIS

10.5.43.   4.15 p.m.

Hallo Darling,

After all these recent days of silence we've so much to say. Tunis has fallen. We've taken lots of prisoners of all varieties, and lots of loot. Jerry is making a final stand in the Cap Bon Peninsula, and our people are gradually collecting him in.

Sorry! We're starting off again! This Campaign is nearly over — our first real victory of the war. D.Y. entered Tunis first in close competition with the 11th Hussars, our Colonel's old Regiment. They are the Reconnaissance of the 7th Armoured Div. 8th Army, Desert Rats. William and I went in next morning early and there were wild excited happy crowds everywhere — cheering wildly whenever a British truck came along. They threw flowers into the car and tried to hug us. Whenever the crowd was particularly dense so that we had to stop altogether the car seemed to fill as if by magic with small boys, each intent on getting a souvenir!

We fulfilled our promise to the Arnauds. We found the address of their son and daughter and told them all was well at home. Since then we've been in a couple of times, once to scrounge enemy cars, and once to exchange some wounded from various hospitals.

Are these things any use? The towels are linen I think. The synthetic ground sheet is something new. [It was about 6 feet square and very thin black plastic. The British Army issue was still a gas cape, which served as waterproof sheet and raincoat. Jerry had been preparing for war so long and their equipment was mostly in advance of ours. This was the first plastic which I had met, and with which we are all now so familiar.]

TUNISIAN VICTORY

165 Brunswick Road,
Ipswich.

10.5.43.

There seems to be an extra happiness about these days, knowing that the great works are being completed. Today has been a super day at school. It's been a wet, windy day, but the kiddies were splendid. They must know these are very special days, bless them. Your letters seem to come through very quickly – fancy your parcels arriving after three weeks.

What a wonderful world this is. And over on one side of it is the loveliest Being, and he's sort of all mixed up with me, and it's all so terribly exciting and happifying. I think I'll go to bed and scribble some more.

10.15 p.m. The world has gone gloriously topsy-turvy since Saturday's news. Perhaps the greatest part of your job is now. I can see you will have lots to do, sorting out after settling down, and getting people to rejoice sanely, and to keep up their hearts for the next push, wherever it may lead.

THE WHITE HOUSE OF TUNISIA

13.5.43.

Darling Appleblossom,

What a pity you can't be here. You'd love it. Last night we arrived at a lovely house on the shores of the Mediterranean in Hammamet Bay. The house is called the White House of

Tunisia and is the poshest in the country, belonging to a millionaire. It has swimming baths and mirrored rooms, and water flowing down the passages, and palms. Just at the bottom of the garden is the barbed wire and minefield, and then the bluest, warmest and saltiest sea imaginable. Last night at sunset there were all the hues, colours and surroundings that one sees in a technicolour film. This morning I had a bathe, and a laze on the white sand beach. This is apparently the house where the Duke of Windsor and Mrs. Simpson dallied. The Germans and Italians have been manning the coast here, and some of the homes are looted, some are alright. What a waste war is. Jerry is fighting to the end, and one by one the Divisions have been giving in.

There are some D.Ys. a bit further down the beach and R.H.Q. is near. So I must go and see them. The sea is a deep emerald and the bay lies round us in a sweeping curve. This morning a few shells burst a bit further round as the last bit of Jerry's Afrika Korps is roped in. I don't think he's got much more punch left in him. Time to swim. Blue Mediterranean sends his deepest blue twinkles. God bless you my sweet, your Bill.

15.5.43.

It will soon be lunchtime, and we've been wandering round the Squadrons. They've had a very good battle and taken much booty. At one place they captured a German Naafi store. William was given 300 razor blades, so we shouldn't be short for a long time! I promise not to thrust all this Itie Army paper with all its propaganda at top and bottom upon you all the time, but the idea of using it amuses me no end! I picked up quite a lot of it, particularly airmail envelopes in one or two Itie Officers' messes, which had just been deserted. I also took a wireless set, a tiny one.

2.00 p.m. Lunch is over and I'm going round the men again. I've just been presented with a large bottle of 4711 Eau de Cologne hairwash from the Jerry Naafi. Sea looks blue and has tiny white horses. When I've seen the men I'll have a swim. We've still got one of the Tunis flowers stuck in the windscreen and a deep red carnation from the Arnaud's garden.

Evening.

Hallo My Dear, There are tadpoles here! Real ones! I found them in a little pit that still contained water in a lily pond that had been allowed to dry up in one of those lovely villas that Jerry has been living in. Two of your airmails, and one from my folk. Our diet is getting very varied. We've just got a tin of spaghetti and tomato a l'Italien! We don't worry about any cooking problems. It's all out of tins here! Tomorrow, for a change, there's quite a round of services, which is a good thing. Soon the sun will be going down. I'm sitting on a grassy dune overlooking the sea – and away behind me the sun is setting in all its colours. Sweetheart, I love you.

VICTORY GUILT

15.5.43.   Very late.

Darling Appleblossom,

I seem to have written a lot of silly and bellicose letters in a very exultant strain lately. I hope you won't be cross at all these Jerry and Italian field post cards and things I've sent you. Please, I don't like war really. I didn't even want to cheer when the last Jerry laid down his arms. There was too much loss and waste and foolishness about the whole thing. No! This war came out of human sin, greed and hatred, and it was necessary, to my way of thinking, to join sides and to fight for what we believe in. But please don't think I'll ever become a fire-eater. True and deep and victorious life must ever lie in that deep harmony of triumphant love. Your kisses and your love and sweetness – your joy and strength and beauty – the love and fellowship that we have in God – these will always be the real things. So my Darling you see that your sweet love will always mean more to me than these excitements and strange horizons. The great day was not when Tunis became ours – nor when Victory shall be ours – the great day was when I met and fell in love with the sweetest girl in all the world.

16.5.43.

Lovely day, but too many flies! Some look just like ordinary house flies but bite through one's stockings round the ankle. Ankles don't have hairs and I suppose the skin is soft. The safest way is to roll one's stockings down over the ankle. The flies get lost in the forest of hair further up and don't have chance of a meal!

Doc. and I are living together at present, and we're sharing the work of cooking. William is very pally with Doc's driver. For lunch we're going to have a tin of German bully beef. Its a very good change from our own; more juicy and rather like boiled beef, when you have boiled beef and carrots!

One of the problems of life these recent days has been all pervading dust! I've been cleaning the car out this morning and came across this diary which I started so well. It was hidden at the back of a pocket so that Jerry wouldn't see it if he captured the car. We're now allowed to talk about the places we've visited, so its a pity I didn't keep it going.

17.5.43.

My Darling,

I've just been given the booty I've always been hoping to get — a pair of Jerry field glasses. They're light and small and the experts tell me quite good ones.

It is now possible to talk about the campaign, so last night I wrote a sort of diary and sent it home, asking them to send it on to you. If there's any more news you want, let me know. Goodnight, my Sweet. God bless you. Your Bill.

D.Y. MESS

I've gone all civilised again and started living in the Regimental Mess. This means meals at regular times, cooked for us, and all the other paraphernalia! Its good fun for a change though I'll be glad when we're on the move again. There's still such a lot to be done. I'm not really a soldier, at any rate a Regular one, nor do I yearn for excitement, but it means a day or a mile or a battle nearer to our time of being together, as the Good Lord intended.

18.5.43.

Half past eight but there's still the lovely morning freshness about. At night it gets cold and we wear woolly things.

5.0 p.m. The weather has cheated today — cold with occasional showers. This morning I called on the Senior Chaplain, and he promised that we can go to stay with the Arnauds for a couple of days. Someone has given William a box of Jerry cigars and he's taking them as a present for Monsieur.

We are to have the Thanksgiving services for Victory on Sunday. The printed service sheets are attractive. The front has the 1st Army Shield surrounded by the badges of all the Army Divisions. A Bishop is coming for Confirmation soon, so we are collecting our candidates together. Our aim of getting men to make their Christian commitment goes on in peace and war.

This morning we got out my spare kit box from B Echelon, and I've dug out my service dress, and my old battered faded purple side cap. William has cleaned badge and buttons, and I'll wear them quite often.

POST VICTORY DEPRESSION!

19.5.43.

Some of our men are returning soon to England in charge of prisoners of war, and I got some of them to say they would act as postmen, but I find its a naughty thing to do, as it doesn't fit in with censorship regulations. No, the time will come for letters with stamps, but I'm living for the time of no stamps at all! All my hopes and dreams will then come true.

Bud Porter (you remember him, a tall chap) and I have been for a stroll along the firm sand avoiding the breakers as they come rushing in. About a quarter of a mile up the beach is an old sailing ship, perhaps a clipper, which has been aground for a year or two. The timbers are in fairly good repair and the masts and spars are lying on the sand.

Tomorrow is the Victory Parade in Tunis. Representatives from all the units will take part in the march. Quite a lot of the rest will be lining the streets. William is going with a party. Somehow I don't think I'll be going. I'm sure its right to celebrate, but somehow it would give me a deep and inexplicable pain. Yes, its right and natural to be proud of what has happened, the first Victory of the war, even to

Pipers of the 51st Highland Division in the Tunis Victory Parade.

parade about the town, but I don't think I'd find any satisfaction.

As we look ahead there are lots of menaces to face. There will be more heroism, more suffering. Yes, we will win the war, and that is certain, perhaps more quickly than we dare dream. But I worry lest it will be just a very worldly victory. There will still be the eternal struggle between the powers of God and the powers of darkness. Man, if he is to be true to his deepest nature, will always have to be a penitent. More than anything else in life I want to get this war over so that we can tackle the job together. Dearest I love you utterly.

THE VICTORY PARADE

20.5.43.

Darling Appleblossom,

It is five o'clock and we've just had tea. The Victory Parade took place this morning in Tunis, but I didn't go. I'm waiting for the final one! Instead I've had a lazy day here by the sea. This morning the Doctor and I did the rounds of the Squadrons. This afternoon we sunbathed on the beach. Just before tea I swam to the wrecked tea clipper. I arrived full of salt water and scrambled up on deck! To show what good form I was in I ran back along the beach.

The men who went on the Victory Parade said it was very impressive. Many newspapers have come today, with great accounts of the D.Y. dash.

It was lovely to get mail this afternoon – seven airmail letters, mostly written after the fall of Tunis – three of them from you.

Yes. My D.Y. have done great things. Ever since the Campaign began they've been on nearly every front sending news back about the enemy. When the first Troop of C Squadron entered Tunis on the first day it was no triumphal procession. There was still scrapping in the streets, and the enemy was still to be pursued to Cap Bon. There are some funny stories to tell. The leading car kept shooting on into the heart of the city. It was a race really, 'cos the 11th Hussars, the armoured cars of the 7th Armoured Division (Desert Rats), were trying to get there first. The German defences were so surprised at seeing British cars in the middle of things that they didn't fire. And so they went on past machine gun posts, and great anti-tank guns that would have smashed any tank at that range, let alone armoured cars. Finally, in the middle of the city the first car met a large German 8-wheeled armoured car, and both were so surprised that they turned round and went off in opposite directions! At one point they came across a barbed wire cage guarded by Italians holding 400 British prisoners, and when the Wops saw our cars they hastily shut themselves in with the prisoners for safety! I hope to go into Tunis in a day or two, but I don't suppose I'll buy much. They say there is plenty of powder to be bought, also ladies blouses, but very little else! Jerry has spoiled any chance of buying things at proper prices. He has flooded the country with Bank of France notes. The other day some of our people sent their laundry into the local town. I was a bit sorry that I missed the day, as I thought it would be a good chance of getting my clothes a few shades whiter! But the average weekly wash came to about 10/-. A pair of pyjamas cost 1/9 to be washed, and other things were just as expensive. In any case as soon as we are able to visit the Arnauds

I'll be able to have them all washed. We'll come away with a box of eggs too.

20.5.43.

Your Tunis victory airmail has just arrived. I can't get anywhere for the whole Regiment to assemble for the Thanksgiving service on Sunday, so its at 9.30, 10.15 and 11.0 a.m. and then on to the Field Ambulance. This is one of the few occasions when I feel a Church Parade should be compulsory. Some say the service was drawn up by General Anderson, but probably it was the Deputy Chaplain General. But General Anderson has a very vital religion.

As soon as this war is over I'm hoping to marry the sweetest and loveliest woman in the world. Be happy my Darling. God bless you. Your very own Bill.

21.5.43.

Its almost lunchtime and I have had a busy morning fixing up Thanksgiving Services for Sunday. I've also arranged a tour of the graves of our laddies who could not be buried with the decency that is their due. Fortunately there are very few.

10.20 p.m. Ten minutes to our 'thinks' time. Would any other earlier time be better than 10.30? I'm sure you go to bed before 10.30 nowadays. At teatime I found four mulberry trees, one of which is just about ripe. Of course I ate lots of them and then found a wee plantation of prickly pears with all their scarlet pear-shaped fruit. I proceeded to eat a few, and then to fetch the Doctor to see whether he would eat any and say whether they were good. The fruit was delicious but covered with tufts of tiny barbs! Each tuft contains several dozen minute prickles which stuck not only into my hands but into my tongue and lips! So Doc started to remove some from my tongue with tweezers, but he removed so much of my tongue that we desisted!! Anyway I pulled some out so there aren't too many left. I shall approach these pears more circumspectly next time.

6.20 p.m. First, Confirmation candidates came to the M.D.S. and 7.30 dinner at one of the Squadrons. Finally an hour or so to stroll down the beach. No moon tonight.

TUNISIAN VICTORY

A letter from my future father-in-law, Canon J. A. Appleton.

Diss Rectory.

24.5.43.

My Dear Bill,

We were delighted to get your letter from Tunis. It arrived at a most exciting moment. We were having a gathering of the clan, Helen, Jay and Iris [her brother, and his fiancée] came on Friday.

Your letter came on Saturday, and was the centre of much rejoicing. It must have been a thrilling time, entering Tunis, specially after all the time spent in the rough country.

The whole of the final attack was an amazing achievement, and we kept hearing of the deeds of the D.Y. on the wireless. I wonder if you heard the bells broadcast on the Sunday morning. Westminster Abbey, Edinburgh Cathedral and Armagh, and then the bells of a Derbyshire Village in honour of the D.Y., a wonderful testimonial broadcast to the whole world!

Your letter and braces came in record time. [My father-in-law's braces were in a poor way, and new ones were difficult to obtain. I cannot remember where the new ones came from. They may have been loot from a Jerry or Itie Officers' Mess!] They were delivered 14 days after leaving you. Ordinary mail seems quicker than airmail, sometimes. I suppose it depends on whether it happens to catch a convoy. The braces are most useful, they came into use at once. My former ones were well nigh worn out. It was nice having the family here altogether even for so short a time.

We've had a wonderful spring with hardly any rain. But today is 'nice rain' which is pleasing everyone who grows things. The garden is full of roses, each kind of flower is ahead of its schedule.

The Guards Padre, David Weigall, who is living here, is away on a weeks leave. He is a great fellow. He won the high jump at the Guards Battalion Sports, the other day, with a 5′4″ in long grass!

Things go on much as usual, though our men seem to be going away, and leaving more and more gaps. Eric Bailey (the curate who joined the army recently) is now attached to the Coast Defence Artillery on this country coast. I hope you are having an exciting and interesting time in more civilised parts of North Africa. It was great finding the son and daughter of the people from your farm, when you entered Tunis. With Love, J. A. Appleton.

29.5.43.   2.45 p.m.

Darling Appleblossom,

I've just taken William to hospital. He's got a touch of the sun, coupled with a spot of dysentery. He's not in a bad way, and I don't think he should be there for more than a couple of days, but he will be looked after much better there.

Today is lovely, and I'm soon going to have a bathe. Last night we saw our first film show since coming to North Africa. It was certainly a thrill. There were two films, one a dancing and singing one, and the main film was *How Green was My Valley*. I'd seen it before, but it was a good film, and well worth seeing again. Out here one doesn't miss seeing a film even if it is an old one! The equipment was very good – a complete talkie apparatus that fitted into a tiny space. Yet it was so clear that the whole Regiment could enjoy it. We sat on the side of a little wadi by the sea with the screen in the bottom.

Last night we had a tremendous bowl of strawberries for dinner. They were very good. It will be at least another month before you have them at home.

Wednesday this week we had a party. This was chiefly outstanding for the food which was up to the usual Derbyshire Yeomanry standard! There were no ladies, of course, though some Regiments are finding quite a lot of Tunisian ladies to invite.

One of our laddies, the Intelligence officer, has got it very badly. She is a French girl, and she lives in Tunis, so he's spent most of the week there! She is to stay down here this weekend, so we may meet her. Which reminds me – I know an awfully nice girl. She is small, lovely and beautiful. She is nice in a flower garden or on a bicycle. I expect she looks nice in a bathing costume. She's lovely too with her far away expression in Church. She's called Appleblossom, and with her red hair she's the most happifying girl in the world, and what's more she's going to marry me.

Wednesday morning there was a Divisional Confirmation by a New Zealand Bishop who has been held prisoner by the Italians for 18 months. He is a great soul. The Confirmation was very real and impressive. I hope my eight will come on well. We have first Communion tomorrow. Just listened to the 6.00 p.m. news. We continue to advance in Italy.

9.00 p.m. We've had a very hearty meal. After a spot of preparation for tomorrow, I'm off to bed. I wish I could find a new colour or flower and name it after you, or find a new mountain and give it your name! I wish I could do something to make you realise how wonderful you are. Beyond my wildest dreams I am happy. Be happy too, Beloved, and continue to fill the world with love. God bless you.
Your Bill.

1.6.43.

Darling Appleblossom,

We've been doing very well with sea post lately. There hadn't been any for about 3 weeks but I've received lots during the last day or two.

I find that there's a special kind of parade tomorrow. [This was an Inspection by the Prime Minister.] You may hear about it on the wireless. Anyway this means I haven't much time to write tonight, as I've been rushing about getting clean clothes to wear.

William has returned from hospital today, after being there for three days. He's not too good yet, and the first thing he had to do was to scrub my webbing belt! Still he took it in good heart and I did my own whack. I washed a pair of shorts, and stitched 'mailed fists' on my last remaining new bush shirt.

Today has been just like the Africa I've always imagined. I went with Ted Phillips, an officer of B Squadron, and four other men a long way inland, to perform the last rites for two laddies who were found by Phil the other day, after having been missing since the end of January. They were shot up in a scout car which had got into enemy lines, and so we never knew their fate. We found one laddie buried, or mostly buried, and the other laddie under the top half of the car – the rest of the car being in bits on the hillside. We made two nice graves, left flowers, crosses and details in bottles. And so we came home. On the way back we came to the town of Zagouan, which was Rommel's HQ for quite a time. Home – we plunged into the good old Med. washing away the dust, grime and heat. I don't think there were any more excitements. Oh, we nearly ran over a 3 ft. snake on the road inland. We thought we'd got him but he still continued to cross the road after! He's only about the third I've seen.

Oh, flowers – I wonder whether you remember my prophesying lilies to come in the wild parts – well, they're here. Great big pink tiger lilies, growing in profusion in all the rockiest and barren places. We put some on the graves. And so I think we know where all the members of the Regiment, who couldn't make it, are to be found. Some of them have left behind monstrously broken bodies in the journey to the Glory Land, and I think only a Christian view of things can make such things bearable. But still we're full of faith and endeavour. One day all will come right.

Meanwhile, my Sweet, I'm very happy and full of the worthwhileness of everything. I'll never lose my bubble 'cos there's the sweetest and loveliest girl in the world waiting for me. I don't think I've ever been fitter in my life, except that my arms and knees are burning as a result of today's scorching! My Darling, I love you with everything. You make me utterly happy. God bless you my Sweet. Your Bill.

WINNIE – THE PRIME MINISTER'S PARADE

2.6.43.

Darling Appleblossom,

Today has been quite a special day 'cos the Prime Minister has been to see us. It was to be a ceremonial lining of the main road with a parade before it. So I got my belt out and joined in. We got to our pitch several hours beforehand, and the heat was terrific. Still, at last, we heard cheering in the distance, and soon the procession came past – the P.M., Anthony Eden, the C.I.G.S. (General Alanbrooke) as well as lots of Generals of all kinds, with an odd Yank thrown in. We were one of the last units, and as we got back to lunch, we saw the whole party in birthday suits fifty yards away from our bit of the beach. Winnie seemed to enjoy his dip particularly. I watched him through my glasses! They had lunch at the big house next door to us – The White House where the Ambulance parked for the first few days down here.

It was so hot waiting in drill formation on the road that the M.O. is having a large crop of patients who were touched by the sun. Winnie came by looking very pleased and happy, doffing his big topee whenever we cheered. He looked very white, and then we realised he was normal and we were brown! As the party came by the D.Ys. the Div. General was heard to remark to the P.M. 'These are the people who have been doing such gallant work'.

The P.M's valet made us all laugh. He goes about with him all the time – and doesn't seem at all worried by Generals and other important people. He stood on the beach with a big white towel. The procession consisted of quite a lot of big staff cars and somewhere near the end a solitary figure

C. Squadron, Derbyshire Yeomanry, on Victory Parade.

reclined in the back cushions, looking rather bored! We wondered if it was Eisenhower or some diplomatic representative, but it turned out to be the valet! And so another chapter closes on the 'Mailed Fist' – 6th British Armoured Division. We've been inspected twice by the King and now twice by the P.M, up to date! But I'm living for the greatest moment of all, when I am with my Darling Redhead never again to part – Dearest Heart I love you eternally. Your adoring Bill.

8.6.43.

Dearest Loveliness, your May 25 airmail has just arrived. I wonder how many of the Jerry and Italian field post cards and airmail letters you'll get from me.

No, my Darling, I don't think I'll be a staid sober-sides when I come home, unless my faith disappears, which I don't think it will. One only becomes flat and disillusioned when one feels that the world is utterly mad, and that there is no way out. Of course the world is mad, but there is a way to a better one, and what is so marvellous is that we're going to have a basinful.

Of course you're a bit of fluff – heavenly and delightful. You've got all the sweetness and tantalising loveliness that the fluffiest people have ever had. But you've also got all the rocklike things and the far-away qualities, as well as the sense of daily things. Oh my Darling you are so indescribably lovely. I love you with everything I've got.

What a funny child you are when you talk about 'the extra special alone' having the real love. I know, too, of so many people out here who have lost their real love at home – people who are trying to seek satisfaction elsewhere. I know all the dangers and difficulties of making a success of things. But I've been certain for a number of years that life would never be complete without a partner. And then you came along, and in a flash I recognised the personality I'd dreamed about, who has all the qualities. How pompous this all sounds. What I mean is Please I love you utterly. In this love I've found all the fulfilment of my hopes and dreams.

Tomorrow night we're hoping to have the most terrific

Regimental concert ever. Lately the Squadrons have been having their own concerts, and a tremendous amount of talent is forthcoming. We've got a huge Jerry trailer, with sides let down for a stage, standing in front of half a huge tent for background. We'll light it up with a 250 volt Jerry lighting set, and decorate it with greenery. The audience will sit about in a kind of natural hollow in the sand. We'll be able to seat a thousand if necessary. On Thursday there is a film show and on Friday an ENSA concert, so we're doing very well now.

There is to be a change of pasture shortly. On the way to the new camp site I hope to stay with the Arnauds for a few days.

The sea sends his deepest blue sparkle and the moon is just getting inquisitive again. He says 'I can see her. She is very lovely, but needs to be kissed terribly'. Oh we have a lot of things in common. Be happy my Darling. I love you utterly. Your Bill.

5.6.43.

Robbo (R.S.M. Robinson) and I have been chatting for hours. He said that I would find it difficult to go back to Parish life, and to get used to old ladies and children, after so long with just men! Oh My Darling, how little he knows! I'm certainly learning much out here, but one cannot live fully in a lop-sided community. I'll never be complete until you and I become one.

Robbo is a Guardsman, as straight as a ramrod, fierce as a fury, and yet a wonderful man and soldier. He looks much younger than his years, and the Regiment owes him a great debt. I have a picture of R.S.M. Robbo, M.M. of the first Army meeting up with his son, of the 8th Army at the end of the African Campaign. He also has a Military Medal.

News has just come through that Charlie Blucher has died in hospital as a result of wounds just before the fall of Tunis. He was lying out in the open for ten to twelve hours with severe chest wounds. He did well to live for three weeks. He was a brilliant and likeable laddie, driven out of his Channel Island Estates by Jerry. At the time of the last push he was

H.Q. Squadron Troop Leader, but he asked to be given a Fighting Troop. His great wish was to lead a Troop in action. He was a direct descendant of Field Marshal Blucher of Waterloo.

[One of the sights that began soon after the end of the African Campaign was the flying over Hammamet of waves of our bombers, as they started the next step, the first landings in Europe. The tiny islands of Lampedusa and Pantellaria were the stepping stones to Italy. It was a sign that African Victory lay behind us, and that the next phase was beginning. Soon the British 8th Army and the American Fifth Army were doing the major assault on Sicily. This was our first indication in the whole war of how all that we had worked for, a major assault on enemy territory, was to be done; Air Force, Army and Navy, all working together as one.]

SPECIAL AND PRIVATE ARMIES

During the Desert War there came into being the Long Range Desert Group. This tough group used to live on its own, making long and deep sweeps behind the enemy lines. Their acts of sabotage, and the intelligence gained, made a valuable contribution to the war effort.

The most unusual group we came across, and worked with, was Popsky's Private Army. This splendid Russian was Major V. Peniakoff, M.C., better known as Popsky. His army of about fifteen men carried out long desert sweeps. When he met up with the Derbyshire Yeomanry he had just completed an 8th Army trip behind enemy lines. Using the D.Y. as his H.Q., and making full use of their system of communication, he carried out a number of spectacular raids.

7

Nine months in an Olive Grove June 1943 – March 1944

11.6.43.

Sadly the Division is leaving Hammamet Bay for an inland destination in Algeria to get ready for the next stage. William and I are making our own way to spend a day or two at the Arnaud's Farm at Le Krib.

It was strange to come down the valleys where our men had fought for such a long time. Where everywhere had been troops and convoys and harbours was just emptiness, with the corn growing and no one to gather it.

The Arnauds are very well, and simply overjoyed to see us. Monsieur and Madame and son and daughter are all here. The daughter's husband is at an aerodrome in the south. The son is very happy pottering about with the tractor and mechanical gadgets on the farm. What stories we had to exchange! I took them two dishes from the Nabeul pottery, like the ones I sent you yesterday. We told our stories and heard what had happened, here and in Tunis during Jerry occupation. There was an enormous meal including William's favourite dish – whipped up white of egg mixed with chocolate. Then we went to bed, sleeping between sheets in lovely spring beds for the first time since we left home. How good it was. This morning we got up very late and had the usual delightful French breakfast, café au lait and bread and honey, cheese and bully! This evening we are to have a dish of Arab Kouss-Kouss. Madame has always promised us one. We gave her some odds and ends, candles and soap and shoe polish, and best of all some needles and thread. For weeks now they have been wondering when we were going to arrive. The day before yesterday the daughter had been saying to Madame 'If we have a wee girl I'll call her Hélène'. To which Madame replied, 'A very nice name. Its the name of M. Le Pasteur's fiancée'. When I went into the kitchen a few minutes ago there was great consultation going on about a couple of Tunisian handkerchiefs. The daughter wanted to embroider your name on them, only they thought that as there was an 'H' in the French version the English one was just Ellen! So I produced your name, and all was well!

12.6.43.   Pentecost.

Here comes a hanky from Mme. Arnaud. Your name is embroidered Hélène by her daughter, Mme. Pugnet. It is about this time last year that the daughter was betrothed, and I think there's a great sympathy with our separation, My Darling. Mme. Arnaud said 'Il vient d'une Maman de Tunisie'.

7.30 p.m. I wish you could be here. Monsieur and the young have just returned from the brother-in-law's farm at Gafour with a great pipkin of wine and a hugh basket of almonds that are just ripe. There was also a huge pannier of apricots. I must confess I'm most likely to suffer tummy ache because of apricots! How our values have turned upside down. Here, in one way, life is very simple and self-sufficient. Its a lovely morning and we've been watching them start the tractor and hitch on the harvester. They had a bit of trouble to start the tractor, and William stood by and very knowledgeably treated me to a lecture on diesel engines! Today they brought in 200 sacks of wheat, an average day's work. Two large barns are practically full.

We've just been invaded by Antoine. He's a jolly good little boy. Yes they're good institutions, though I fear they need constant supervision.

Whit Sunday afternoon. What fun to be in one's own room, and to have sprung mattresses, and proper floors, and windows to open. The bathroom is just next door. It's heaven. No not quite, because it isn't England and I've no sweetie pie here.

This morning we went 30 miles to Le Kef to see the men in our Reinforcement Depot. After one or two stops to fix the carburettor we arrived for tea break. Poor laddies, they are so far from the sea, and there's no shade. It's so hot that they sleep in the afternoon and work morning and evening.

I saw lots of D.Y. whom I haven't seen for a long time. It is a depôt which supplies men and machines when necessary. They haven't had a service since Palm Sunday, so there was a good turn out. Keith Leslie, a very rotund D.Y. Captain excelled himself this morning. He is a very good organiser. He used to be a Borstal Housemaster. Anyway he took over the spacious Officers' mess tent and turned it into a marvellous church, with a very large altar and lots of bowls of pink lilies everywhere. First we had a service for Pentecost, and then Holy Communion.

We got back to the farm for lunch. Madame had killed a cock in honour of Pentecôte, which was boiled and served up complete with head (a great delicacy here), and a pile of potatoes, carrots and onions. The trouble was that the cock was only one of four equally large courses, hence the need for a sleep now!

[The last Christmas card which I can trace came from the Arnaud's in 1952, so we had managed to keep up a link for 10 years.]

While I was snoozing Keith Leslie was writing to his wife as follows:

'Dear Ruth,

. . . Padre Cook came and stopped the night, and this morning, using the "captured" Italian mess tent as a chapel – one end being open – we had the Victory (in N. Africa.) service. He gave us such a nice address on the meaning of Pentecost – Cookie has come 'on' and his services are a delight, so informal and sincere.

He has made a great name for himself out here

amongst all ranks as he is so absolutely sincere and nothing is too much trouble for him; he has been all over the place — Kairouan — Pichon, etc.; checking up on graves and so on; I have a great admiration for him.

I had arranged a lovely altar for him with masses of flowers in coloured Arab jugs, and with his Altar frontal and Cross it looked a real picture. I wish you could have been there, but in spirit my darling you were, and at Communion after, I felt you by my side . . .'

KING'S PARADE

The Regiment left Hammamet on June 14, and arrived with the whole of the 6th Armoured Division, on a large salt lake plain at Morris, near Bône, to be inspected by H.M. the King. Flying weather was bad, and His Majesty was delayed for 24 hours. This low lying plain proved to be extremely unhealthy, and full of mosquitos. There was great jubilation at the King's arrival, and he was cheered all the way. No mepacrine tablets or mosquito nets had yet been issued, and eighteen days later 20 per cent of the Division was down with malaria.

The King passing down the lines of the Derbyshire Yeomanry.

TO EL ARROUCH

17.6.43.

8.15 p.m. Here we are in our new Camp, an Olive Grove on a hillside. The Arabs have barely finished cutting the corn which is between the trees. The main part of the Regiment arrives tomorrow, so there aren't many of us about.

This afternoon we went to Philippeville on the coast. It is quite a large town, and a strange mixture of harbour and cliff, wide and narrow roads, and Arab and European buildings, all jumbled up.

Generally it seems much more European than any of the other parts we've been in.

We are really very isolated, and there is no cooling sea or sea breeze. Philippeville must be 20 miles away. I fear that a forty mile round trip to swim would leave us hotter than when we set out! My Sappers aren't far away, and here the Regiment will all be together. We shall have good centres for worship, and I can see the need for getting canteens and entertainments going as soon as possible.

18.6.43.

Darling Appleblossom,

There was great rejoicing when I received your airmails of June 5 and 8. Don't I know about longing for you too. What fun to have some tennis.

Energetic you to cycle home to Diss from Ipswich. I'll write up seventeen extra hugs in the big book. I hope you decided to post your letter about war and Christian principles. We've certainly got to hold this Rule Britannia stuff at bay. We've got to think sanely about this better world. There's no real change of heart in the world to bring it about yet. The Christian job is still a missionary one. One reason why I enlisted in this war was that my manhood just couldn't stand aside and not share all this suffering that is everywhere. I do, of course, passionately believe that we have right on our side, and that is probably my chief reason. Always I want to keep judging everything by Christian principles. We must be true to our mind and conscience.

And now we've moved far away to an olive grove at El

Arrouch. There are infinite varieties of bugs and beetles, large and small of all shapes. There are some round black tubby beetles which fly and are about an inch long or larger. They go about in pairs and when they spy a bit of manure they bite off a lump as big as a marble, and roll it into a ball. Then with one pushing with a backward motion and the other pulling with a forward motion, they take their booty away with terrific speed, uphill and down dale. They're fascinating to watch.

The air is heavy with the sound of grasshoppers; a breeze is coming through the trees, and in this lazy atmosphere I'm going to dream of the loveliest girl in all the world. I love her smile and the colour of her hair, also the shape of her eyebrows. I adore the things she says and everything she does.

20.6.43.   Trinity Sunday.

It is nearly lunchtime, and I fear that this present midday heat will grow as the summer progresses. We are having a rest after a busy morning.

Just across the path men are levelling a bit of the hillside to pitch the recreational tent. Poor men, they've all stripped to the waist, but its too hot to work in the midday sun.

Dearest Heart, your latest picture is the best you've ever had. It seems to reflect so many facets of your loveliness. Could you send me an enlargement? The dimple has come out well.

Helen in 1943.

21.6.43.

We've had a meeting tonight to fix up the usual entertainment programme – concerts, whist drives, debates, etc.

This afternoon I visited the Field Ambulance. As they're so far away now, the Padre from the big General Hospital next door is looking after them. So I commended my Confirmation men to him. The General Hospital was terribly civilised with Nissen huts and tents and paths and nurses – real English ones.

Coming back I called at the only pipe factory in North Africa, and got 200 pipes for the men, as there is a great shortage in the Regiment. I've been thinking of taking to a pipe so I'll probably try one when they arrive tomorrow.

I really can't think of much to say tonight. All I want to talk about is your lovely picture. Darling it is such a wonderful You. I introduced you to the mess this evening – they were all thrilled – Bud Porter and Ian Dolan, who'd met you, said it was jolly good. They also said lots of other lovely things too. I'm certain that we've got a great work to do together when all this destruction is over. Perhaps it won't be too long now. At any rate all life looks to that time when we can be together.

It's twenty five minutes to ten and soon it will be too dark to see to write. Then there will be washing of feet and a chasing away of gnats, tucking in of mosquito nets, and so to dreamland. No, I think I'll wait and come back to you in England. It's rather warm and mosquitoey to cuddle in these parts. We'll have a honeymoon in the Lake District or bonny Scotland, where we can cuddle very closely to keep warm. Or we'll come here in wintertime. What fun to half open an eye and peep over the corner of the pillow, when the morning sun begins to come in. And if the brown eyes are still closed, I'll give them some lovely, lovely kisses, and then go down to make a cup of tea! Behind our thinking and working – our loving and cuddling, there will be that great and wonderful knowledge that we are doing the best with our lives – serving and helping God in His eternal fight to renew human relationships. Dear, dear heart I love you utterly. You make life so wonderful. Thank you for the picture. It's wonderful. You're beautiful. Your very own Bill.

ORDINATION

During the war years I collected a number of men who seemed to be facing up to the Call of Ordination. After the North African campaign we had nine months of regrouping and retraining. In particular the Derbyshire Yeomanry, who had careered all over Tunisia in their armoured cars as the Divisional, and often Corps, Reconnaissance, had to learn to perform this same task in Sherman tanks instead. A learned Senior Chaplain, Dr. S. G. F. Brandon, from Bône, produced a complete course of Ordination study, Old and New Testament, Greek, Doctrine, Liturgy, everything. And week by week six or eight men would meet to study. In particular it was good for my Greek!

26.6.43.

My Dearest Helen,

What a thrill. A lovely letter from your Papa and three from you. Today is very warm. We had too large a luncheon, fried potatoes and a pie stuffed with sausages and eggs, followed by grapefruit out of a tin. I'll probably soon be asleep. As it is I'm sitting on my bed with only a pair of Jerry shorts on. Occasionally I pause to flick a spider off my back or to deal with a big black ant.

We've got a recreational tent going once again. Last night's debate on the cinema went on for hours! Tomorrow night is my community hymn singing, and question time. I hope we get a good crowd. I don't think I'll feel very shy about tub thumping when the war is over! I hope one of our parishes is a very tough one so that we have lots and lots of friends to make, and things to do. Pause! We've just been invaded by black ants, and about 100 of them have been manhandling an enormous spider about an inch across. I can't alter the course of nature, but I do object to these holocausts on my doorstep! What a silly letter when there's you to talk about.

9.25 p.m. I've just had an enormous meal, including a ham originally from America which the Colonel brought back by plane when he went to Cairo recently for a holiday. I've made a nice altar in the recreational tent for the 7.30 a.m. Eucharist.

The trouble is that I have to pack it up for the 9.30 service at the Engineers, and then set it up here again for 11.00 a.m.

The inspection light is on in the car or I couldn't see. Outside it looks like a Christmas card! What else is there to say. It's all so wonderful, we get so many opportunities to do great things. I've shared about faith and life with so many people, sadly many don't see the connection. Rarely do I have to get into involved argument. We've got to keep drumming away at the elemental things of our faith in Jesus and sin and salvation – our aim in life – our eternal destiny – the Christian community as the hope of the world. Salutations and fondest love, my Darling. May the peace and joy of God grow in your heart. I love you my sweet. Your Bill.

7.7.43.

Darling Appleblossom,

The Spring is lovely out here too. I wish I had your words to describe it. But here it turns into Summer and then into Autumn almost at once. I always connect you with the beauty and splendour of an English Spring.

Darling thank you so much for putting such wonderful thoughts into words. I haven't got that letter with me but the last line was 'I went out into the world and loved mankind'.

Your very springy letter written in the woods with Tony and Mrs. Reid, has just turned up together with a letter from Mary. This batch has taken almost two months to come. It would be nice to know what sorts of adventures this mail has had to arrive. Yesterday was breathlessly hot – in fact it was the Sirocco, a wind straight off the desert. Today is much cooler, thank goodness. Malaria, yellow jaundice, sunstroke and dysentery still send a lot of our men into hospital. I visited about 50 of them this morning. The General Hospital is only about 5 miles away, and has been put up hurriedly to cope with the situation, as the two on the coast are full.

Yesterday I started some ambitious sewing – though I doubt whether I'll have the skill to finish! I took three pairs of pants to make two new ones! Well two pairs of these were beyond darning but the elastic was good. When we had to leave our bombed hospital in a school at Kasserine Pass and go out into the fields, William and I had so much kit stolen from our car the Army gave me a couple of pairs of the straightest, coarsest pants you've ever seen! The Army is particularly unimaginative about underwear! The cloth is best Aertex but the size and cut are Victorian!

What joy – there's a lovely breeze and it is quite cool. Mary, my sister in the ATS, makes me very jealous by talking about her course. It was nearly held up by the mud – lovely mud and rain. How nice it will be to have to put woollies and thick coats on in order to keep warm. Lots of love, Bill.

3.8.43.

Darling Redhead,

More excitements at lunchtime. Your July 25 airmail, July 8 and 9 letters. Day by Day the wonder of your love grows more and more, till I think I'll bust with pride and happiness.

Thank you very much for the new rubber sac for my fountain pen. I'm sorry you had such a hunt for it. It fits well, and I had to cut a bit off the end. The old one had perished, and no longer had the strength to draw the ink in.

Dearest one I'm so lucky and so happy about this burning love. There were times during my winter in Diss when during Evensong or back in the Rectory where he usually offered me a bit of supper, your father would have a far away look. Often at home his eyes would be resting on your mother's picture, as his love went out to the Glory Land. And I would be wondering what Papa would say if he realised that I'd fallen in love with his daughter. It was so wonderful and exciting and terrific when she really became mine. Be happy my sweet. Your own adoring Bill.

165 Brunswick Road,
Ipswich.

9.7.43.

My Dear Bill,

I have just written 'un tout petit mot' to Mme. Arnaud. I told her I would write a longer letter when I have my French dictionary. I hope she will forgive me; I can't remember the French words that I want to use. Mrs. Read is out and Tony is in bed, he wanted 'MAAAAAAAAmeeee', but he soon fell asleep.

After School I went to see a poor wee mite from my reception class; she has pneumonia. She bawled when she came back after being absent; now she begs the Doctor to let her come to School. She lies between the dolls on which she has spent much affection and the great unknown beyond – there can't be so much margin between the two areas when a five-year-old has pneumonia and a heart still weak from rheumatic fever.

In what ways can a child's life fit in with our idea of the next life? One child is happy and 'good-natured', another is a little cross-patch and is all nerves and repressions and stunted because of unsuitable environment for good development. Our responsibility is terrific if the influence of our lives helps or hinders a child's completion. How unbearable the possibilities of death would be if death were unconquered; and perhaps the lives of other people would scarcely seem our concern if Jesus didn't love EVERYone so much that we find ourselves all mixed up together because He loves us all.

Once I didn't know if I loved you enough to want you to go on unhampered by me or if the hope that perhaps I might help you . . . were true – anyway I love you. T.C.T.C.A. mille fois! Hélène.

MY BROTHER JAY

Once I went to London to see my brother while he was part of a Bomb Disposal unit. Their task was formidable as bombs could dive into London clay making them even more difficult and dangerous to recover. Once, having rendered it harmless, they lifted a 2,000 lb. bomb from a narrow, shored-up 30 ft. shaft, only to be told that the Colonel, who had planned to be present, was late . . . So they were told to lower it again and repeat the lifting process for him to record!

After our day off in town we found our way about Eltham in the blackout. Round one darkened corner was a dimly lit convenience. We hastily arranged to whistle the first few bars of Beethoven's 5th Symphony on coming out, so as to find and identify each other. We were by no means the only ones to use Beethoven's music in our wartime need. All over the world oppressed people were hearing the first bars of his 5th

(V) Symphony ··· — ··· — *(v) the B.B.C. identifying signal,
reflecting Churchill's famous V for Victory finger sign.*

*Jay was on leave at Diss, when I came home bringing Iris,
a fellow-student friend with me for a holiday. Here they met
. . . at the moment in time that was to change life for them.*

*Their romance blossomed, helped on by leaves and
holidays. They were married at Hatfield Broad Oak on 5th
August, 1943.*

*It was a very happy wedding which our father took from
his book of 'uncommon prayer'. Iris's late father had been
Rector and her mother had died when Iris and her brother
were children. Bob, on leave from the Scots Greys, gave her
away. She looked lovely in her blue crepe dress, with brown
hat, shoes and gloves and a cascading bouquet of white
carnations and fern. Jay's friend Hum (John Bliss) on 24 hrs.
leave from Evesham, was Best Man. Jay had a fortnight's
leave for their honeymoon in the Lake District, at Rydal
where we were to spend part of our honeymoon, two long
years and 3,000 letters later.*

*So many wartime newly-weds had no home of their own
to go to, and were either temporarily parted after their
marriage on leave, or had to live in rooms, or with relations
or friends. For Jay and Iris the answer was Diss Rectory
where Granty's former room (where I slept when Bill had my
room) became theirs.*

ENTERTAINMENTS

During our Olive Grove sojourn units settled in their own
areas; Sunday mornings were usually a split-second timing
rush between abour four different Camps. These services would
be in the open air, or later, in large canteen tents. Now that
peace-time conditions prevailed I was dismayed to see the
spit and polish parade rearing its ugly head, here and there,
before my men came to worship. Roads were usually dry
earth tracks, and by lunchtime I was ready for my afternoon
siesta, and a letter for Helen, written under my olive tree.
Sunday evenings were always enjoyable, with a free and easy
voluntary service in the canteen. Often there were Discussions,
and slowly a Regimental choir was formed. Invariably we

finished with the D.Y. hymn, number 773 in the old *Ancient and Modern* book, 'O My Saviour, lifted from the earth for me, draw me in thy mercy, closer unto thee'.

Already many family problems were coming along as husbands and wives failed to take the strains of separation.

Occasionally the units were entertained professionally by visiting ENSA parties, and several nights a week we had film shows, and Bingo sessions. Increasingly each Regiment and each Squadron began to form its own Concert Party. Basically it was my job to see that boredom was kept at bay. It was pleasant to watch a show in the cool of the evening, but soon we were to take a real hammering from the mosquitoes. So shorts were changed into long trousers after tea, we were issued with plenty of anti-midge concoctions and mosquito nets. By the time we had to take the yellow mepacrine antimalarial tablets, much of the damage had been done, and our army hospitals were full of cases of malaria and dysentery.

As time went on evenings were spent in crazy but cosy messes or the Regimental Entertainment Tent. On August 3 I took our Regimental Concert Party to give a show at a Canadian Hospital. There the canteen was run by the Salvation Army. Each Canadian Regiment had several ancillary workers attached, and each unit had its own film projector. Next week we had a film show in our Camp on Monday, a concert on Tuesday and our own Party went out on Wednesday and Thursday to other units. I have mentioned our voluntary services on a Sunday Evening in the canteen. It was from these contacts especially that I began to build up a little group of men who were seriously to consider ordination after the war.

LIFE IN OUR OLIVE GROVE
7.8.43.

Dearest Helen,

Saturday afternoon — siesta time — its very hot, so what better than to lie on one's bed writing weekend letters, and preparing tomorrow's sermons. There are two in the morning and an evening one in the canteen. Sermons and letters to my sweetie pie all get mixed up on a Saturday. But then they're always mixed up really 'cos life and faith and love are all mixed up in the Good Lord who is love.

I wrote to the senior chaplain the other day and said 'cannot you get chaplains mixed up with the Prisoner of War escort business?' At any rate he wrote back to say that as we weren't armed we couldn't act as guards, but he would write to some higher authority to see whether we couldn't have some share in a convoy back to England. He was sweet about the marriage business. To quote his letter – 'Your reason seems an extraordinarily good one! I will do all I can to help'!

Oh my Darling, don't be cross. I didn't mean that it was even likely that we would get married in the event of such a leave. It would be an awful scramble to rush round making hasty arrangements, and then being together for a few days, and trying to see all the family. The war is going well now, and there's lots to be said for being patient.

Last night we had a meeting of the Regimental Concert Party and decided to do a review. The concert party insist that Charles Anderson, who does lighting and the technical side of things, and myself shall do a turn! But that remains to be seen!

Two nights ago we had the best concert ever. It was done by the Rifle Brigade, a London Regiment, and so it was full of cockney humour. There were crooners and sketches and people singing while standing on their heads. It was terrific. I've never seen a bunch of people with such team spirit. Someone started by telling a joke, then they all burst into song quite spontaneously. Afterwards more jokes, then someone sang 'The Holy City' and they all became serious and sang the choruses in harmony. What other news? We're still getting lots of fresh fruit. The grapes are getting better every day and water melons are more plentiful. We have them at nearly all meals.

I've found an ordinand, Norman Balshaw. His family is Methodist but I think he is drawn to the worldwide Catholic tradition, the threefold ministry, and the liturgical necessities – beauty, dignity, reverence. He is also drawn to being a regular communicant. Praise the Lord. I have a list now of men who seem to be called to the ministry, and our study course is very good.

This period of inactivity is a godsend for serious study; once we are on the move again it will be difficult to meet like this. All my love. Bill.

REGIMENTAL THEATRE

9.8.43.

This morning I went scrounging for paint for our entertainments tent stage. We've got 3 artists who are all keen to help. The present stage backcloth is canvas seascape with islands. For our review we need a room, an office to be precise, so that will mean still another backcloth.

The car stopped about six times through the plugs oiling up. In Army parlance we've had it! Poor old car, we send her into workshop tomorrow, but I'm afraid the only solution will be a new engine, and I don't think there are any. So I'm taking to a smelly dusty motor bike again.

We've a film show tonight, called *Oh Johnny* – a singing one, I think. I'm just waiting for the man to turn up with his apparatus so that we can fix a site. He's giving half an hour's recital of classical records before the show. What an odd variety of jobs I get. We've all got to smear ourselves liberally with anti-mosquito ointment, because the mosquitoes seem to like the cinema screen too. How silly to talk about mosquitoes and cinemas when there's the sweetest girl in all the world to talk about. So many of our laddies are getting lonesome for their sweeties now. This time of inactivity certainly doesn't help. I get the backlash of their loneliness so much. How lucky I am to have you my Darling. All my being cries out for you, but your love is all sufficient, even though we are separated. I love you – darling lovely woman. Your very own Bill.

19.8.43.

My Darling,

Red letter day again – two lovely letters, and the Missionary notes, and Mrs. B's sweet letter. Dearest Heart, you are lucky to have such nice people to look after you. Mrs. B. thinks you are looking better now. She thought you weren't too good a while back, and hopes my Mum and Dad will be able to visit Diss 'cos she wants to show them the 'Room of Romance'.

Still my dear Heart the mills of war are getting up steam for one last grind, and then it will be all over and I will kiss you lots and lots.

I was planning to go on leave on Monday with Arthur Phillips, the RASC Padre, but he's in hospital. I went to see him this afternoon. He's been regraded to Category C and in a day or two he will be on his way home! He is 35 or 40 and not too strong. He underwent some tremendous strains during the battles. Once his car was peppered by shrapnel. I will be sorry to lose him, but it is better so. I met him first in the Troon days when he joined the Division. We came out here together, and were often together in battles. He's from London and has given me his address in case you're in London and would like to go and see him. He'd love to meet you and would be able to give you any news you wanted. For such a long time he's been of a bachelor frame of mind, but now he feels an aching for a companion.

I've been rushing about on a motor cycle all day. I started off with clean shirt, shorts and stockings, but they're filthy now! Still William is doing wonders with the car. The cylinders got so enlarged that oil came through and choked the sparking plugs – so I went to Bône and got hold of an engine from a crashed car, together with doors, seats and springs. We are in high hopes of an efficient car again. I'm writing this in the hospital tent. Tonight there is a debate which should make feathers fly! 'That in the opinion of the house woman's place is in the home after the war'! Of course the answer will be a compromise – home life and still the opportunity for expressing one's full personality. It will be interesting to see which way the voting goes – I expect those who speak against the motion will have a thin time! We all miss our women folk so very badly.

Yesterday and the day before we spent in Constantine, our ancient Roman city thirty miles further inland, looking for a piano for the entertainment tent. We paid £100 and got an undertaking that the people would buy it back again for £60 when we had finished with it. The piano lived on the sixth floor of a block of flats, and we were few, so we sent a gang of men over this morning. The piano is now covered up (I hope well enough) on the stage and needs tuning.

I forgot to say that the Phillips' address is – The Rev. A. H. Phillips, C.F., 50 Derwent Road, Palmers Green, N.13. Do go and see him if you get the chance. He'll tell you how well I am.

21.9.43.

Its been one of those tiring days. I think I've felt more tired than usual, so I spent the afternoon reading on my bed. I read C. S. Forester's *The Ship*, and now a book with a gay but insipid cover *The Heart is a Lonely Hunter*. Is there something for me here?

Last night our show went off very well at the Hospital. They've got a good and sensible stage, with an enormous concrete floor. There were no lights, so we took three armoured cars. They played their spotlights, and the effect was very striking. There must have been 600 or 700 patients in the audience.

Good news still. Allies advancing all over the world. The latest is the landing in Corsica. Gradually we're building up our link of air bases.

JAUNDICE

23.9.43.

I've been holding this precious airmail form until I hear from you. The mail has been very lazy lately. I expect nearly all the ships go straight to Italy or Sicily. But today your airmail arrived, and one from home too. The Harvest Festival news made me feel homesick! We are hoping to have Harvest Service next Sunday, but now I'm not sure how I'm going to turn out. I'm feeling a bit off colour 'cos I've survived malaria but collected jaundice. I've been feeling tired and lackadaisical for days. The official answer is to spend a few days in hospital, but I can look after myself just as well here, so I'm trying to keep out. News is very good – poor old Hitler. He's full of headaches now. William got me some grapes in the village this morning, lovely large green ones, but they're nearly over now.

25.9.43.

The old yellowness has won, and I'm yellow all over – my tummy looks the funniest. I refused to go to the local General Hospital even though there are nurses and all the other civilised parts of hospitals. I came to the coast to our 165 Field

Ambulance and they've made me very comfortable. One of the nursing orderlies was a chorister in one of Arthur Philips' churches. He was an Ambulance attendant during the battle. Jerry mortar bombs began to crump from the side. He was the coolest cheeriest laddie I'd seen!

Yes, it's good to be here. I know everybody, though one or two of the Doctors have changed. Next door are two General Hospitals near enough for any specialised treatment that anyone may require. My temperature has behaved and I am lying in bed looking out to sea. About 50 yards from here the Ambulance choir is rehearsing for tonight's concert. They just play the tune and the Welsh (mostly) put in their own harmony. Tenor predominates so much that its difficult sometimes to guess the tune! But it's a good effort. Half the repertoire is Welsh tunes. At present its Cwm Rhondda! My diet is slops and tea and marvellous Horlicks milk. I still have some sickness, but I'm much better.

This morning I was talking to some of the men who have been home as prisoner of war escorts. They all said how lovely it was, but what a terrible strain to come away. Dearest Heart I think we're better this way. Jerry's doom is sealed. Then I'll come home and we'll be married with bells and bridesmaids and honeymoon, and our work together, and our furniture hunting expeditions, and our home, and our living together. Phew!

27.9.43.

I had a good night. The yellowness is slowly going. I've a tent to myself and a German spring bedstead and SHEETS. We have luxuries like Horlicks and Bovril. There are lots of visitors, Doctors, Bob Martin (Padre 17/21 Lancers who is trying to get Prim, his WREN, to make up her mind!), and Father Dommersen who shared a cabin with me from Scotland. Six Sappers have just looked in. They have been admitted into Hospital with sores. The time of year has come when the smallest graze or sore festers immediately.

Its 5.0 p.m. and the loads of Italian prisoners who work at the Hospital are going back to their Camps. They work very well and are always cheerful. Beyond this road the ground drops 100 feet in 150 yards to the sea. Its lovely to be by the sea.

29.9.43.

Lots of sea and airmail today. Good old William went back to D.Y. for ours. There's a Gunners Chaplain here. He came to the Division just before the last push when Tunis fell. He hadn't a car and couldn't join his very scattered Regiment, so he stayed at the Field Ambulance for the day. Then he got fed up, and so I told William to take him to his Regiment. By that time Tunis had fallen, William got wrongly directed by the Military Police who'd only just arrived, and didn't know how the battle was going anyway. They reached a crossroads and Powell got his map out, thinking something was wrong. A German tank came up the other road followed by several big troop carrying vehicles full of Italians. William and Powell jumped out and stood by the car and gaped! The enemy then turned round at the crossroads and made off again, only about ten yards away. The only explanation seems to be they were all too intent on escaping to Cap Bon than to capture a parson's car!

The Senior Chaplain now has jaundice in the Canadian General Hospital. I'll be up first and go and visit him! I've just censored 20 airgraphs and 100 airmails and letters. Having lots of time I've done it properly. Goodness there are so many men just pining for reunion. Just to read these letters makes me realise how lucky I am, My Darling. Today has gone really cold. I only had one blanket up to now, and mostly none at all. Now I have two and will probably have another. During the last two months I've lost most of my fat. I'm probably quite a reasonable shape again. There's a 110 volt lighting set going in the Ambulance. All the tents are lighted, and no one closes the openings at night. With the two big Hospitals next door great beams of light go sweeping out to sea, but no one seems to mind.

30.9.43.

A good night again. Colossal breakfast, with porridge, Horlicks and more to follow. Then a wash down with a change of pyjamas. I'll get up today. Doctor has just been in. I can go back to D.Y. soon to convalesce. I shall be yellow for a little while. I've been hatching a plan to go on leave for a few days.

6.45 p.m. A neighbouring concert party has just arrived and is giving a show in the tent about 100 yards away. They're singing a Flanagan and Allen song at present. Two men have called in for a chat – Chemistry, Holy Land, Colour of Divisional Gunners Berets – even religion! Sorry to have gone on so much about myself. Anyway I've avoided malaria! Colonel Philipson, the OC of this Ambulance comes in every morning to ask about progress. During the Campaign he was the world's greatest 'Swanner'. In his Jeep he was always out in front, positively looking for trouble it seemed! Completely mad, I'm afraid, but a marvellous Doctor, and a real charmer.

ITALY SURRENDERS

My Darling,

I went to Philippeville to take my surplice to be washed. Then I had a haircut and a very smelly shampoo. It's lovely to have your hair washed in civilised luxury after life in an olive grove! On the way back I bought a kilo of pomegranates, picking 3 lovely big ones, each about ¾ lb. William got through his very quickly, driving with one hand, and spitting the pips through the window as we came home.

I've fixed up a very ambitious entertainments programme for the coming week – two concerts, a film show, a debate (that in the opinion of this house wartime marriage is to be deplored – luckily I'll be chairman), a quiz – both the last two against the R.Es., also a whist drive and nightly allocations to the Ensa show which is playing on the Divisional stage all week.

Sorry this letter is so scrawly. It seems a hotter afternoon than ever, so I am lying on my bed. Next Wednesday we're having a holiday to celebrate the fall of Italy. Isn't it fun to hear that the Italian fleet is joining us! Poor old Musso. Time to think about tomorrow's sermons. The R.Es. are having a tremendous spit and polish parade. I love you utterly. Bill.

A COOKS HOLIDAY

15.9.43.

Bill's parents came to Diss for a short stay in September 1943. We sent a joint letter: Mrs. Cook writes first:

> 'My Dear Billy,
>
> We have spent a few very delightful days at Diss. We think it is a lovely place. This afternoon we went blackberrying; your Father was delighted, he was so busy he did not speak a word to us! We go home to-morrow, and we shall take with us very happy memories of our visit to Diss.'

Bill's Father's contribution:

> 'We have spent a very pleasant evening. Helen has delighted us with funny stories of Norfolk life. Mr. Appleton read us a few poems, very clever, written by his son, Jay. Your Mother related a very funny story about three young preachers, and I recited the yarns about John and the cow. We have enjoyed the kindly hospitality. They have done everything to make our brief holiday a happy one. We have had mushrooms and blackberries galore. Diss is a lovely old town. Mr. & Mrs. Burlingham have been very good. They picked a big basketful of mushrooms for us to take home, for which we are very grateful. Last night we all went to see the film 'The Rose of Tralee'.
>
> God bless you my Son.'

My Father:

> 'Now comes my turn in this mutiple letter. We have so enjoyed having your people here, but their visit was too short . . . We've just had a visit from Pte. Baker of the D.Y. He last saw you in hospital. He has been sent home as unfit for foreign service, and expects to get a job of driving in the Army here. He has followed your example and found a young lady in Diss. He is staying here for his sick leave, and came up to tell us the latest about you. He certainly has a high opinion of you. He just

missed your people, such a pity as he knows Earl Sterndale. Best wishes and love'

My bit . . .

'Pip, it was so lovely to have your people here. It all felt so family. *I think they are happy about things. I wish they could have heard Pte. Baker tonight, talking about their son. But perhaps they would have been so proud they would have said "Yes, of course he is far too good for this child". Of course he is, bless him, but queer things happen in this house, don't they? It is lovely to hear of you from a lad who has been in it with you. Goodness they do realise how wonderful you are, my love. It's good to hear it from a laddie who seems a bit shy of saying his thoughts, yet he couldn't restrain his tongue about 'The Padre'. Darling, they love you too. They feel a lot of encouragement because they know you are close to them even in the thickest – because you come after their isolated groups and chat to them. "Ah, he's a Boy, he is!" – That means so much – it means – "He's one of us – like his Master he doesn't just preach . . . he goes thro' it with us, and he lives what he gets across to us". Yes, all that one could hear in what he said. Darling you must never, never feel that there are other places where you could do more useful things. For all the Pte. Baker's sakes, and for our sakes too. Thank God for you. You are so lovely. God bless you . . . I adore you. I love your people too, very much. Be happy. T.C.T.C.A. Helen.*

Pte. Baker also told me . . . 'to comfort and re-assure' me . . . that, when they were going into action he looked back down the column and there was the Padre's van following them. Surely Bill and his driver, Bill Penn, were a couple of 'BOYS'! It was wonderfully re-assuring to meet one of Bill's chaps – my first living contact for over a year. I was truly grateful to Pte. Baker for making the effort to come to see us on his sick leave.

Diss Rectory.

23.9.43.

Dear Bill,

I have had a most industrious day; this morning I cut out pyjama legs and finished them this evening. I invented a method of keeping them up . . . a broad waistband ties at the front, dispensing with the need for elastic or poppers, etc. (not obtainable here). All this was interrupted by a great sort-out of 'linen', with Mrs. B. finding old sheets with two good sides to put to middles, with a flat seam down the centre, and one holey pillow case to patch another. Dad's blue suit has also been renovated; patched, darned and pressed; it looks quite smart!

It must be difficult to give a picture of your life without saying dangerous things; you manage marvelously.

We did have a good time when Catherine (Domestic Science mistress at the High School and my lodging mate) and Dad and I were at Fenn Cottage. We bought half a cod from a cart in Aldeburgh, caught that morning by a local fisherman . . . and off the ration! We went to the part of the beach between the sea defences, and paddled. We also shampooed our hair in boiled up well water, as it is so much softer than in Diss or Ipswich. On the Sunday we went to Aldeburgh Church at 11 a.m., as the service was not until 3 p.m. in the modern Church at Thorpeness; it is like Troon Church, but not so big or so posh! Our Landlady was a milliner and enjoys cheering up old hats. When we came away she was turning a red hat for which she had purchased a new feather . . . so we bought a picture P.C. of the beach and composed a verse for her:

> *She said, as she turned her red hat,*
> *'With a stitch and a twist and a pat,*
> *And a red and white feather,*
> *Whatever the weather,*
> *I ought to look stylish in that!*

She did approve of our flippancy! We were on holiday. I wish you were here to help you recover from your jaundice. Nancy's doctor friend says you need plenty of rest. Do please be kind to yourself and get really fit before tackling your demanding work again. Sea breezes and love, L.M.P.

A SEASIDE DISCOVERY

31.9.43.

On a leave to Herbillon after being in hospital at Philippeville with Jaundice.

Beloved,

This precious airmail has been waiting for a week, because we've been away from the Army Postal Services. Each day I have written you a surface mail, but this weekly airmail will tell you how we have had a completely civilian week, away from all things military! William and I set off, a week yesterday, with a week's rations, lots of books, writing paper and a swimming costume. We spent three nights at the Arnauds, taking most of the first day to get there. They seemed very pleased to see us and gave us comfy beds and tremendous meals. The son, daughter and her husband were all home. The husband is in the Free French airforce and shortly is going to England for training. I've given him a few addresses. Top of the list is Diss Rectory I'm afraid! Best French please, if he does turn up! He has a book of useful English words, and lots of O.K's and gestures, so he is very easy to communicate with.

After baths and beds and French food we went through Souk el Arba (I've got a feeling that Saint Augustine was born here) north to Tabarka, and the end of the mountains where so much fighting took place.

From Tabarka we went laden with grapes and melons, eggs and onions, to Le Calle, the next town along the coast. We got stuck in the sand as we left the road, and we took an hour to get out. So we bathed and took ourselves to the hills towards Bône. The Arnauds had given me a bit of leather for a new watch strap. I made half of it before we slept, and the other half in the morning.

We reached Bône for lunchtime, and whistled along the twisty road out to the lighthouse at the end of the bay, about ten kilometres.

Coming back into Bône we wound up the most precipitous road imaginable, around a steep mountain 2000 feet high at the back of the town. The view was terrific. On we twisted through a boulder strewn cork oak forest road for 35 miles to a tiny French town called Herbillon. After a bit of persuasion we got a couple of rooms at the local inn, splendidly named 'Le Grand Hôtel de Beau Séjour'! It was rather primitive, as one would expect, with good cooking and a very friendly atmosphere. The town was clean, and French houses and people very much in the majority. There was a tiny and lovely church, with a very old and saintly priest. They promised to take me to Low Mass on Sunday, but somehow the arrangements broke down. We bathed twice a day and splashed about on the rocks looking for pebbles and shells. We had given our rations in, and ate large meals, and read lots of books. The splendid fact was that we had escaped from all things military. In the hotel was a Doctor and an R.A.F. Officer, both very friendly. So I dreamed of my Sweetie Pie, and forgot about the Army, and William thought of his little Brian who was a year old on our second day there. Of course everyone had to meet my Fiancée. They all loved you.

Six of your letters were awaiting my return. Darling your letters mean so much. I'm glad you don't have to come home from school at night and to cook your own meals. You would not have time to buy food and cook it properly, and I'm sure you would not bother to eat enough. Yes, I'm glad you're being mothered. Dearest Heart, I love you so much. I'm glad you've Miss Fordham to look after you.

Life can never be life until we are one. The holiday has done William and me very much good. We both feel very fit. Your Bill.

SETTLING IN FOR WINTER
26.10.43.

Darling Helen,

Today has been such fun. The airmail has burst. Whoopee! It's the first for weeks. There were four from you and two from home, all wondering about the jaundice. Well, it's gone altogether, and I'm very fit now, though jaundice is still a fashionable thing to have!

How can I answer all the lovely things you say in your letters, I love your sweet drawings. Home letters were all about the garden and fruit bottling and jam making. They're always talking about their visit to Diss. They love you very much.

We've made a huge theatre-cum-canteen by joining four huge store tents side to side. It slopes down to the stage which we've put indoors. The top tent is normally the canteen, but it can be cleared and used to provide seating for 600 or 700 when needed for a concert or a Church Parade. The great thrill has been the visit of our Welsh Guards choir, consisting of 55 or 60 great strapping Guardsmen, nearly all Welsh. The Padre, who started the choir, came with them, Emrys Hughes by name. They gave a concert here on Sunday, and then stayed two nights while giving a second concert elsewhere. The Padre and I had a great time together, a fellow spirit.

R.H.Q. have a new mess. We've got a large greenhouse-like structure, roofed in with the old tent. One of our bricklayers is building a fireplace, aided by two Italians. Everywhere in the camp similar erections are going up, made of tins, wood and canvas. Roads are being covered with stones, and we seem to be settling in for the winter. Next Monday I'm going to live with the Sappers — the other half of my Parish. It is not enough to bustle over for Sunday services and just occasionally in the week.

Wednesday. Noon. The mess fireplace is growing gradually. By tomorrow we should have a fire. It was rather cold last night so we had another evening of parlour games. Normally I'd have pottered off to bed at 9.30 or 10 p.m., but last night it was midnight.

8.11.43.

 y Darling,

I've been very busy trying to do my own bit of settling in w that the winter rains are upon us. I took a pile of timber, a bag of nails and two alpha grass mats for my house — my mosquito net tied to an olive branch over my bed no longer suffices! William and I made a framework of the main part, the bed/sitting room, and put the roof on. It looks crazy but I think it is going to be snug and waterproof. I move back to the D.Y. from the Sappers where I'm now living, next Monday, so my house must be ready.

This morning I went to see the Senior Chaplain. He has recovered from dysentery and jaundice, and has his new vehicle, a Ford 15 cwt. truck with an eight cylinder engine. He's trying to get one for me as my old bus is just about worn out. I seem to have done more mileage than anyone else in the Division. The new truck would carry everything, and would serve us as an office and bedroom too.

The first choir practice with my Sappers brought 17 altogether. I was thrilled at the way they got going. Hymns are the easiest to begin with, and they finished up with Cwm Rhondda, Aberystwyth and 'While Shepherds watched' (anticipation of Christmas!). I've found a conductor and a pianist, and the aim is to try to beat the Welsh Guards' choir! The General came and stayed for a meal afterwards. Wherever you go in these camps round about there is a feverish sawing and hammering as tents and shelters, messes and cookhouses go up.

Starting this week we are being given a second airmail letter for the next five weeks. There is a funny system whereby the second letter can be sent free. It has to be marked "free" and the authorities will keep it in England and deliver it at Christmas!

It is so difficult to think constructively about the future. There will be a future, but it does seem a long way off. Meanwhile I dream of your lips and your utter loveliness. I need you so much. God bless you my Sweet. I love you utterly. Your Bill.

A PRE-CHRISTMAS CHAPLAINS' RETREAT

15.12.43.

Darling Appleblossom,

The 6th Armoured Division Chaplains make up quite a good number. We must be about a dozen altogether. All these Quiet days, all these services and meditations seem to be so connected up with you that I almost feel that we are sharing them together. You seem to be so much a part of me that you fit in with everything. Often I think I know what your thoughts and reactions would be to many circumstances. The Conductor has some good thoughts and a wonderful command of language, but I fear he's too immature yet to make us really sit up and listen. We really need an old greybeard who has spent a lifetime thinking about these things.

5.30 p.m. Back in the Common room. We're not used to kneeling in retreats these days! The floor of our chapel is cold, hard, pottery tiles, and with nothing in between, during Holy Communion and Litanies etc., my knees have gone quite square! Andrew Stewart (Church of Scotland and Chaplain to the Lothians and Border Horse) is less used to kneeling than we are. This afternoon he went to sleep and snored during the talk. Luckily he was in the back row and the Senior Chaplain just in front kept pulling his trouser leg! At last he woke up with a reverberating snore and a look on his face as if to say 'I haven't been really asleep! I was just closing my eyes to concentrate'! Today has been good. The Conductor said some lovely things about the childlike mind.

10.00 p.m. I started to scribble before supper but got stopped, so now I'm in bed. Andrew Stewart is sleeping in the next bed and has just given me an airmail letter form. I am feeling very happy tonight. This evening's talk was terrific. I wish I could tell you all he said but I cannot remember. Religion is a force that binds us together in our search for God. But our faith is different. It is a revelation. It is God finding a way of remaking His World – giving people eternal life. In these war Christmasses you cannot talk glibly about worldly peace and happiness. but we can talk about the Father's love in intervening dramatically into His sin-drenched world by sending His Son to be born among lowing cattle and scurrying mice. Peace on earth, goodwill to men, is secondary, and can never come in isolation. It must always follow the response of creature to Creator – Glory to God in the Highest.

Be happy Dearest Heart. I don't suppose this sea mail will reach you for Christmas, but I'll be with you in spirit. God bless you. Your Bill.

HOME CHRISTMAS

45 Woodville Road,
Ipswich.

20.12.43.   9 p.m.

My Darling,

We had Christmas pud for lunch and went to the Congregational Kirk to the Carol Service at which Miss Fordham my landlady, was singing. I've also written 8 letters so please, I've earned a few scratches to my Billy.

The party that Miss Neal (Head) gave for the K.G. and Transition went off very well. Only about 30 children were there as the rest were away with colds, etc. Catherine had made a wonderful tea. We had a tree with lighted candles, a Father Christmas and a present for everyone. Oh, it was a REAL party. But still the war goes on. Folks have switched over from the hankering after the things that we had before the war and longing for their return. We don't look for returns any more, we accept what is, and hope for things new. So the kids have the best Christmas festivities folk can make, and the best is always satisfying since it seems to get better as time goes on. Flour from soya flour makes 'almond paste' with a little almond essence; jellies are lemonade with gelatine to stiffen. But children are children, and they seem extra good specimens. There's nothing ertsatz there.

Yesterday I took Prep for an absent mistress. When senior school staff are to be away they just set work for their class!

I also got one or two oddments for Christmas, but I've still to get my cards – disgraceful but unavoidable. [This was when I found greeting cards for specific people, e.g. 'to my dear Uncle . . .' and thought how wasteful when paper etc. is scarce. It would be an economy to have only the general cards we had always been used to] *Anyway as long as my Bill gets told I love him in time for Christmas that is really what I care about. You make me so happy. Sometimes it all seems too wonderful to be true, then I remember the way you bounce on your heels against the fender, the way you look over a teacup, the way you brush my hair, and that 'thinks' look, and the way you stoop and envelop me in strong arms. It's all very real and timeless.*

I saw a khaki back with a Sam Brown and 3 pips and a forage cap that looked purple on top in the town yesterday. I feel sort of offended when I see that as if it was such cheek of anyone to wear my Bill's uniform.

It's really the sort of night when we ought to sit and chat and embark on the first stage of a Preparation for Christmas Service in a Church dimly lit by Heath Robinson lights. Maybe we'll have a Nativity Play before so many Christ-masses have passed. Then we'll have to insist on the blacked-up 'heathen' staying in the kitchen until it's time to go to church (if near) so that they won't smear black all over the angels — you know how it is. Oh, and we must see that the tiniest angels pay a visit before they get dressed — but that will be my job. You'll have to dash off in the middle of testing the lights to show the Rural Dean to his pew — what a lovely mix up it will be! I'm ravenous for you and the life ahead of us. God bless you Darling. Your L.M.P.* loves you.

[*This was an old family joke. Some said it meant 'Little Miss Pussyfoot', others averred it meant 'Lady May Paget'!]

Diss Rectory.

24.12.43. Christmas Eve 9.30 p.m.

My Darling One,

It's Christmas once again. What lots of people will be spending it in misery and loneliness — the hungry and cold in France, Greece, Norway, Germany and all over the world, where there is cruelty and the darkness that brought God to Bethlehem 2,000 years ago. But all over the world, too, are hearts where tonight He will be born afresh. Darling how I long to journey with you, past the complications of reason, through the mists of doubt to that very understandable mystery, and there in the stable to kneel, lost in the joy of realising God is, God cares, God loves.

My Billy, you have taught me so much of life and Love and God. You feel so near tonight. Do you think the time is meant to come when it is like Christmas all the year — when people want and expect God to come and be in them? Can His Kingdom ever come on earth? Christmas is wonderful . . .

Christmas Day.

Billy you are here all the time. I love you utterly. We've had pheasant for dinner with all the fixings, and Christmas pud with holly on top, and we drank to you and we drank to Jay – in sherry. Now we are sitting all cosy round the fire and happy at having washed up. Mrs. B. has appeared with a tray of coffee and biscuits! Trust Mrs. B.

Now darling, there's something very big to say – too big for me to say at all efficiently: first I want you to feel very thanked for the lovely bag and all the parcels you have sent – dates and lemons – all your letters and airgraphs. They make me feel so very very happy. Apart from that I've never seen a nicer bag – Bill it is a 'masterbit' as they say in these parts. All the folks here were so glad we had good news of you – your December 10th air letter came today! Marvellous timing. Perhaps this will reach you soon after New Year's Day. Anyway I send you lots of happiness and wishes and hopes for the new year. I feel about 1944 – not just HOPE. Maybe it means we SHALL be here together next year – or somewhere together anyway. Now H.M. the King is going to speak to us all. Billy I love you – no Kings or Archbishops or anyone could happiness anyone by their message as one wee kiss of yours happinesses me – even to remember. You are my everything.

God bless you and make you happy and someday bring you home, if it fits in that way. I believe it does. T.C.T.C.A.* Lots of love Darling – thank you for all your lovely gifts. Helen.

[*Latin! Te cum toto corde amo – I love you with all my heart.]

CHRISTMAS DAY 1943. EL ARROUCH, ALGERIA

6.0 p.m.

My Darling,

Part of the Christmas Joy is to scratch a few lines to the most beautiful and wonderful sweetie in the world.

After lunch I went to bed for a couple of hours. The last

12 hours had been an awful rush, and I was a bit dozy. Besides I had to prepare for tonight's party. Remember how I was hoping to be so proud of my special Guest in the Regimental Party two years ago! Then you went down with measles and mumps! So my heart was in the Rectory that night.

Yesterday William and I went to a smallish and lonely unit about 20 miles away. After tea we had the Christmas Service at 7.30 p.m. in a brilliantly lit tent. As soon as it had gone dark they illuminated a big Christmas tree which they had dug up in the hills. The service was specially hearty and a few had got a bit merry, but they soon calmed down. Afterwards we had Communion. They subscribed £13 for the Waifs and Strays.

It took about three quarters of an hour back to Derbyshire Yeomanry. I put a long table up in the recreation tent on the stage for an altar. The white frontal and shiny brass with white, cream and pink roses looked wonderful against the black curtains – we lit the whole thing up. Then we went to the R.E. canteen for our midnight communion at 11.30 p.m. Ten came from D.Y. and about 45 altogether. We sang carols, and it was a good service.

This morning I got up at 7 a.m. for 8 a.m. Communion here. The D.Ys. were all tee'd up for 10.30 a.m. The Colonel read the lesson, the first time in his life. He has a very quiet voice but read quite well. Mighty warrior that he is, he got a fit of knee wobble towards the end! Nobody noticed it though! H.C. followed at 11 a.m. Before and after the service Henson Maw (the cinema organ man) played a Christmas medley – bits of the Messiah and carols, bells, Jingle bells and White Christmas all mixed up! Last services were at 11.45 with a small unit in a local village in their own hall. Meanwhile at D.Y. the final of the Inter-troop football had been played off. Christmas collections for Waifs and Strays came to about £37 for all these services.

The men had their Christmas dinner at midday. Pork, turkeys, plum pudding, and it's the officers turn this evening. Cocktail party in the Q.M's office at 7 p.m. and Dinner at 8. All the Officers of the Regiment are coming to R.H.Q. to dine. They can just be squashed in. The miller in the village gave me some lovely roses for the altar. I've given them to the mess now we've finished with them.

Boxing Day afternoon. Paterson (Y.M.C.A.) and I watched a cracking inter-squadron football match. Soon we're going off for a stroll up the hillside. It goes a long way up. Phil has just taken a picture of my house. So by the time the film is completed and has returned from England the war will probably be over! Christmas mail has just come in. How splendid. Last night we had a wonderful Christmas dinner. Soup, pork and turkey, Christmas pudding with flaming brandy, and mince pies, cheese straws, crystallised fruits. Goody!

Tonight I dined with 'A' Squadron. We had chicken and tinned plum pudding, from Canada I think. It is now 11 p.m. and bedtime. All round songs and choruses are coming from the various canteens. I fear that Christmas is just the great opportunity for drinking a skinful of liquor for most people. Dearest Redhead, I've a feeling this coming year will see you in my arms. Anyway be strong and happy, my darling. Our time will soon come. Happy New Year and lots of love to everybody. Your Bill.

A SECOND LEAVE TO HERBILLON

25.1.44.

My Darling,

I'm afraid your Birthday airmail will arrive a bit late. Anyway my Darling I send you all my love. You make life extremely full and worthwhile. Next Birthday I hope to give you all the kisses and hugs that you need so much.

William and I came back to Herbillon by the sea. Today is the end of our leave — we've had a lovely winter holiday. We return to camp tomorrow. It is afternoon and we are sitting in the sun on the beach. The rocky hillsides are covered with green bushes, red rocks and sea like a millpond, blue and sparkling with a blue sky.

This morning I had my second bathe of the holiday. The local people are rather scandalised by our bathing in winter! They reckon to bathe in June and July. The water was rather cold today, so I swam half way across the bay to one of the little quais, past the moored fishing boats and back to the beach.

We came in the new Ford 15 cwt. truck which can carry lots of people, so William brought his friend, Jim Shawcross, the Doctor's driver for company; we have also brought two more friends, Bert Swann, a possible ordinand and Eric Hadley, a fine Christian and orderly room clerk. They slept two in a room, and I had a room to myself. It is the first time the newcomers have slept away from the Army in North Africa so they have been specially thrilled. There is nobody else staying at the hotel, so we have had lots of attention — including fish every day. I'm hoping to take some fish back to camp tomorrow, but a wind seems to be getting up and this means no fish. We seem to have made very good friends of lots of the local people. The village carpenter Jean Sposito, an Italian, has a wonderful workshop. He makes sailing boats, houses, furniture, everything. Bert Swann broke his pipe a day or two ago and the carpenter mended it. The local grocer is a great character — a very patriotic Frenchman. We always used to pop into his shop to inquire about the news. On the last leave he said the war would be over by Christmas. I haven't reminded him of this, but he's still very optimistic. You should see his eyes light up when he tells of bombs on Berlin! 'Ah, les Russe avançent toujours', he says every day. For the last few nights we have gone to his house for the 6.0 p.m. news. Sometimes we get coffee and buns.

The local Curé is quite a young man and home on sick leave from the Army. We took him along with us when we visited Bône the other day, as transport is very difficult. When we returned he asked us if we would bring back some mosaic tilings for the Church. So we loaded ¼ or ½ a ton of tiles on the wagon!

Sunday we had communion in my room at 8.30 with marble mantel shelf as altar. At 10.00 we went to listen to sung Mass. In the evening the Curé had dinner with us. Afterwards we had coffee and buns 'chez lui'.

Eric Hadley is musical and we have been playing a lot of recorder duets together. As he is more musical he has had to play the second part most of the time! He has been very patient when I have made a mess of it! We have learned a great deal. Darling we must do lots of this. It will be such fun to play together. You will? Goody. Goody.

Now we must come back to your birthday. Dearest Heart it was a great and wonderful day when you were born.

3.45 p.m. Hello my Darling. We conked out halfway back with an airlock on the carburettor. We got back just in time for lunch. The mess said that hardly any mail had come in during the week, so I didn't dare to expect any – but there was a great pile waiting for me – your 11th Dec. onwards. How lovely of you to send the pen. It looks a good one, but I'm waiting to get some proper ink to put in it. Bert Swann is giving me a bottle of decent German ink at teatime. This French ink causes all kinds of stoppages and corrosions. I have managed to keep my two pens all the campaign. Neither were new when we started. One was very old in fact, and they're just about finished now. So it is lovely to have this other one. Love and kisses. Your Bill.

ENGLISH SPRING FROM HELEN

30.1.44.   *Diss Rectory.*

Spring is sprung! It's that Spring day when you feel you'll never lose the joy of sunshine – whatever weather comes you'll surely never forget this sunshine, this birdsong, that little orange starred crocus patch under the boles of smooth grey beeches, that yellow carpet of aconites or the fresh frailty of the first pale iris. But we do forget, and thats why it's so great when Spring comes again to remind us.

We're lucky people, Darling, you and I. We're going to be sad people when we come across folk who aren't happy. We're going to have great joys and great tasks, and great disappointments and great sorrows and struggles because you see we're going to love very much.

I love and long for you. There's a very deep quality about love across the seas isn't there? I think this will have made our life extra life somehow.

Now up to the Cemetery with some winter jasmine and catkins to put on Mother's grave.

Your huge box of sultanas, raisins, onions and 2 lemons

came yesterday. MANY, many thanks Darling. Uncle C. (Burlingham) was excited about the onions, and needless to say we all rejoiced about them all.

> *Aconite gold carpets the sod,*
> *Crocuses hold tidings of God.*
> *Jubilant notes sung on the breeze*
> *Past smooth grey arms of arching trees*
> *Rising up high 'gainst a deep blue*
> *Blue of the sky . . . I am dreaming of you . . .*
> *— You and your love that will always sing*
> *Deep in my heart — a perpetual spring.*

30.1.44.

After shepherds pie and Canadian Christmas pudding I'm having a pipe out of doors. A laddie should be here soon from B Squadron to talk about ordination. Sometimes I get frightened about all these possibilities, and the way God seems to be touching these men's hearts. How many splendid opportunities I have with these men if I've only got the grace and insight to use them. It is good to know that God touches people and says 'I want you to do this for me'. Sometimes I feel that a sermon is a conscious effort on my own part. Sometimes I know that it is more than myself speaking, and I think my hearers sense it too. Its part of our calling, my Darling. You have got this ability also, to be a channel of the Divine Grace. I felt it at our first meeting. It was for this that I wanted you for my wife more than anything else in the world.

I've a feeling that the Army is a useful experience for afterwards. For the last four years I've lived outside the church, except in the Diss days. I'm beginning to see what the needs are. Most feel in their hearts that the new age will come with the destruction of Hitler and his gang, but it will only be when men's hearts are changed. Men believe this wistfully, and shake their heads and say 'No' to the church. Its ceremonies are often dull and unintelligible. Where is the link between the church and the better world? There seems to be growing in me a burning message for our dull and unimaginative church members. We are the one universal society – Divine and human, hope of the world. What are we going to do about it my Darling?

12.2.44.

Darling Appleblossom,

Frank Hartree (Quartermaster) has just lit a fire of coke and logs. The logs are pine instead of the usual cork oak, and are blazing away with the bark crackling like a gun going off. George Trollope, our happily-married Adjutant, comes off best with airmail. His Missis only writes airmail, so he gets a lot. I do better than most, but when it comes to sea mail I leave them standing! Five of your sea mail and a postcard came today. There were letters from Iris, Mary and my Papa. Mary has just refused a commission and I've written to tell her she's very silly. Apparently each gun site has just one A.T.S. officer, so she lives a lonely life with very little to do other than to see that the blankets aren't damp! At present she's more or less her own boss, and has a lot of responsibility (radar, ack-ack, gunlaying etc.). Anyway I've given her a brotherly rocket.

Last night was another squally, blustery, wet one. We all have a rum ration tonight, a tablespoonful is the official dose. Dick Witney has spent the last two days on a survey of our local stream. Apparently it is full of malaria. If we get a week's sun the mosquitoes will hatch out, so 200 Arabs are starting to channel the stream. We've had a lot of clothing pinched by the Wogs lately, also there's been a lot of selling of clothing by the men, so Phil took a gang of chaps this morning to strip a few Arabs. They went into several villages and stripped the Arabs of all Army clothing. Some were left completely naked, I'm afraid, including a shepherd on a hillside miles away from home. Rather sadistic I fear, but I suppose they need a lesson.

What a lovely picture you give in all your letters of Flat life. I'm so glad you're well settled in. I did think that you'd be too tired or busy to cook and look after yourself properly but I think you'll be alright.

13.2.44.

My Darling,

THE PHOTOS came today. You're lovely, tremendous, wonderful and very, very beautiful. Please may I have a larger print of the Dimply full face one? About four times as big. I want a large one to have around as the typical Appleblossom.

Yesterday the last week of sea mail rolled in. There was a letter from the Bishop of Derby. He doesn't think it is a good thing for me to work in Diss when I come home in the near neighbourhood of my Fiancée until I marry! He concedes that I may marry when I come home, but that I should not commit myself to any post-war plans. He says leave it to God. 'When the time comes', he says, 'I certainly want you to come back to this Diocese. Derbyshire has a primary claim on you, and I shall do my best when you are demobilised to place you where you can work happily and fruitfully, under God, with all your military experience as a Padre to enrich your usefulness.' So now we have the Bishop's reply to your Dad's idea of my coming back to work with you at Diss!

William didn't feel well when he came to wake me this morning, so I sent him to bed. Doc. says he will have to go to Hospital if his temperature doesn't drop. I wanted to go out this morning so I took the truck out myself for the first time. Pat (Y.M.C.A.) came with me. The gears are like a lorry, and don't slip in automatically, like a car, but I did fairly well. Coming back I turned off the main road and ran into the water truck. There wasn't much damage as we weren't moving fast — just a wing a little buckled. The Y.M.C.A. are to move on elsewhere so we shall have to run it Regimentally. I shall miss Pat very much.

Tonight there is a Canteen Service and Pat is to give the farewell address.

Frank Hartree (Q.M.) has invented a marvellous new bath house, with canvas screens. So far we have had an ingenious shower fastened up into a tree top. Now we have a real bath, with very hot water from a large brass tap and cold water from a large brass tap also! There is even a gadget to hold the soap. It began to get dark and there was even an electric switch to light us up!

14.2.44.

I went to Philippeville today to see William who seems to be improving.

Now that we are getting ready for our move to Italy I've been reviewing my clothing stock. The plan is to take a box with me, and to leave a complete set of spares with the baggage party. The Officers' shops are ubiquitous and excellent. Shoes are 16/- a pair, and very good woollen shirts are 12/6, about a fifth of the prices back at home. I even got a dog collar and stock.

15.2.44.

News of the bombing of Cassino. There is a racket of selling army clothes to the Arabs. Everywhere are posters 'The stuff you pilfer helps that !!! Hitler!' I got a bunch of French papers and posted them today. They are papers of Fighting France. 'France is in the valley of the shadow looking to a brighter day': 'Ce Journal est né en exile et en combat.' Here the French are real Patriots: especially had they been offended by Marshall Smuts, who a month earlier had declared that France was finished as a great Power. Even more intense was their undying scorn of, and hatred for Italy, a traitor, a jackal, and a coward.

We have a Film Unit pottering round the Camp, taking pictures of meals and parades, and getting up in the morning, and buying eggs from the Arabs, and donkey races. The film is to spur the people of Derbyshire on in their War Savings Week.

Sweetheart it really is time for our next chapter to begin. I've been trying to ask myself Who I am? I'm head over heels in love with you, and that's certain. I got on well with my men in our first battle. I've been a useful part of our life in our olive grove during these last nine months. But Who am I? What am I? A Priest or a Soldier? Have I forgotten the past? Am I a different person? Have I changed? The answer comes through again and again. I'm not different. I haven't changed. I'm still a Priest. Dearest One I hope you've felt this all along. I ache so much to get back to Parishy things. It's not a wail about this sometimes rather lonely Priest in an Army existence, but life is so lopsided. Goodness I've learned a lot, but

I dream of being in a Parish again. One thing I'm certain of — we don't need learning and great powers. We need love, a great big burning overpowering love in the heart of everything. I think I made sure of this when you came along. The kind of love that grew up inside me was just an echo of the love I'd learned from God. Your love and my love, My Darling, is God's love. Its the love that burns down barriers and gives people a new vision. It is all embracing and all patient. It is our Pearl of Great Price. It is God in action.

I've had a letter from George Mackenzie, our Senior Chaplain. He is in 56 British General Hospital, with a duodenal ulcer, and he was writing to say Farewell, as he did not think he would be fit for active service. When we first met I was enjoying life, and being useful, I think, but George was a wise man and could see the tension that exists for me as a chaplain to a County Yeomanry Regiment. This I think may be seen in his farewell letter.

> 'My Dear Bill, I am afraid that it must be assumed that I shall not return to the Division as S.C.F. I am making progress but it is very slow, and there is quite a chance that they may send me back to U.K. for a time anyway.
>
> I want to thank you so much for your friendship, loyalty, hard work, hospitality and the many other things I appreciated greatly. It was good to know that, though in my opinion you had one of the hardest jobs in the Division, it was done, and there was no doubt about the way you tackled many of the problems that you came up against, and of the influence for good you exerted. I was hoping, if this had not fallen upon me, to see a lot more of you, particularly with reference to your Ordination Candidates. Please continue to keep an eye on young Cheetham if you can. I was sorry I did so little for him. I hope all goes well with you. If by chance I do go to the U.K. perhaps I can do something for you in a certain direction, in which I believe you are interested! Seriously though, if I do go home, let me have her address and I will drop a line, or do any other necessary action for you.'

It was an encouraging letter, but it did not turn me any more into a soldier than a priest. George did go home, and in due course Helen got a lovely letter from him.

17.2.44.

It is weekly NAAFI ration day. I got two tins of Three Nuns Tobacco, two bars of chocolate and a couple of 'Life Savers'. In the evening the mess was very cosy. The fire of charcoal and wood glowed brightly. Colonel Peter had invited some friends in for dinner and poker. For dinner we had a creamy soup, mutton and asparagus followed by one of Charlie Chef's famous fruit concoctions all whipped up and covered with spun sugar. Finally a savoury of tinned crab and sauce. During the poker session Colonel Peter took £50 from a visiting and very reckless Major.

Dick Witney and I take it upon ourselves to keep flowers in the mess. We have pots of mimosa and daffodils and jonquils.

18.2.44.

This is the twelfth day of almost continuous rain.

Three more Greek New Testaments have arrived as free gifts of the British and Foreign Bible Society for some of my ordinands who have not yet had one. The Y.M.C.A. have moved out, and the Regiment has taken over responsibility for running the Regimental canteen. The problem has been that the supply of fresh bread has gone too! However, we've managed to get it through the Church of Scotland canteen, with the Lothians and Border Horse. Sgt. Teasdale the provost Sgt. has taken it over, and everybody is trying to decide what to call it — Teasdale's Tearooms, Cook's Cafe or Bill's Beer Garden!

21.2.44.

I have taken my friend, Reggie Snaith to Hospital with malaria. William is a little better, but will be in for another week or two. My truck driving is improving and I'm getting used not to have synchro-mesh gears.

I have just reminded the mess that it was Shrove Tuesday

and there was a discussion as to what to give up for Lent. Sir Ian suggested I give up letter writing! In the evening about four of my ordinands came to my tent for our weekly study. We talked too much after our study, about theological colleges after the war so that I was quarter of an hour late for dinner. I sat at one end of my bed, a Sergeant at the other end, a Sergeant and a Lance Corporal sat on two car seats. Norman and Frank can translate 'The Slaves threw the tables and doors into the market place', without turning a hair!

They also dealt with ὁ λαος ἀει γιγνωσκει τους νομους ἀλλα ὁι δουλοι ὁυ γιγνωσκουσι τους νομους – The people know the laws, but the slaves do not know the laws!

23.2.44.

The Ordination Candidates were to have an official interview with Dr. S. G. Brandon, the Senior Chaplain back at base at Bône, the learned organiser of the Course, but it was cancelled at the last moment.

24.2.44.

Frank Hartree, our Quartermaster, one of our few regular soldiers, and about the oldest man in the Regiment, stayed in bed this morning. We're hoping he isn't brewing malaria. He's one of the few with the proud record of having stayed out of Hospital since coming to North Africa. The Arabs stole a couple of B Squadron kit bags during the night, so I expect there will be another expedition to mount. Powell, one of the Chaplains came over this morning to say that his concert party would come next week. I gave him a Pelican Book on comparative Religion. He's a Baptist and a Scholar.

Q.M. Frank sends his love, he complains that you don't return it often enough! He's not looking very spry though he refuses to see the Doctor.

Diss.

25.2.44.   Half Term.   Friday 8 p.m.

Lots of letters at Ipswich and more waiting here. Your Mother had a pin put on the silver D.Y. badge . . . it is lovely

. . . thank you. I am proud to wear it. We had an Army Half Hour this evening; six 8th Army men came in to practise songs for Sunday. Dad has roped in the other Ministers to help in making the Corn Hall 'an outsize home' for Sunday nights 8–10 p.m. This week there will be card tables for people to be chatty or write at, songs and music and cups of tea.

Jerry comes and tries, but he gets what he deserves . . . the Ack Ack is terrific. No damage here or at Ipswich.

25.2.44.

Your Jan. 17 airmail arrived – first from your Ipswich flat. Also a bouncy letter from Mary. [My Sergeant-Major sister in the A.T.S.]

Mary's letter was written from home on Jan. 22. The Battery had a marvellous time at Christmas, and did lots of good deeds. They had 9 lessons and carols on Christmas Eve, and made and took toys to the Crippled Children's Home. Officers and Sgts. took cups of tea to men in bed on Christmas morning. They waited at table and did Guard duty! Mary and two others took the first prize as Tom Mix and horse at a fancy dress dance. They also held a party for local kids and gave them toys they had made.

Bedtime. One of the canteens is in the middle of a sing song. They always sing when they're a bit merry.

25.2.44.

The Colonel has been reading Alan Moorhead's African Campaign book, *The end in Africa.* He gives the account of the race between D.Y. and 11th Hussars to Tunis. He also says that the 6th and 7th Armoured Divisions are the finest of all British Fighting Divisions! Could you get a copy? I'm off to hospital to see William and so many others. Sir Ian has just read out a personal notice from *The Times*: To exchange 8 bottles of whisky for a Pre Utility pram!

Coming back from hospital along the coast road I picked up an Arab laddie who'd had a foot crushed by a French Military truck which hadn't stopped. He was one of the orange sellers, and in great pain. I'd got about half a dozen chaps in the back for a lift, so we got out and applied field dressing, and took him into town to the French Civil Hospital on top of the hill. The hospital was a most modern building to look at, but seemed to be completely chaotic and unorganised.

When we got to the hospital and found the admission department, which wasn't marked in any way, French men and women started gesticulating and fighting about where he should go. There were other Arab street accident cases sitting about on benches, and nobody seemed to be interested. Have I mentioned the storks before, this spring? They've been back for a few weeks now. You see them everywhere. They'll soon be building.

4.3.44.

William comes out of hospital this morning and Alf Buddell has gone to fetch him and anybody else who is due out. Sgt. Brown, the Officers' Mess Sgt. went in with his fourth bout of malaria. I wonder if he will be sent home after this.

5.3.44.   Lent II

There were some wonderful Services this morning. B. Squadron is far away the most enthusiastic Squadron. About twenty of them stayed for Communion. Then I went to collect some more army comforts (what a word!), a football, Sunday newspapers, scarves, cigarettes etc. Finally a very late service at 12.30 so we got home and had a late lunch.

6.3.44.

William is starting back to work today. Doctor says he ought to have his tonsils out. Thank you for the Bible Reading Fellowship notes for Feb. and March. Our ordination course starts with Mark so the two fit in well. These evenings we're seeking to become better people and are thinking about the things in us which make such a mess in the world – but first we're looking to Jesus. We all respect and love one another – Rank doesn't count. Sgts. and Troopers and L/Cpls all use Christian names. I'm never 'Sir' but Padre. The latest Ordination notes from Dr. S. G. F. Brandon at Bône are

'Parson as Prophet Pastor and Priest'. The notes are so good that many of our Chaplains are seeking them. How marvellous it will be my Darling when we can start to try to work out this love business together.

My snug little home in the olive grove is now in pieces and quite a lot of it is stored in my truck.

Now I'm off to bed. I'm starting to keep a diary on the same thin paper bits that I used on the last convoy.

SOLDIERS AND SOLDIERS!

[The northern coastal strip of Africa is surprisingly green and fertile. One has to penetrate thirty or forty miles inland to come towards the desert.

It was the 1st Army which landed in North Africa in November, 1942, fresh from England, mostly new to war and traditionally clad. Uniform was khaki, vehicles were freshly painted and camouflage was green.

In due course the men from the desert came north and there is the story of these bleached tatty Desert Rats catching sight of the new army and saying to one another 'Look there are some soldiers!'. These were hardy reliant men bleached by the sun, uniforms faded to the colour of sand, and with camouflage the colour of sand. The officers had ceased to wear ties, and in the shops of Cairo had bought brightly coloured scarves. Their trousers were corduroy, and they wore desert shoes. These are still very popular, rubber soled with sheepskin turned inside out as the uppers.

When victory in Africa ended up with the capture of quarter of a million enemy troops, the 1st Army was merged into the 8th Army. Henceforth, honour having been satisfied, the men of the two armies became one. Some of the seasoned troops went home to prepare for the second front. But both armies had new lessons to learn.

The wars of desert mobility were over. Italy was to prove one of the hardest terrains of all the theatres. It is true that there was much sunshine, except for winter mud, but where else could there be endless mountain ranges, some many thousands of feet high, roaring rivers delivering mountain snow and water into the sea? Where could there be such a terrain of mountain tracks with tiny villages perched on hill tops, providing perfect observation posts? Where could there be acres and acres of vineyards with vines strung ten feet high between poplar and later, mulberry trees?

When the last winter came with British and American Armies decimated by the needs of the Second Front and the landing in the South of France, there can have been no braver slogging than the continuous warfare up in the Appenines almost within sight of the Po valley and victory.]

8

Italian Slog

MARCH 1944 TO VICTORY 1945

———◀━◆◆◆◆◆━▶———

A DIARY FROM AFRICA TO EUROPE

EL ARROUCH TO NAPLES – MARCH 1944

A journey with the Derbyshire Yeomanry advance party commanded by Major Sir Ian Walker, from a North African olive grove to Italy.

Sunday, Lent III, March 12 – evening. Dinner is at 7 p.m. The Asconia is slowly turning round from her berth in Bône harbour to pass out to the roadstead. We are the Regimental Advance Party for joining in the Italian campaign at Monte Cassino.

The crew have lashed and battened down; everything seems ready. There is another ship, the Léopoldville, which has moved out too. We were up at 5.45 this morning. I had 6.30 breakfast, and scrambled into all my kit, until I looked like a Christmas tree!

7.50 p.m. I've just been up on deck. It is cold and wet with a few lights showing from the mainland. The ship is rolling slightly.

8.30 p.m. Had a talk with the 2nd Navigation Officer – two gold stripes, and from Liverpool. He says we're bound for Bari. The coast is slipping by with lights of some towns here and there. The Asconia, 15,000 tons, built in 1925, is one of the smallest of the Cunard ships.

Monday, March, 13, 10 a.m. Ship rolling a bit so I'm on my bunk! What a pooey I am. Went down to breakfast and started on some puffed wheat, but couldn't make it. During the night the other ships had joined the convoy. We are steering east, hugging the African coast. At breakfast time we passed a larger convoy coming from seaward, perhaps it's going home. The steward has just been in, and he says that quite a few are under the weather. He's a Cockney and hasn't been home for a year.

Tuesday, March 16. Italy. 5.45 p.m. The sun is beginning to set across the bay from Vesuvius. We arrived at Naples between 10 and 11 this morning, passing the Isle of Capri on our left. Vesuvius, 4000 feet high, was wreathed in cloud. To seaward Capri is a small square island with precipitous cliffs going down to the sea. In the Bay the view was impressive. Naples spreads out for miles, with Pompei to the south. The harbour was full of ships, our own and enemy ships bombed, burnt out and lying in all positions.

Wednesday, March 17. Vesuvius has a plume of white smoke, and the sky is continually full of aircraft. The last few days have been wet, but now it's lovely. Last night there was a raid over Naples. Our baggage party was unloading the last of the gear and got caught in the alert, and in the smoke screen!

This morning I wandered round the other units' lines. There are four Chaplains so far. Today the advance party goes across the Volturno to the new camp.

Our first impression here is of the hunger and poverty of the people. In peace time the standard of living of these Southern Italians is low enough, but now it is pitiful. Here the Ities have nothing but fruit. They come round with tins for scraps, which they wolf greedily. Goodness, there is no glamour here.

Vineyards stretch for miles. Poplar trees (I think) are planted at 15 yard intervals with all the branches pruned except the top ones. The vines are strung across in festoons. What an awful country to fight in.

The Ities come and cut hair and clean shoes. An Itie will do anything for a tin of bully.

Thursday, March 18. Went into Naples with Father Dommersen. Wandered round the city, especially Via Roma, the main street — very long with shops full of everything, mainly watches at fabulous prices. Had a cup of chocolate and a chocolate nutty cake in mid-morning. Bought some flowery silk stuff for summer dress for Helen, costing £4.10s.

Visited the field cashier and got tied up with the Lire! Bought Easter cards (very pagan ones!). Visited the Cathedral, large and cold.

Lunched at the Officers' Club. 2.30 p.m. went to the opera at San Carlo theatre. We saw 'Cavalleria Rusticana' and 'Pagliacci'. Orchestra wonderful, chiefly strings. Leading soprano flat, but with a lovely voice. Caste indifferent! Theatre large, white and gold. Main seating on ground floor with five tiers round the walls.

Vesuvius snow covered after last night's rain. Got a lift back with Sir Ian. Had a large meal of mutton with onion sauce and cauliflower and potatoes, prepared by Smudger (S.Q.M.S. Smith). He's a crafty old chap, and can turn his hand to anything.

Friday, March 19. We'll soon be on the move again. This time forward to our new camp. The sky is full of our bombers and fighters. It is very reassuring. An old priest, a tiny little man, is rushing about with a collecting box and a grin on his face.

We went into Naples to collect the N.A.A.F.I. supplies this morning, and took the opportunity to have a good look round Pompei. Here was an ancient town that was unashamedly Pagan. I got cards and a tiny water colour of a street with famous villa at the end, framed in Juniper trees.

PIEDEMONTE D'ALIFE
1st DERBYSHIRE YEOMANRY C.M.F.

24.3.44.

My Darling,

This is our new address. C.M.F. stands for Central Mediterranean Forces. You should have got my airmail posted when we landed in Italy, by now. The hills have a slight covering of snow. Last night several of the tents were torn to shreds by the gales, but the local people say it is a sign of the end of the winter. We are living on smallholdings, farms with a wee house and a few vines and olive trees, and an acre or two of land.

One of our farmers spent 20 years in America, and became naturalised. He returned in time for the war, poor man! He often helps us with problems and local customs. When the Germans were here he had to flee into the hills because he was marked down as an anti-fascist. Our camp is about two miles from the tiny walled town of Piedemonte d'Alife, and the women walk up to ask for washing, which they do in the same day, and return next morning. The town has a little cathedral, filled with small chapels. Each chapel is decorated with gaudy waxed saints. Caruso is supposed to have been born here. The whole countryside here is like I imagine Switzerland to be. Certainly the air is very invigorating. We can see Vesuvius' eruptions from all this way off. It is offically the biggest for 200 years.

Your March 12 airmail came today and Mother's of the 9th, yesterday, both via North Africa. It was a thrill to get letters again.

This morning I held a service at the Field Ambulance in a little town a few miles away. They were in a school which used to be a monastery. We held the service in a corridor place, and the acoustics were terrific. There were only about 25, but we sounded like a choir of 100!

Nearly teatime. I've just been up the hillside for a stroll. It is great 'walking stick' country. Many of the men have made themselves sticks. I found a wonderful one, but I should have cut it with a knife. Instead I pulled it and split the root end, spoiling a good knob handle.

7.0 p.m. Our temporary Mess was a small ridge tent. Now we've been given another to put at one end. Then we laid a crazy pavement, with bricks from a shelled house. We gave the old lady some bully beef and soap for her bricks.

We are not likely to be here long, but we did toy with the idea of a fire place, like we had in Africa. Frank (Quartermaster) got one of the local army stoves for us instead. It consists of an empty oil drum with one or two necessary holes, and a flash pan on to which is dripped water and diesel oil. We enjoyed rigging it so that the mixture was correct. The stove pipe had to go safely through the canvas too. After flames and smoke in all directions we made it work beautifully. I believe that this Heath Robinson stove was invented by the New Zealanders in the desert.

Two years ago, My Darling, it was my most wonderful Easter, when we shared it at Troon, the deepest I have ever known. My knowledge of the fulness of our Saviour's Resurrection came with the wonder of sharing it with you. Dearest we're soon going to begin our Adventure together. We've so much to do, and so much loving to make up. But please it is more than even I dreamed of to belong to you. Be very happy and certain that God has a wonderful work for us to do together for Him. I love you.

We're slowly getting organised. Sir Ian bought half a dozen Italian-made carbide lamps and let me have one. They stand on a table and give a white naked flame, or we can hang them on a hook in a tent, so we're well illuminated.

I'm beginning to take an interest in your new clothes in a new exciting kind of way. You see I've a feeling that I'll be there before they're worn out!

Charles Ridley, my new S.C.F. turned up today and had lunch here. I think he'll be alright. We were at college together. He was very much older, and had been a regular soldier – a bluff Yorkshire man. We talked a lot about old times and the time to come. He's married now, and has an infant whom he has never seen.

Reggie Snaith joined us yesterday. The people in the city are in a bad way. The war has made them hungry and has made them lose a grip on things. Three girls came up to Reggie to sell, or rather to try to sell their bodies to him for food or for money during the course of two days. One was very attractive and well dressed. Darling it is so pathetic. Ideals and everything seem to go when war comes along. There are more soldiers in hospital in Italy with V.D. than battle casualties, I believe. We've had films and talks from Doctors on the subject, and I'm always harping on the religious side of it, and I'm waiting to see how the Regiment is going to stand up to these temptations.

Always these things bring me back to the wonder of our love, Darling Woman. God's love and the family seem to be the key to everything, and you fit in so wonderfully with all my hopes and dreams, and also light up the gloriousness of our task. Religion can't grow old or out of date when this new frightening scientific world emerges out of the present chaos. Religion is concerned with human nature which also needs God before it becomes whole.

Bedtime. Reggie and I both talk about life as we see it. He has told Muriel about his accosting. We've both agreed that the great thing is to try to understand human nature. Reggie lost his bed a long while ago and so he has been sleeping on the floor ever since. I've been telling him how to make one out of branches and telephone wire, but he says he prefers the ground. We've just been giggling at the thought of him saying 'Goodnight' to Muriel and then curling up on the mat or going to the bathroom floor to find a firm unyielding surface! Geoffrey and Dick have appeared and are undressing – so I'd better follow suit. We are four in this square tent and have a quarter each. There's not much room so we have to be tidy.

EASTERTIME IN ITALY

12.4.44.

Darling Lass,

I collected some smirky pictures this morning. Think I'll risk sending you an advance one in an airmail. If the Postal Authorities disapprove they'll bung it in the seamail. It shows me wearing an Africa Star anyway!

Easter Day was a great rush. Early Communion was well attended, especially by the officers. The Colonel and two Squadron Leaders were there. Then came two spit and polish parades with two Squadrons each. We collected £17.16.0d. for the Prisoners of War Fund. Another Communion, this time in the open air.

The truck has been off the road for a few days. William has been putting long hours in and we might have it on the road tomorrow again. Italy is much greener than North Africa. Lots of jolly hedgerows are coming out. There are fields of onions and green stuff.

5.5 p.m. I called in at the Field Ambulance this afternoon and passed the Dental part. I popped in to ask the Dentist to file down a sharp tooth, which had lost a chip the other day. He said he'd better examine them all and found a bit that needed filling, so I had that done as well, all at the Army's expense!

After the emptiness of Africa, one is very tempted to go to the town to buy all sorts of knick knacks and presents just because they are there, and it is silly really because it is so unnecessary. I ought to be saving lots of money. George Trollope found a black market the other day and spent £30 on silk stockings and black undies for his wife.

I called to see Bob Martin, Chaplain of 21 Lancers, this afternoon. His prayer book came by the same post as the one you sent for him! Prim (his fiancée) has been pestering him for a picture, so he's off to the picture shop tomorrow. This afternoon we passed the local R.C. seminary out for a walk in a crocodile. There were boys from about 10 years upwards, all in flat black 'Holy Joes', black cassocks and shiny celluloid collars. My dog collar must have created a good impression because they all bowed and doffed their hats as we flashed by!

EASTERTIME IN ENGLAND

2.4.44.   Palm Sunday.

I got up at 6 a.m. at School, after Fire Watching (clocks put on); went to 8 a.m. Church, and back to the flat, to get breakfast and clean the place up — ready for the teacher-owners to come for their holiday. On Friday, on our Nature Walk, one atom threw another's glasses up into a static water tank . . . about 20,000 gallons of water are kept there for emergency use . . . incendiary bombing.

7.4.44.   Good Friday.

We had a Three Hours Service 2-5 (double time) the most convenient time. We sang the D.Y. Hymn: 'Oh, my Saviour lifted from the earth for me.' Tonight the Choir sang Stainer's Crucifixion. Dad is saying that his only bother is the lawn . . . it is woolly and tufty . . . he needs 3 gallons of petrol for the

mower, for the whole season. He has asked the Education
Committee for a chit to get some as so many Youth, Scouts,
Cubs, etc. use the lawn!

10.4.44.

Easter Day was lovely, with a hectic evening – the Corn
Hall was fuller than ever – Mrs. B. and lots of valiant souls
dished out tea and dried cups while I washed up. Yesterday a
crowd of men, passing through, appeared at the Church Hall,
while a Bridge Drive was in progress . . . wanting tea. They
drank 900 cupfuls before the Canteen was officially open!
At 4.30 Dad brought five Officers home – there was only a
tiny piece of cake, so I cut sandwiches – honey/cheese –
and gave them quarts of tea. Then I was at Canteen 5.30–
10 p.m. men queueing all the time.

Tomorrow a soldier's wife and daughters, aged 7 and 8,
come to the Rectory for three days. Mrs. P. (evacuee) is still
in Thorpe Mental Hospital – she got involved with a Canadian
airman, I think, and is mixed up in her mind. Douglas, her
four year old son has gone to a children's home temporarily,
a friend has taken little Barry.

We had an I.O.M. mother and little girl, and one on the
way, staying here, and now a quiet Welsh girl, also expecting.
It makes me look forward! But I'm a very happy girl . . . I
have the best man in the world and he loves me; and he is
doing the very most a chap can do for the Kingdom, he is
giving everything all the time. Do you realise how happy that
makes me, Bill? To know what great things you are doing just
by being you! It is nearly three weeks since I got your
'landed in Italy' airmail, so there should be some news to tell
all the folk who ask after you each day. God bless you my
Beloved. I love you always. Your L.M.P.

22.4.44.   Saturday 10 p.m.

The News . . . England beat Scotland 3–2 and Home Guard
exercises – 'Germans' with blackened faces! Home tomorrow,
St. George's Day Service for Scouts, Guides and Cubs at 3 p.m.
Dad took the Scouts, in a U.S. truck organised by a Padre, to
a Base where they explored a Flying Fortress. What a thrill
for Dad as well as the boys!

We are only 'on call' tonight i.e. we stay in our cosy camp beds until a bomb drops!

Sunday 12.20 Ipswich Station. Another very hot day. A little boy, across the table, is amused at the view from the train window . . . a soldier is shaving from a bucket of water, outside a back door and dry garden dust is blowing all over him . . . off we shunt. Here's to the exhausting journeys when we take our family to see the Grandparents . . . sticky-fingered, bouncy kids! So many dreams . . . so much to long for but so much more to enjoy – just the being and knowing – your love lightens up every moment of every day, until . . . perhaps it won't be so very long until . . . It is when the sun shines on a wakening earth and the countryside responds – when trees burst their buds in a few hours and daisies open their eyes while you look at them – it is then that it seems only right that you should be back to enjoy it all before another Spring has passed. So I think you will. There may be Autumn fogs and rains first, but we will see the best Spring of all together.

6 p.m. Sunday. Your April 12th air letter came today with the most truly you picture. Thank you very much T.T.C.A. your L.M.P.

21.4.44.

I came to spend a week with my 8th Field Squadron R.E. Across the valley is Million Dollar Hill, a brute of a hill, which cost the Yanks dearly. Cassino is about seven miles away to the north, and we are on the fringe of the war zone. Both our Sapper Squadrons and the Indian Sappers are well up, preparing for the next attack. There are lights galore and mobile open-air cinemas, where two thousand men may congregate within reach of Jerry's long range guns.

Yesterday afternoon the S.C.F. took me forward a bit for a tour. Everywhere is war, like the last war, with every town, house and village blasted, roads up and bridges down. From an Advance Dressing Station we saw a German sign to their dressing station.

By day traffic is discouraged, but as soon as night comes the guns start, and supplies go up. The bravest men are the porters who climb the bullet swept hillsides, across bridges under smoke screens to Cassino, to the Guards, and back again into Cassino. The place is just a pile of rubble and smells through lack of sanitation. The Welsh Guards' H.Q. is in a crypt of the Gaol. In the Prison chapel are the Coldstreams, and the Grenadiers in the Church crypt. We hold two thirds of the town. Jerry holds the rest and the Monastery hill commanding the town.

Last night I went out in a scout car with Sapper Officer Winkle Watkins to see his men laying tracks for a regiment of guns to move up.

Friday, April 22. Evening. Returned to D.Y. after seeing quite a lot of the R.Es. Went with S.C.F. to the Guards Echelon where the Q.M. took us up to the Grenadiers Reserve company. We started at dusk when the mists began to fall, rushing down Route 6 and turning off at the Cassino straight, about a mile from the town. We followed a sunken road to a corner near the house, then walked the last bit so as not to show a vehicle. This followed up in the dark. We had dinner — a very good one too — by candlelight, and afterwards went

Bill Cook listening to the Band playing to the troops in the concentration area at Mignano.

round to see the men. They had come out of Cassino the night before.

Quiet night at Cassino with occasional shells popping off. Jerry had planted two flags on two of his houses in honour of Hitler's birthday! Some reports say we tried to shoot them down. Others that we just ignored them.

PREPARING FOR THE SPRING OFFENSIVE
AT CASSINO

28.4.44.

We got back about an hour ago having been on tour with the Sappers for three days. I wish I could tell you all about it but I fear it must wait until afterwards. Everybody was in good heart. Here life is very static and comfortable and civilised again. There was a sea letter, and an air letter waiting when I got back. You are a Darling. I've been overwhelmed with mail for the last two or three weeks – mail every day.

Bishop Woods of Lichfield is coming out here next month for confirmations, and to meet ordinands. Yesterday I saw one of my ordinands for the first time for three months. The ordination lectures keep rolling on in an ever widening scope. The latest is a series of lectures on Greek culture – the gods and heroes and philosophers. I'll try to keep copies for our own parochial ordinands. Darling, we will keep our eyes open for vocations.

7.45 p.m. Mess. I don't suppose much will get written now. People are arriving and talk is brewing. The Colonel is trying Phil's new homemade fishing rod. Neddy Baring is reading an old Sunday newspaper. Cliff Jones and Dick Witney are lighting the oil stove – talk, talk, talk!

This morning I ran into a company of colonial soldiers ('Basutoland Boys'), black, and in the charge of a splendid broad Yorkshire Sergeant who had himself recuited them from their home 2½ years ago. They are very martial people (Christian too, though some of them have three wives!). They love being in uniform – in fact they wear all the uniform they possess at the same time. Today some of them were wearing scarf, cap comforter, balaclava, tin hat and side hat!

They love castor oil so much that the Doctor has to ration it severely. Once when the Doctor was away on leave they crowded round his Locum and drank him dry in three days. [These Basuto boys manned the smoke screens that were kept perpetually burning on the hills in front of Monte Cassino. Jerry had every bit of land under complete observation. So all supply roads, bridges and sites where troops tried to dig in on rocky mountain-sides had to be hidden away by smoke.] It is a wonderful sight to see all the members of this great Commonwealth and of the United Nations doing this great thing together here – British, Free French, Americans, Jews, Poles, Greeks, South Africans, New Zealanders, Australians, French Goums [who were to inspire as much fear in their enemies as the Gurkhas].

TUNIS DAY

7.5.44.   Sunday evening.

Dearest, Do you remember a year ago today? We ought to have had a Regimental Party to celebrate, but alas nothing is static anymore. William and I came to the Sappers tonight for evening services. They are so nice and friendly. We had a happy service, and communion, at the foot of a little hill. It's all rather devastated here, yet spring has come with fields of poppies and flowers of all colours. There are even a few Italians wandering around. At one of this morning's services a woman and a girl carrying baskets of soldier's washing stopped for communion time, and when it was over they silently replaced the little roll of towel on their heads, then the basket, and went away. It was touching.

Another heartbreak tonight. A sapper's sweetie had pressed him to get married before he came away from England. They have known one another since they were 15, so they ought to have known their minds. Anyway she has decided that the marriage can't go on. Her letters are vicious. She doesn't want him to come home. What people can do to one another. It will be much easier to beat Hitler than to win the peace and to seek to rebuild in this wreckage of broken towns and homes and lives. Our task is coming clearer and more urgent every day, Sweet dreams, Darling Redhead. I love you always.

Diss rectory.

24.4.44.

Many thanks for a big box of dates and figs, a sweet little Eastery card and 2 letters . . . crossing sea, and after.

The Officer's family who have been here for a fortnight, went today . . . just as a telegram arrived, asking if Mrs. Weigall and David could come on Thursday. So now we are trying to get the big room ready for them; Jones came to fumigate it today.

On Sunday night the Cornhall was packed. I arrived ten minutes after it had begun, and could only get one eye over the shoulders of the audience. At the end a Yank, who was standing near, departed when the Epilogue began. I saw him afterwards in the street, with a companion, so I tackled them about his exit, it was silly because I think he was a Jew, only I didn't connect looks and religion then! Anyway they both came home and we gave them lemonade and biscuits before they did their 4½ mile walk back. They were obviously very impressed by the house and garden and being allowed to sit on comfy chairs and feel at home. I think they were struck by the jollity and hospitality of the parson too. One may return to take photos of the garden. Dad likes to have chaps dropping in.

Trees are still flowering; chestnut, may, laburnum. It's lovely in England, now that April's here . . . but it will be lovelier by far when the birds have the sky free from bombers and children can go to school and not to shelters. It will be rather surprising if the land doesn't spring into flower under your feet when the triumphant armies come home.

Time to get tea as we are going to a flick . . . Deanna Durbin in The Amazing Mrs. Holliday.

God give you courage and joy. I love you muchly. Helen.

ITALIAN PLOD
8.5.44.

Sunday afternoon ought to be rather a snoozy time, but I've been pottering in the Jeep and now its teatime. An 8th Army Educational leaflet on Florence, with all its sights and a street map has just been circulated! Sadly we've not quite got that far yet! But it shows how on the spot all our various departments are! Melons are coming out now and we've had some lovely ones for lunch.

I talked with a nice Doctor today who had been away from home for over two years. He's engaged and even the minister is fixed for the wedding. I didn't tell him that we'll be able to fix our own quite easily too! We're to have a hymn sing-song in the hospital tonight. I must go and prepare. Be happy my love. You're infinitely precious.

8.5.44.

The B.B.C. announcer said that we are sweltering in the sun and he is right. I dream of fog and fireside and windy hilltops and the breeze in your auburn hair. We came back to the Regiment this morning. Carol Levis, the talent spotter, is coming with his wife to entertain us this evening, and staying to dinner afterwards.

Bedtime. Well, the entertainers didn't arrive. They're coming tomorrow instead. The night is rather close. Last night we were away from Camp and my tent, so I slept under the stars – first time since last Autumn. I slept very well. Goodness, how we all dream of our Sweetie Pies. The easiest way to a man's heart is to ask him about his missis or sweetie. In no time you are deluged with pictures of wife, girl friend and family. I've looked at hundreds in the last few days. I wouldn't have known all this joy and wonder of being in love if you hadn't come along.

12.5.44.

My Darling Lass,

Things seem to be moving now. The B.B.C. said at midday that the attack has started in Italy. Its a lovely day and I'm sitting in a field of red clover. The farmer is cutting it as quickly as he and the family can manage. There is broom here and acacia in large quantities – a pleasant green valley with scrubby hills on both sides.

CASSINO ASSAULT – FOURTH AND FINAL BATTLE

14.5.44.

Three days after the initial Infantry assault B Squadron, D.Y. crossed the river Rapido, just under Cassino. After many attempts to capture the Monastery by many very brave men it finally fell to the Polish Corps. This victory for Poland seemed so right. Hitler brought us into the war by obliterating Warsaw and Poland. Now the Polish flag flies in the rubble of the Monastery.

18.5.44.

I think it's Wednesday today, but its rather difficult to keep up with the days of the week at present. The news is good and we're wondering whether the B.B.C. will have it on the bulletin. A Canadian Padre by the name of McClean came along this morning, and we gossiped for half an hour. I'll scribble a proper letter if I get the chance. Meanwhile I'll put this in the post to let you know that all is well.

19.5.44.

Our mail still gets up to us, and we even have 8th Army News daily. Here, whatever happens, the nightingales sing continuously.

Eager Brundell, C. Squadron Leader, was killed a couple of days ago, charging several machine gun nests, in the top of his tank. Colonel Peter took his place, and the Troop achieved its objective. Eager was a very brave man. The Squadron will miss his leadership sorely. Peter Liddington, a troop officer, was wounded and captured, and freed the day after. He will be alright after a stretch in hospital. What a waste all this madness is. Will we ever learn the gentle way of Christian love? This is terrible fighting country. The farms are tiny and very simple, all deserted and in ruins. It is a very primitive part of Italy.

25.5.44.   Whitsun Eve.

My Darling,

The sun is getting quite high, and it will be another hot day. Yesterday was the hottest day we've had so far in Italy.

Refugees come straggling down the roads. God what a pitiful sight. Old men and women, boys and girls, carrying a bundle on their heads, or a wee tot with a hen clasped tightly, or a couple of goats, or an old woman with a holy statue under her arms. They're past being terrified I think. They raise their hats, and keep saying 'Buongiorno' all the time. I suppose they're afraid we will maltreat them. Any surplus food we have we give them as they go down the roads.

The African campaign was a picnic to this grim, close, relentless battling. We've just heard that Bob Martin (Padre of the 17/21 Lancers) had a chunk of shell in his head. He's in a very bad way, poor lad. [After he died, his replacement was also killed.] I have just opened a Cemetery on the banks of the river Melfa, under the shadow of the Monastery. Poor Harry Johnson, one of Tom Caldwell's Gunners, was killed instantly. There will sadly be more to follow. But Jerry is finished and soon it will be over. By then the kindly muse of forgetfulness will have blurred over all the horribly tragic memories. Whit Sunday tomorrow. I hope I'll get a service in. Blessings, my Darling, we're fit and well, and I love you with all myself. Love and kisses, Your very own Bill.

FLASH BACK

Frank Elkington, one of my North Africa confirmees, vividly recalls his experience of battle on his late wife's birthday, May 25th, 1944.

'I was drafted from H.Q. to No. 4 Troop, B. Squadron as co-driver of one of the four tanks that crossed the Melfa, by a makeshift wooden bridge. We climbed the steep bank to a very large flat open field, and were picked up by enemy artillery fairly quickly. Despite vigorous evasive action by the commander and driver, we were hit after some near misses . . . I later learned that Tpr. Johnson was killed, and Sgt. Walters injured. After some difficulty in opening my hatch, and with burning ammunition showering my shoulders and arms with a golden rain, I found Tpr. Paige outside with leg injuries, and helped him down the slope to comparative safety. I left him to summon help, my shirt falling off my back in two halves . . . I only had the will power to retrieve the contents of one shirt pocket . . . I was picked up by a turretless Honey tank, and having told them where I had left my companion, was helped into a clean denim jacket . . . We were left on stretchers by the river until towards dusk. The infantry being unable to get through, it was decided to burn the remaining tanks and M.10s . . . the first time I had seen one . . . and retire on foot, an M.10 having been blown up on the bridge, which had also burned. We waded through the cold, swiftly-flowing water almost waist deep, and climbed the steep bank. I was sent to a dressing station, after a hurried look by our medical orderly, and thence to a field hospital, where, although I was maggot infested I had skin grafts. After two months in field hospitals and a converted monastery in Naples, I was shipped to Liverpool in the Dutch H.S. Oranje. After more operations and grafts, at the end of the year, I was discharged from the Army.

25.5.88

WHIT SUNDAY,
AFTER THE CROSSING OF THE RIVER MELFA

28.5.44.

May your heart be full of peace and joy and holy fire to-day, my Darling. I think it will be. We sorely need the power of the Holy Spirit.

I've just been to the roadside to give packets of biscuits to refugees. There is one village upon the hill which has escaped shelling, and the Whitsuntide bells are pealing.

11.45 a.m. I've had two very simple and real services.

29.5.44.   Whit Monday.

What couldn't we do with a day like this? The night was moonlit and dewless, and now the sky is cloudless. The almost daily slog goes on. But we keep advancing, and slowly Hitler's Empire shrinks. Always there's a trickle of refugees, patient, frightened, white-eyed people. What a mess it all is. I gave a hungry old lady some bully and sardines, biscuits and margarine this morning. In return she is doing our washing. So clothes should go up three shades cleaner! The car has had a spring clean.

Last night I had a long talk with some American Ambulance Drivers. They are usually Quakers, nice men and pacifists. We had a go at the question of evil at the root of war. The better world depends on the change of heart in the individual. One man is a genealogist, so although he has never been to England he knows just where all his forebears came from, Lancashire, Derbyshire, West Country and Wales!

8.55 p.m. One of our men came up in great distress this evening. He has a wife and child and money saved up for a home, also the prospects of a good job after the war. He had a most hectic battle. I can't tell you about it, but he was lucky to come through, and when he came back to harbour a couple of nights ago there was a letter to say that his Missis had been getting fed up and bored, and playing about with another man. Goodness, this separation is making such a mess. If only he could go home for a leave.

31.5.44.

I've been dreaming about you so much today – you seem very close. We are resting and its been a lazy day, but I've done my best to keep in touch with all the units. My box of books is much sought after.

Tonight some of the men are going off to an ENSA Show, and we have a film in Camp, *Road to Morocco*. We really are looked after very well. I collected some free cigarettes for the Regiment. There are cards to the school children who have worked to send these 'comforts' in each box. There were also footballs and bladders and newspapers and bundles of books and magazines. More books for my library!

This is a lovely rolling farming country. The grass is lush and full of clover, and shoulder high corn in the valley, with oak trees and garlic all mixed up.

Dear Bob Martin died, and the whole Division seems to be mourning for him. Poor Prim, his fiancée.

1.6.44.

We're still at rest and how nice it is to lie about doing so little. At a Chaplains' Conference this morning we had a memorial service for Bob. Tea time news spoke of further advances in Italy. It is a continual slogging match – inch by inch – hill by hill – village by village. But these men of ours,

keep on battling, constantly under observation, slogging day
by day, always willing to have a go at what they are asked to
do. Then a day or two of rest, whilst someone else takes over.
How I admire them.

3.6.44.   Saturday.

My Beloved,

We moved into a jolly farm this afternoon. There is the
farm family and one or two evacuated families, too, with lots
of clean wee atoms. How good to see the children. I gave them
chocolate and they brought us lettuce, so we gave them bread,
etc. The entente is going quite well. A charming spot in fact.
Jimmy Simpson brought in a beret full of cherries at teatime.
The great thing today has been your Whitsun airmail arriving.
Your Papa seems to have had his hands full on the Day. He
certainly beat me. It was only possible to hold one service
and one Holy Communion all day. Your description of the
Church makes me very homesick. Now you seem to be
surrounded by Yanks. Perhaps they're at Uplands and the
Old Rectory. You're a good child about your security, bless
you.

Here, the countryside is quickly losing its greenness and
turning brown and dusty, also a little too hot. Darling you're
much too energetic cycling home and back to Ipswich. I'll
have to go into training if you make me do these things.

7 p.m. The sun is about four inches above the skyline —
quite a long way to go yet. I stood with a towel round my
tummy in some lovely red earth and corn, having a wash.
I'm rather like a zebra, stripes of different degrees of tanning
(only my very middle part is white). Now for a preparation
for a Trinity talk. The only message that seems to matter at
present is the Pentecost one — wherever we go, whatever we
do, He is there, in us, with us, guiding, inspiring and strength-
ening. So I don't think there is much danger of my going
into a discourse on the parts of the Blessed Trinity — Three
yet One, Incomprehensible and Indivisible!

Trinity Sunday. Midday. Still in our farm. I've had two
services and two communions, good ones. At both farms, the
locals came and stood at the back for Communion. They

knelt at the Consecration. One farmer seemed particularly pious. 'Of course I'm not Protestant – me Catholico', he said when I tried to say I was Anglicano. His eyes opened wide as I prepared the altar on the tailboard of the truck, crucifix, candles and robes. 'Good heavens, I thought only Catholics had these things. He even believes in Jesus Christ' – or so his mind seemed to be working! Goodness the world knows so little about itself, let alone the Christian Church.

There is a trail of little boys contentedly marching off from the cookhouse, one with an empty bottle (very precious) and a bundle of biscuits, another with biscuits and a bit of chocolate. We have some very good fresh meat, even though we are on the wander, with lots of good white bread.

Let us talk about my Appleblossom. Dearest Heart you'll never know the tenderness I have for you in my heart until we are 'us'. Darling, I ache for you and long for you. You are the light and inspiration of all life. God bless you. Happy dreaming. Your own Bill.

5.6.44.

It's 7.40 a.m. and I've been up for a half day already, or so it seems! I got up soon after 5.0 because Sgt. came up and said 'You really ought to be getting up Padre'. Breakfast at 6.15 and I had 20 minutes to spare. This place looked quite clean and attractive by moonlight, but it is very drab really. Our present pitch is dirty, and Jerry has occupied it. Old papers, uncovered latrine trenches and well, just a Jerry smell – so well known. The people look poor and starved.

Fifth Army seems to be in Rome now. I hope the Krauts will not fight there.

8.0 p.m. 5th Army well and truly in Rome. Its taken three weeks, this last drive.

The people are thin and frightened and starving. They hang round the cookhouses begging pitifully. This used to be a prosperous farming area with plentiful bread, meat and vegetables. Now they've come to this.

6.6.44.

Things are going very well at the moment, but I mustn't

say more than that. Last night a nightingale sat on a tree by the car and sang for a long time.

GREAT NEWS OF THE INVASION

4.30 p.m. What heart-warming news, and at the anniversary of Dunkirk. We've just had lunch, and breakfast was at 5.30 a.m. We haven't slept for 24 hours, and I'm off to sleep now. Its been a bit like Piccadilly Circus in a traffic jam! Since Cassino we've seen very little of Jerry planes. If there were any we should be in a bit of a pickle here!

7.6.44.

The Invasion seems to be going slowly but surely. Good old Second Front. Quite a lot of the 8th Army are there. It really has been a great tonic to us all. At the moment all that we are likely to see at present is the world's largest dome on the skyline. These are Great Days, My Darling.

Ipswich.

5.6.44.

One sea mail — and news on the wireless of the occupation of ROME!

Another major objective reached after months of bitter fighting. Rome is the Allies' — the first great Capital in Europe breathes freely again. You are part of the great liberating force. We are so proud that you are doing such great things — I don't mean slaying the enemy or taking lands — I mean carrying on the goodness of life through all the badness of war. In all the madness of peoples great things, like our love, seem so vital — it almost brings its own peace. Sometimes your love and God's Being seem the only right things. Tousle your Tuft for me! Boo to dictators! I love you always. Helen. P.S. Our silkworm's an inch long.

INVASION DAY

Ipswich.

6.6.44.   Tuesday.

Beloved,

It is all happening — the beginning of the end!

Today they swarmed across the sky and sea; men dressed for war, with weapons of death (made from pots, pans and railings! our contribution!), with a nation's heart and strength behind them. It is all such a mad necessity. A relief – that all the pent-up energy and polished proficiency is at last focussed on the real target . . . a suspense – because everywhere, everyone is feeling part of the great moments when history is made. As the King told us at 9 p.m. in his broadcast, everyone is in it – we all have our part to play . . . it is our job to pray . . . I hope you heard him. New, dramatic attacks help to intensify the significance of the older Campaigns – North Africa, Italy, Burma, The Pacific – there is a feeling of oneness and purpose shining through it all. It must reach the prison camps in Malaya and homes in Greece, and Germany. There is unparalleled joy and strength when man realises he is powerless and yet can do all things through Him who strengthens . . . NOW we understand why roads and lanes to the ports were so crowded with convoys, and all kinds of transport; and all the aircraft above . . . lots of things fall into place. God speed you all.

8.6.44.

Its a lovely evening, and nearly dinner. Our view is over red rolling country, smiling with corn and fruit and tiny farm houses, with an occasional town or village on a hill or brow. We are in a kind of Aviation Museum in memory of a couple of Italian flyers, 1923–1930 time. There are cases of flying relics and models round the walls, and a real live aeroplane taking up the floor space. Its a funny old plane. We have a Mess in the building, under a wing! It's quite nice in the grounds except for the slight Jerry smell of recent occupation. I don't know what it is, but the whiff is always the same.

Lots of these villages are shelled, yet the people wave and clap and really seem glad to see us. I think they hated the Germans. Good news of the Second Front. It seems to be building up strongly and surely. Good old Invasion Armies. Tonight the Germans say the Russians are attacking on a wide front with tanks and infantry north of Jassy.

ROME

9.6.44.

We've done it today. Apart from the Doctor who went there almost by mistake a night or two ago, I think we are the first D.Y. to go into the Eternal City. Hugh Waller wanted to buy wine for the Mess, so we got into the truck and packed William in the back, and whistled straight down the road. It's officially out of bounds, till the city is organised, so there were hardly any soldiers there. I bought you a wad of stockings and I'll send them by Registered Post, a couple of pairs at a time. I'm a bit worried about the colour and the size. One pair is real silk and the other artificial. The shopkeepers say the stock will be gone in 10 days, when the Allied soldiers get loose! In the first shop, a kind of Gamages, we met a man who had rowed against Oxford at Lucerne. Then we met a man, a big jolly, hale and hearty banker and we went in search of wine. We tried Vermouth and Marsala in all kinds of shops, but it was very dear. The Germans have taken most of it.

What a pooh to have been in Rome, and to talk only about wine and stockings! We didn't really see very much. It's population is now trebled by evacuees.

The second man began to talk about Scotch whisky, and said that a bottle was worth 2000 lire. I pricked up my ears because I had hardly any money on me, but my emergency bottle was in the car. He paid me 800 lire for it, so I made 30/- as it only cost me 10/-! He took us to a little Restaurant where Hugh and I had quite a good meal. I lost all my good deal because the dinner cost us 600 lire. We saw a few ancient buildings. The only one I recognised was the Colosseum. I wanted to get out and look at it, but Hugh said we hadn't time. So we turned south for 15 miles where our wine-bibber had told us that we could get wine for the mess. We bought an enormous pipkin full of white wine – a great green bottle holding 60 litres. We packed it among the bed rolls, and William sat with his hand on top as we came home.

But much more exciting was your June 2 airmail which awaited my return. You make me wildly happy – Happy beyond dreams or deserts. June? Well, I don't think you will be in my arms this June, but what about next year?

9.6.44.

I had four services this morning, small but good ones. The Visitors' Book has caught on. It's an 8th Army idea. Men are invited to sign their names and addresses, and we send off greetings cards to the local parsons.

11.6.44.

6.0 p.m. We've reached a hill top and are concealed (I hope!) among the vines, tomatoes and olive trees. I've a Service at 7.0 p.m. with a couple of Squadrons.

All around this present tragedy is bloodshed and horrible waste. But it is redeemed by deep comradeship and countless heroisms. I never waver about the elemental things. The great eternal Fact in the Universe is the God who loves, and lives through His Spirit in our hearts. There are so many external things which make this loving such a dream, and all over the world now there are great deeds of courage and heroism, through all this hate and killing. But still our God looks down in His great Love, and offers us the forgiveness for the things we have to do, and for the things we fail to do.

It is time to wash and take a spade down the hillside. We only dig a latrine if we are at a site for at least a day!

12.6.44.

We had a good Service last night, and many stayed for Communion. It's difficult to see when we shall get our next Service in. We have moved into a lovely valley, with brilliant sun and the ground drying out. I've been wandering by the river which is broad and running swiftly, and from which there is no turning back — the river of fate (The Rubicon). The valley is thick with corn, and on all sides are red and green hills with fresh looking towns perched along the skyline. A lovely spot.

We were up early, and had a cup of tea at a quarter to three, but no breakfast until seven-thirty! The waiting time gave me a chance to wash some clothes. Then I darned last summer's stockings which were getting rather thin.

Good old Second Front. They are doing well, and it is such

a comfort that we are no longer on our own. The Russians are starting a great thrust into Finland.

1.45 p.m. We're moving now, and still in rolling country.

16.6.44.

Good morning my Dear. We've just had the 8.0 a.m. news. The long arm of Yankee bombing is starting to reach over to Japan. Second front settling down well, and Russia too. We have a wee pussy now, a sweet brown and white, who is just old enough to take a wild interest in things. She bounces after flies and claws great holes in our stockings. We call her Nebel. Her full name is Nebel Werfer. [This was the name of the Jerry multiple rocket launcher.]

17.6.44.

We didn't have much sleep last night. We spent most of it trying to catch up with Jerry. Harry Hearsey (Chaplain 12 Royal Horse Artillery) was hit by a bit of shell, but I don't know how badly. What a good thing it will be when Hitler has the sense to give up. Anyway Darling we're fit and well and very happy, waiting for the Great Day.

18.6.44.   Sunday evening.

We've a room in a large square house as a mess, and the staff haven't taken long to organise it. It's easy to find a likely room because most of these places have just housed Jerry. Again his peculiar atmosphere! I've just been talking to an old Jew (you couldn't tell his race) who was a Viennese lawyer before the Anschluss. Life became so intolerable that he came away. I don't suppose he'll ever go back again as he is too old to start again. My collar produced the usual whispers and smiles. A woman brought a two year old in her arms clutching a red carnation for me, so I had to produce a bar of chocolate in return! Harry Hearsey will be alright, but it was touch and go. Jerry is slowly retreating but he's still got a terrible bite.

19.6.44.

I had a service with some of my Royal Engineers last night. Communion was rained off afterwards. They had been building a Bailey Bridge, and the locals gave them so much wine that the Bridge was christened Vino Bridge! Whoever makes a bridge gives it a name, which is carefully painted, and fastened up, at the entrance. The local people do seem happy to see us. They fling flowers and stand by with glasses and a bottle of wine for anyone who wants to stop. Jerry's last act of unpopularity in each place seems to be to strip as much food as he can, also local transport.

20.6.44.

This Italian weather is a proper how-do-you-do. It started off with a thunderstorm three nights ago and it has rained ever since. William is sleeping in an undertaker's shop, and Roy Hodder (R.E.M.E.) and Jack Oatway (D.Y.) and I are in somebody's house. We have a room to ourselves, though I don't suppose we'll be able to stay here long. The locals are very friendly, so there are great sing-songs each night as the men get plied with Vino! Ugh, the mud! Its thick and slushy on the roads, and every passing vehicle throws up a spray. Yesterday I went out on a job, and got completely covered.

22.6.44.

Arezzo is beginning to breathe again, though Jerry is still very interested in the suburbs to the north. Some of the shops are open this morning. There are services this afternoon, so I'd better start to be thoughtful. It's no question of producing written sheets of flowery language built round a high flown subject with headings and subsections! Its usually a matter of thinking of one point and sharing it.

23.6.44.

Its nearly supper time, and I've had a long talk, in French chiefly, with the owner of the house, a Banker, and his many sons. We've discussed the differences between Roman Catholicism and Anglicanism, local beauty spots, and whether Florence is better than Rome! They could even discuss Libya and Cyrenaica without regret. They want to take me for a tour of this lovely town tomorrow. I'd love to go if I can. It's full of Giotto and Cimabue. Further north we come to the home of Leonardo and Michaelangelo and Raphael.

16 Framlingham Court,
Ipswich.

18.6.44.   9.25 p.m.

Dear Pip,

It is wonderful to read last week's papers and then to look at today's Sunday Times *map and find a different bit of Italy. We get direct news from the Cherbourg Peninsular – Frank Gillard, standing at the Front, chatting about what he sees, over the wireless. It is keeping us informed in the most direct way ever. What advances in these last few weeks: the push in Italy until the weight of Jerry yielded and could only with-draw . . . . thousands of men swarming over French soil (getting garlanded and kissed, I bet). We heard parts of the Sir Henry Wood's Jubilee Promenade Concert Season this week; I wonder if you have been able to listen.*

Last weekend we had a Conference of our local Christian Auxiliary Movement. The theme was 'The World Church of Jesus Christ' and we had C.A.M's. Travelling Secretary to lead our thoughts. Sessions were about 'The Rise' – 'The Challenge' – 'Servants of The World Church'. On Saturday evening we prepared for Holy Communion next morning, which was a united Service in St. Mary's. In the afternoon we had 'Music and Poetry Reading' for which I was responsible, and relieved that so many joined in so happily. Our Speaker was allowed into the Town as she had papers to prove that she was on lawful business! Now that we are a Restricted Area we have to show identity cards on busses or at the Station barrier, even on the trolly busses.

JERRY PROPAGANDA

Field Marshal Carver states that in the Italian theatre of war the British soldiers faced severe problems, military and psychological. We were subjected to the greatest amount of propaganda in the many leaflets fired over us during the Summer of 1944. This was at its height when the Second Front opened two days after the capture of Rome. The aim was to prove that the Second Front was failing.

The second great wave came a little later when Jerry tried further to undermine morale. His final flings of propaganda were about the flying bombs (Doodle bug) and the V2 Rocket. I have many examples of these leaflets.

Liverpool Street

26.6.44.   Monday.   10 p.m.

My Dear Pip,

Today I had my second teacher interview. I went to Fulham Town Hall, and met five quaint and friendly officials who seemed loath to draw me from Ipswich to London. They more or less offered me the job, then asked 'Can you start Monday?'. When I told them I would not be free until after the end of term, in August, they were very distressed! They chose the only other applicant as she was available, and provisionally offered me a new Nursery, which they are building, to be opened in August or September. The need of somewhere for the women in factories on war work to leave their children gives rise to this crop of Day Nurseries. It is rather nice to have a post 'up my sleeve', in case I do not get offers from Worksop (where Great Grandfather went to be Vicar of the Priory in 1843), or West Malling, in Kent.

After the interview, I tubed to Charing Cross and had supper in the Strand Corner House. A Canadian Officer came to my table; afterwards he insisted on paying for my meal . . . the waiter had put everything on one bill . . . I tried to ask for a separate one but my supper partner was too gallant! I had no lunch, and a bun for tea, so had settled for a later train, and some food, first! The people were tucking up for the night in the tube stations on their bunks and on the floor. Some of the kiddies looked thin and pale. It is awfully hot and noisy and stuffy down there. The Monument and Liverpool St. ones were full by 9 p.m. I walked out from Charing Cross on to the Embankment and heard Big Ben toll nine. Its slightly cracked sound fits in with the cracked and broken buildings across the water. The north bank seems pretty complete.

9.45 p.m. Tuesday. A letter from Kent was waiting for me. The Vicar wants to know more about me. He was a College friend of Dad's. It sounds quite hopeful and also rather nice.

ASSISI

26.6.44.

It has been a memorable day. The Senior Chaplain and Andrew Stewart and I went into Assisi. It was liberated with Perugia. We saw the house where St. Francis lived and was imprisoned by his father. It's now a church. Poor Francis, simple-hearted, most loved Saint of all times, who needed nothing, yet had everything. In spite of his great desire to possess nothing, they built the great Basilica in his honour. It is most unusual. There are three churches in one. Below is a large vaulted crypt which is really St. Francis' Tomb. The Friars came down, chanting, and kissed the steps of the Tomb.

Above is the second Church, at ground level, with the High Altar directly over the Tomb. On top is the third part, a really spacious lofty church. The church and monastery dominate the hill on which the town is built. There is a lovely view across the very fertile plain to Perugia, an ancient university town.

The churches are painted with Biblical scenes and stories from the life of St. Francis. The artists are Cimabue, Giotto and Lorenzino.

Jerry has only just departed, and so we had a field day in the shops. They are full of lovely souvenirs. We bought wall tiles and crucifixes and postcards. Most exciting I bought several of the famous Francis carvings.

Tomorrow after services I'm hoping to take a truck load of men back to Assisi. It's so important to go there.

From the Basilica we went to St. Clare's Church. This was already 200 years old in St. Clare's time.

Clare had been buried in a stone coffin for hundreds of years. In about 1850 she was exhumed. Now she lies in a glass shrine for all to see.

Today we did go back. The Men were thrilled, and there was much buying of souvenirs.

1.7.44.

Very hot! This morning I had two very good services in a modern school which Jerry had been using as a hospital.

Some of the men have had glowing accounts of D.Y. episodes from the local Derby Papers. The details have been sent in by the Divisional Press Officer, who is a Derbyshire Yeoman. The articles talk about our tanks, so I suppose it's a secret no more. The Regiment now fights in American Sherman Tanks fitted with a 75 mm gun. Armoured cars would have been useless in this formidable country. That is why we spent all last summer, grilling in our Algerian Olive Grove, learning how to use them.

Goodness these men have done impossible things, bless them. Surely there can be no more terrifying country in which to have to fight. But it shows how good our security is that only now is it known that we have tanks.

[During July and August the Division laboured up through central Italy, pressing towards Florence. The Regiment was often the flank guard of the Pratomagno, as the Division fought its way in very close countryside.]

7.7.44.

Confirmation is on Tuesday so I've just had a lot of letters to write and arrangements to make. I have 6 candidates. The Divisional Commander has ordered that men shall be allowed to go back from the front and spend the night with the Bishop even if there are great excitements forward. This is very heartening. Good old Commander.

CONFIRMATION BY THE BISHOP OF LICHFIELD
AND
CHAPLAINS CONFERENCE IN ROME

11.7.44.

Darling Helen,

There was your July 6 airmail on my breakfast table this morning. How lovely and civilised! It came in last night so it only took four days.

I'm waiting in the car, all packed up and ready for Rome and the Confirmation by the Bishop of Lichfield. One laddie, Kenneth Ingham, Congleton, Cheshire, is aboard. Soon the other two should arrive and then off we go.

It's good to get away for a week. Last night there were lots of military excitements and noises, but I didn't hear anything,

Confirmation by the Bishop of Lichfield.

being sound asleep! I'm not usually 'tough' like this! The men will return after Confirmation, and William and I are going to the Chaplains' Conference in Rome.

8.15 p.m. Here we are camped by the roadside half way back to the Eternal City.

We've just exchanged ten cigarettes for a couple of eggs for supper.

Wednesday evening.   Rome.   9.0 p.m.

What a change it is to be in a building, but how hot it is after the fields. Oh, there's so much to tell you. First of all, the Confirmation was terrific. At 2.30 p.m. the Bishop of Lichfield turned up and confirmed 207, his largest number so far. He is a tall gaunt man with white hair. He has a challenging and yet fatherly way with him.

The whole affair was very well run. We went to an out of the way place which turned out to be a health resort, with every house a hotel. There are hot mineral springs. Anyway we took the largest place in Bagni di Chianchiano — Albergo Grande. The candidates spent last night in the guest rooms. The service was in a large downstairs room. You should have heard the hymns rolling round and round. A mobile canteen turned up, and there was to be a cinema show in the evening and first Communion this morning.

After the service the Bishop shook hands with everyone, and then stood on the steps while the Army Film Unit clicked away. The Deputy Assistant Chaplain General made some announcements and talked about the film show. The Bishop asked the title and was told *Heaven Can Wait*! 'Ha, Ha', said my Lord of Lichfield, and everybody roared.

We had to be in Rome for the course by 5 p.m. this evening, so William and I set sail last night. On the way we called in to have a dip at the luxurious marble baths. I tried to wash my hair but the minerals curdled the lather! The water comes out of the ground at 102°.

THE CHAPLAINS' COURSE

We made quite a few miles and soon afterwards ominous noises began to come from the truck, but we arrived without mishap, though it was half past three. We charged around until we found Piazza Cavour, where are the Waldensian Church and Seminary. The Waldensians were a reforming sect before our own Reformation. They are Presbyterians, and about 50,000 strong, mostly north in the Alps near Turin. They seem a very fine type.

Their Church is plain but solidly built, and their motto is 'Lux in Tenebris', Light out of Darkness! It seems as though they looked around for a plot as near to St. Peter's as possible and then set about trying to bring light to the people of Rome!

Here we have devotions and discussions, and tours to places of interest, for 6 days. The Conductor is Robin Woods (son of the Bishop of Lichfield) – so we left the Father yesterday for the Son today! He is very good.

After tea another chaplain and I prowled about the Vatican walls, but the Swiss Guards indicated that it was closing time. We wandered round St. Peter's to anticipate our conducted tour. It is large and marbled and – Italian. It is difficult to compare this setting, and the sheer size of St. Peter's, with our own Cathedrals with their traceried windows and vaulted roofs. Anyway more later. We just stood and felt very humble before Michaelangelo's Pieta – created by him when he was 20.

Round the walls were monuments and busts of Popes.

There is one of James II of England. St. Peter's Square is very large with a pleasing view. A long obelisk is the centre with two fountains.

After 7 p.m. supper we had an introductory talk by Robin and Evensong. Now it is bedtime. I'm sleepy — there is a proper bed with a white pillow case and one sheet. What fun!

Thursday   6.20 p.m.

Busy day. We haven't had a spare moment yet. Supper is at 7 p.m. so there's no chance now for much writing. We had HC and Mattins at 7.45 this morning. The gearbox of the truck needed seeing to so William and I careered round Rome looking for a workshop. This made me late for our Bible study session — The Biblical doctrine of Judgement! At 12.00 a nice lady Professor came from the University to give us a talk on Roman history and culture. She stayed to lunch and took us round Roman Rome this afternoon. There are 14 chaplains on this course, but one went into dock with malaria today — a couple are Canadian, one from Newfoundland.

William stays in the town with the other drivers, and he should have plenty of time to see the sights.

19th July, 1944.

We discussed the Army of Occupation. The 8th Army Assistant Chaplain General has sent in lots of suggestions. We shall have to think in terms of a Parish or District, rather than a Regimental Unit. He suggests that wives be allowed to go out with their husbands. You will marry me won't you, and come out with me if I have to stay for a long time after the war? Somehow I don't think I could be a peacetime chaplain for long. anyway!

We had a good journey back. It is good to be with the men again, and in the fields.

20.7.44.

I've had an office day today, dealing with an ever increasing amount of Welfare mail. Also I have written to some more next-of-kin of recent casualties. It is so important to do this. They do write back such brave and wonderful letters.

I'm glad you are wondering about the traditional services

of the Church, and the Parochial system. It will be so good to get into an organised and orderly life when all these present noises have ceased, and the last shell has been fired. But there is only one thing that matters – the love of God for His children. Our love is a special part of this, oh Darling we've got to be fools for Christ, breaking down accepted standards and prohibitions to get this across.

We do believe this don't we? I've got a fire in me about these things, and you have your genius and all the depths of your faith which will grow and grow.

BATTLING ON

23.7.44.   Sunday.

Darling Redhead,

The usual tangle of warring things, I'm afraid. I love you very much. I'll explode with pride when I can introduce you as Mrs. Cook!

Things are so mobile, and so little can be planned. I must wander round to see if I can get in a service anywhere.

8.30 p.m. I found some of my sappers, and we had a good service, with vehicles going past all the time. We got on to the topic of love and fidelity – quite a usual topic I fear. We thought about Pompeii and Pagan Rome, and how the Christian faith alone survived the break-up of the ancient world, and then we tried to see how this same Christian faith is the only link in the world which hasn't snapped in this war.

Have you heard about the brave new union of the churches of South India? I'm sure it will come about soon. What a shining example to us all.

There were more names in my Visitors' Book tonight. We send them back to their home Church. It does seem to be a good link.

Last night William had to attend a parade where Sgt. Sutcliff, the Troop Sgt. read out a lot of pootling orders, pootling as far as the sharp end of things is concerned!

One was that army drivers are careless at level crossings, and were being run into by trains! Here roads are full of bomb holes, bridges don't exist, electric railway pylons are lying across the rails. Rails themselves are in fantastic shapes, and bashed coaches and wagons are everywhere! They'll be like this till we've advanced another 200 miles! Anyway, whenever we go over a crossing, I tell William to go carefully! Once this afternoon a bashed truck was still on the rails at the side of a crossing. 'Shsh! Don't show Sgt. Sutcliff that' says William, 'or he'll have a baby!'.

The men here are very friendly. One man was sealing an airmail to tell his people to start divorce proceedings for him against his wife. They've been happily wed for 14 years, and now she has a baby by another soldier. She's very sorry but his parents say she hasn't changed. I told him to wait till he gets home, and to be willing to forgive if he finds he's any love left.

24.7.44.

Our Camp is in an orchard with lovely plums, and the ripest and most succulent figs. Another good thing about the site is that it is a little hollow with low hills around that makes it so private. The sappers always keep up at the front. They're looking for mines in likely places. Quite a few lovely fruits have been booby trapped.

Four Partisans came into the Camp today and we gave them biscuits, cigarettes and chocolates. None seemed to be over 23. German brutality to the local population turned them into Partisans. They live in the hills and swoop down on Jerries. They claim to have dealt with 100 Jerries and Fascists so far.

News continues good. The leaning Tower still leans in the Jerry bit of Pisa. I hope it will still do so when they leave!

Trooper William Penn,
1st Lothians and Border Horse,
Bill's Driver/Batman for six
years.

27.7.44.

William is sitting shirtless on a tub, reading *Readers Digest*. He's quoting a page of interesting facts about marriage, which he insists on reading out! June is the best month for marriage, say the experts, and March is the best month to have babies!

28.7.44.   Friday morning.

Sightseeing all yesterday in Siena so no time to write. Some of our men had a special clean and polish and went down to the King to receive decorations. His Majesty seemed to be in very good form.

Wednesday evening, my military genius was to the fore! I'd had the chance of a film show, so I recce'd a place that just hid us from sight. So we gathered and saw Gracie Fields in *Holy Matrimony* and a Popeye film about tanks. It was a great success, accompanied by the usual bonks of the usual shells falling in the usual place a quarter of a mile away.

7.45 p.m. Yesterday was enjoyable. We emptied the back of the truck. S.S.M. Frank Powell (one of my ordination hopes), three more Sgts. and a Cpl. (two newly confirmed) piled in, and we shot across the countryside for about three hours to Siena. We clattered into the Square in the middle of the town where there was a fountain with running water, so we proceeded to have a wash. The others stripped to the waist but I was more modest! You should have seen my towels afterwards. Siena is lovely and medieval, with a large cobbled square where the ancient Palio is held in August in honour of St. Catherine. The Cathedral is black and white marble with mosaics and paintings everywhere.

Curiously there is no Cathedral in honour of St. Catherine – instead her house is preserved and fitted out with religious knicknacks so that even her bedroom looks like a church!

William produced the stove for tea. Halfway through, a boot repairer invited us into his shop and gave us wine. We loaded him with food and he took us on a tour round the town. The Senior Chaplain came here a couple of days ago and ordered me to go as part of my education.

Darling they're all showing me new photographs of sweeties and families. It is such a long time since you sent me one.

I want to see if your hair is greying, and to relive the kisses from those lovely lips of yours. Do be a good lass and send me some more.

ADVANCING NORTH OF SIENA
GERMAN ATROCITIES

29.7.44.   Saturday evening.   7.30 p.m.

And so for a story of grimness and gallantry. I went to one of the wee mountain towns this afternoon which we took yesterday. We've got a few tanks keeping watch there. The people were pale and haggard from their terror, and praying that we don't go away again. The Germans went completely mad in the town, shooting and destroying right and left. In the small square there are still the ropes dangling where they hung three people for three days, one old man of 87 and another of 77. A man took me into his house where Jerry had been in residence. The furniture was systematically smashed – a piano had been pickaxed – two marble washing table tops shivered in little pieces. The bridges were blown and some houses still smoking. Mothers were frightened and worried lest they should return.

Paul Clark, the Troop leader, with his handful of men and two or three tanks, was terrific. He organised the Partisans. He settled squabbles between women who accused each other of looting. He directed the civil police, got the town swept, arranged food for the Partisans, gave all his milk and bread to kids, and all the cigarettes to the men. All this was in addition to coping with the battle. I went to collect two of his men for burial. One was far forward, and so the Partisans took a cart and fetched him, with a grizzled old man in a torn shirt in charge. They brought him in triumph wrapped up in a white sheet (a most unusual sight) and covered him with flowers. As we put the cover over the Jeep trailer to take them to the cemetery, the women came and tumbled flowers all over it. God, it was touching.

I've told the story very badly. A journalist could have made a good one. But this war is grim. The Germans seem to go mad in these little hill towns, they loot, murder, sack and kill as they will. They've got it coming to them.

HOSPITAL DUTY

31.7.44.

8.30 p.m. and a lovely evening. My writing is better than usual. I'm by an open window, and using a small marble topped table, and sitting on a round iron stool!

I'm doing a week's Hospital duty, having relieved Evans the Chaplain, and I've been very busy ever since. We are in a civilian Hospital, with one wing still civilian. It's modern with shining glass and plaster. It's not quite as good as it used to be, but it makes a marvellous hospital.

Your July 23 arrived yesterday. You have just started your new school at West Malling. The village sounds a real family, but with the R.A.F. so near I don't suppose life will be quiet!

I will tell William that Brian [his little son] is settling down in Diss again. Julie, William's wife has been bombed twice in Tottenham. [They came up to the Rectory during the blitz and back again because of the flying bombs and rockets.]

1.8.44.

Second day of Hospital duty. A chap from the Ambulance Orderly Room popped in a few minutes ago with my Siena walking stick which I'd left in the Orderly Room! He stood at the window and said, 'What a lovely view of those blue hills'. And when he started to quote 'I'll lift up my eyes' I said 'You must be a poet'. Whereupon he departed to return with a notebook crammed with his outpourings, some of it not at all bad. He meets nightly with three or four others for Bible study. I invited them here tonight. It was heart warming.

A jeep and a trailer go with this job. The trailer is used when the cemetery is in operation. I do all my running about in it. They're so small and handy on crowded, cratered roads.

After lunch I popped over to the Regiment. They are in good heart, and there were air and sea mails from you and home. Each had a packet of lighter flints. Thank you so much.

We are still rationed to one airmail a week, so I'm trying out one of the Doctor's tricks. His wife and mother live together. Folded (against the rules!) into the mail he inserts a very thin sheet that fits exactly for his mother in his wife's letter. Let me know if this one gets through and we'll pursue it further!

We have a gang of Ities who do quite a lot of the cemetery digging. When we met this morning I said Buon Giorno, Luigi. Luigi stared in amazement ! It was his name! I muffed the second challenge but was right with Pietro for the third! They thought I was a wizard!

My present hospital establishment has grown from one driver and Ford truck (my own) to include a jeep, trailer and grave diggers. We organise a little central cemetery when it is necessary.

I'm glad your arms are brown. Sometimes I look a really deep brown, until I have a good wash and half of it comes off on the towel!

I'm still buying post cards whenever I get the chance. What a sight seeing tour of Italy – Pompeii, Naples, Caserta, Capua, Cassino, Orvieto, Perugia, Assisi, Lake Trasimene and Rome – so far.

Friday afternoon. Life is busy and hectic, and everywhere the armies are rolling forward relentlessly, triumphantly, though often with great pain, courage and loss. I grumble at red tape and some situations, but here there is this marvellous comradeship. We need one another. We rely on one another. These shared experiences will always be a great memory, and a continuing reality.

We are using this present chance of being near to civilisation to have our washing done really white! Everything was clean and rather grey, but now everything is shining white and pressed – not least my surplice and altar linen.

2.8.44. (Sea mail)

We moved to the other Field Ambulance this afternoon, my North African one. It was like going home to meet so many old friends.

I'm sharing a room in a larger modern civil hospital with the new R.C. Chaplain. He's very nice, considering his Papal blinkers!

Along the way a piano is being tuned very laboriously by an amateur. There's a soirée here tonight so that the Doctors and ambulances can get together. I'll clock on.

This morning we called at our Advanced Dressing Station in a farm which is surrounded by fruit trees. Most were dripping ripe peaches. The old laddie kept filling our tin hats full. Whenever he pulled one off many more fell down. When we started to pick them up he said 'No'. There are lots on the trees. What a waste! How I wish you could have some.

One of the daughters of the house, a sweet shy girl of 16 or 17 has red hair. Its very uncommon among the Ities. I told her I liked it, and said 'Mia Fianciata' had 'Capelli rossi'. She seemed pleased and blushed, poor lass. So we left it at that.

Mind you its not awfully common in England, and then it has to be a very special shade! Is it Titian? Dearest Heart I love you so much.

HOME FRONT – AUGUST 1944

In Kent school terms were between the main harvests so that children could be with their families at the cherry-picking and hop-gathering times. I began teaching at West Malling C of E village school on August 9th. My digs were with a friendly Mrs. W. (and her cat), whose Methodist ardour brought biblical authority to her mealtime pronouncements. Garden cuttings fuelled the copper to boil the water for my first ablutions in the zinc bath in the scullery. It was not far to the outside loo, but quite far enough in lashing rain! Mrs. W's baby grandson shared the name of Michael with her cat. Malling was the last fighter station before the London barrage of balloons. Planes chasing flying bombs had to hold fire, and peel off over Malling to avoid having wings sliced off by balloon cables moored beyond. One pilot crashed his damaged plane into a field to avoid wrecking a school. Local people were moved with gratitude for this brave sacrifice. Fire watching in the Control Room was below ground; my duty sessions were overnight. Reports were phoned in and bombs, damage etc. plotted on a chart and necessary help summoned – relief after one night when, unusually only four incendiary bombs were reported in one area; a few chickens the only casualties. One morning, at 7 a.m. an R.A.F. Officer came down, . . . st . . . st . . . stood on the st . . . st . . . step and st . . . st . . . stammered . . . 'I've l . . l . . lost a b . . b . . balloon'!

— a most serious emergency as the trailing steel cable might damage by drag or whip.

At school, traditional ways with very old apparatus left little scope for a teacher. New materials were scarce and very hard to obtain.

Teachers were on duty, and responsible for their charges, from before the first child arrived, until the leavers were safely through the school gates. At playtime — over the trees — a sudden shatter of sound — 'chug, chug' — doodle bug d-d-d-d machine gun fire from chasing planes . . . by this time the children should be indoors! No room for plane-spotting interests at these frequent emergencies. Little wonder that managers, staff, authorities and many parents decided that the children must go to safety.

EVACUATION

24.8.44.

Beloved,

This is to be a much-travelled weekend edition; with additions as time goes on. Tomorrow we board our bus at 8 a.m. for the first few miles to the appropriate station, and then we get into our train and off we go to the home of 'Jesu, lover . . .' tune! It will be nice to see the hills. I hope the children find good homes. Now I must collect my tin hat and my supper, and go on my firewatching stint. Good night my Darling, I love you always with all myself.

26.8.44.   Sunday evening.   Aberystwyth.

My Darling, all the bairns have got billets now, some of them lovely ones, some of them went where the house was already well-occupied, and after three or four trudges to different places with a policeman to push them in they came back and went off to try again, feeling very unwanted. But there has been a lot of kindness and hard-working good-will. There are some splendid people hereabouts and they should do well if only the kids try to fit in. I saw a couple off to chapel with their foster Ma just now, and they were smiling and skipping along.

We had a fine day for our travels which made things much easier. But it has been a real bit of war experience. We were on the bus by 8.0 a.m. yesterday, went to a station and we got the 9.0 a.m. (special) train; Cardiff was reached by 4.0 p.m. Here we waited a very long time, and later there was another long wait, before we got to Aberystwyth by 11.30 p.m.

Buses took us to the Rest Centre, which is a school, and it was 12.15 a.m. before we got the poor bairns into bed. Today they had a medical test at 10.0 a.m. and ever since a very decent and energetic Billeting Officer has been getting them homes. Oh, Darling, to see these poor babes sitting about waiting, waiting, and it is all so vague we couldn't take some out for walks or anything in case they were wanted. However, we got them down by the sea this morning for a breather. They were pretty good, but goodness, that journey! When it got dark we really felt it was time we arrived! There were two lots of milk for them (a.m. and p.m.) on the train and the W.V.S. gave them tea and buns at Cardiff and Carmarthen. Its so full up here in the season too, so we, the escorts, are sleeping in the Geography room on camp beds with stacks of chairs and piles of rock, and bottled specimens all round. Spam has been our diet — morning, noon and night. Oh well, we'll be off tomorrow on the 7.40 a.m. so I hope to get home tomorrow, but it may be Tuesday!

There have been some good jokes, but my word its a strain. I hope our bairns will never have to be evacuated. Oh Billy, this is heavenly, the others have gone for a walk, but as I'm trying to quell a bit of gastric trouble — I'm 'tired'. I've already been to the station to see about trains so now I'm being lazy and having a lie on my bed, and I'm going to dream of my Billy. God bless you, My Darling!

Liverpool Street Station

28.8.44.   Monday.   8.30 p.m.

My Dear Pip,

We have seen some lovely country, and glorious Welsh hills, that we couldn't see on Saturday, in the dark. I do hope the children will be happy, then it will all have been worthwhile.

This morning we rose at 5.30, and made our spam sand-

wiches, for the journey home! We got to London at 7 p.m.
I made a bee-line for here, to find, to my relief, that there is
a train tonight . . . change at Stowmarket . . . arrive Diss
2. a.m. I rang home. I heard Iris answer, faintly; Dad had
gone to Fen Cottage.

Tuesday 7.45 p.m. When I stepped from the train at Diss
at 3.30 a.m. this morning, Uncle Charlie (Burlingham) was
there to meet me. As he escorted me on the mile walk home,
I tried to express my gratitude; he said he wouldn't let one of
his daughters come alone and he knew my father wouldn't
like me to, either! He is a sport. I had a poached egg . . . and
a bath before dropping into bed. Love galore and more to
follow – or precede – in an air letter! Your L.M.P.

PERUGIA

10.8.44.

My Darling,

I didn't write at all yesterday. Baldy Porter and I went
with a couple of Jeep loads to bring four laddies in from a
brewed-up tank to a central cemetery. After the tank was hit
it was a week or two before anybody could get to them, and
just cover them up. Anyway they're at peace now, bless them.

Coming back we called at the Officers Shop in a town that
was front page news a week or two ago. I bought shirts, tooth
brushes and a sleeveless leather and khaki cloth jerkin. It will
be lovely for the cold weather. We didn't have time to explore
though the churches are very famous. The town had been a
shambles, but was looking much tidier today.

Night before last there was a terrific thunderstorm and
again it rained yesterday. The tracks and approaches to
temporary bridges were made of earth bull-dozed into position, and many of these were swept away. The R.Es were
very busy. We had quite an adventure to get back. We tried
all the known bridges and had resigned ourselves to the tail of
a long queue. Vehicles were being winched over a hole in the
river bed at the rate of about one vehicle every ten minutes.
Then a corporal appeared, and told us about one bridge further forward. So home we came as it got dark.

There was a lovely fruit salad for lunch today made in a

hollowed out melon. We had pears and peaches, though the red glacé cherry was obviously missing!

I sorted out my clothes trunk this morning and came across two pairs of thin pyjamas. Silly poot, I've been wearing thick ones till now!

Will you be fussy about my wearing my winter woollies? You won't get it all your own way even though you are a copper knob.

Good old Redhead. Darling, God has made you wondrously fair, and you're such a happifying Darling Darling.

North of Florence.

19.8.44.   Saturday afternoon.

Darling Helen,

After breakfast we went out box hunting for keeping the library in. We found a dump of metal ammo boxes and brought 6 away. Two are 5′ long by 1′ 9″ and lovely for books. You can put them in rows with titles up and see them all at the same time. We had a clearing up of the car, throwing wooden and cardboxes away right and left.

Two wooden boxes are full of prayer books – three of library books (nearly 200), three of tins of food, one of my books and knick-knacks – ditto William's – my German ambulance box clothes chest, as well as sundry sacks of clothing, maps, respirator, cooking stove and a small folding table.

Grapes are getting ripe, but usually you eat half a bunch and toss the rest away. How wasteful, but there are probably hundreds of square miles which will not be gathered this year.

Last night's news from France was surely the most exciting of the whole war. German line in France crumbling and in disorder – Darling it can't be long now and you'll be in my arms.

Sunday lunchtime. We called and collected our pictures. William says his will go faster in the Green envelope, so they're all ready to send off. Please don't forget will you? I'd love a large one, and a wee one. Perhaps one of all of you too. Anyway I'll love what I get.

This afternoon we're going back a long way to our baggage party. I've only seen them once since Cassino.

Monday teatime. I'm sitting in the station-master's office outside an old walled town on a hill. The station is rather bashed, and they haven't got the line working yet. So our B Echelon has taken possession.

Most of the men have got their feet under the table, and go out to the various farms in the evening. Food may be short in the towns but seems very plentiful here. All the men are talking about the binges the locals have when the harvest is in, a real harvest home. The men had to eat solidly for 2½ hours.

Last night we got to Arezzo where we hunted up the Banker's family where we stayed earlier on. They seemed very thrilled to see us. I had dinner with them – Father, Mother, and two grown up sons, who are studying to be engineers at Rome University. But first we went for a walk down the road to gossip with the neighbours, and for me to tell them the latest B.B.C. news. There was a retired Admiral, and a Doctor, and a Turkish Count with a French wife! A couple of them spoke a bit of English, but my French was better, so we talked in French. The Countess had brothers in Paris and Marseilles, and she is very worried about them. They have a son who is a Turk and who is away doing his two years of military training. We had cold vegetables and thin flakes of ham, then soup to which we added shredded goat's cheese, and finished with fried meat cakes and more vegetables. The evening was warm and the stars bright, so we sat outside and talked till midnight – very pleasant. This morning we came away at about 9.0 a.m. dumping Signor Bussoni, the Banker, at his office in Arezzo. Before 10.0 a.m. we were in Assisi, where I couldn't resist buying some more photographs.

Then we turned south, and after an hour or two the truck developed a nasty rattle, the transmission case working loose. So we dropped in at a workshop and they tightened it up. This made us late for lunch so we opened a tin of steak and kidney and a tin of beans which we ate cold. Now its teatime and I'm tremendously hungry, so I'll toddle off to tea. The chaps here lead a lazy life, bless them. There's nothing to do but guard the baggage, and the locals seem too friendly to want to pinch it!

8.30 p.m. The sun is setting and there's a rosy glow in the

sky behind the city on the hills, and everywhere seems so quiet and peaceful. I'd love a fortnight here so that I could dream of my redhead. Dearest Helen you make me so happy.

28.8.44.

My Darling,

Tuesday afternoon, Warm, warm day. Service and Holy Communion with one of the Squadrons. They live in a village with about four houses and a church built in the middle. The whole district is rather bashed, including the church roof. George Trollope, the Squadron Leader, took it into his head to ask if we could use the church for our service. The priest was an old, old man, who had been hunted by Jerry for being anti-Fascist. We had talked yesterday, and been the greatest of friends. Of course it was wrong of me to allow George to ask for the use of the church knowing how things stood. But here was a war and everything in confusion. Soldiers and civilians all living together in the ruins. Anyway he refused, as I had known, and he tried to find another room. But I found a jolly spot under a tree. Darling, I cannot think of anything in the world that will ever bring us to be recognised by the R.Cs. There is a great gulf — war does not overcome it. Nothing will.

1.9.44.

My Darling,

My summer stockings are lasting well. I haven't had to buy any this Summer. I bought some pairs at the end of last Summer from the Officers' Shop which I've hardly worn. The original ones which I bought with my tropical kit in Glasgow before we came away are so nice and soft, but are getting a bit darned. Could you send me a wee hank of grey darning wool? Only a wee one, mind you, 'cos I don't intend to darn my socks much longer!

Last night I had a service with the Royal Engineers, and the truck was very sluggish coming home so William has had to strip it down. Two cylinders weren't firing so they fitted a new distributor. Of course the hose connection between the cylinder block and radiator, the cooling system, broke, so that had to be patched up as well. Nuisance, as I wanted to go out tonight. Anyway they're just off to test it now.

William's lunchtime airmail from the Missis said his home had been bombed (Tottenham in London). Poor lad. It is the second time this war. He is waiting anxiously for more news – whether the furniture is gone, etc. If it is, I *think* he can claim compensation. Perhaps your Papa will know and will be able to advise Mrs. Penn.

It is my sister Mary's birthday on Sunday, also the 5th anniversary of the outbreak of war. It has been a searing time for us all, but it has given me my beautiful Redhead, and I've known her for well over half that time. And what a difference that has made to me, my darling Beloved.

We have a day of Prayer on Sunday and I had the first service last night. There is one tonight and one tomorrow too – then a couple on Sunday and I will have covered most of my Parish. Last night I stayed on at the Sappers for supper. They're a very friendly lot. One of them, a South African, had seen an old vellum and leather book, hand painted and printed with board and leather covers, with rivets all over in a bashed church. He nearly brought it for me. I was fighting my' conscience as he said he would produce it next day. Fortunately the local Priest went in among the ruins and retrieved it, so there was no temptation! Two of our Squadron messing trucks – the ones which take rations and cooking things around – have church bells hanging on them as gongs (one is beautifully chased and marked). They came from ruined churches somewhere. I've a good mind to confiscate them when we leave Italy, and to return them to the Italian Ecclesiastical Authority. Sweet dreams, My Darling. Your Bill.

1.9.44   9.30 p.m.   *West Malling Control Room.*

Dear Bill,

   Our skies are quieter now. The balloons seem to be winning and flying bombs less frequent, but the dreadful screeching ones that drop suddenly from above must be worse for our brave Londoners. Roll on the Peace . . . but how shall that be won?

Our weary world is split by useless warfare
How can man rest if suffering abound?
Where is the light and wisdom for our counsel?
When will the way of peace be found?

Though wars may cease and clash of arms be silenced
What shall we find to bind us into peace?
How can we love the race that smote our dearest?
How shall our aching hatred cease?

The God who made us is our Re-Creator
And in His love His only Son He gave
That He might bear the pains of sin and hatred,
Living to life beyond the grave.

This God who saves us, saves us for His loving
That we might be His family on earth,
Deep in His heart He shares in all our struggling
To bring His Kingdom-life to birth.

God of our joys, our tears, our hopes, our struggles,
Take our whole lives and lift them up to Thee,
Move our proud hearts and warm them to each other,
Only Thy love can bind and set us free.

. . . and so to camp bed . . . may you have the peace that
passes understanding. All my love, Helen.

RETURN FROM A HOLIDAY IN ROME

Podenuova, near Consuma.

11.9.44.

Darling Beloved,

I have been a bit worried about you and the buzz bombs, but it looks as though we won't have to worry any more now. Whoopee! We returned this evening to our railway station where we spent the night on our way back from Rome. At 9.00 p.m. I heard the news. The first real news since I went on leave.

Here up in the hills mornings and evenings are very cold indeed. I'm wearing a pullover tonight. We are in a house — a nice house with the people just coming back. I have a tiny room all to myself. There is a woman here who is English and escaped from France at the beginning of the fall of France.

Goodness, there has been a reign of terror, my darling. There's a little cubbyhole leading off the main kitchen where people were herded in, and then the Germans threw hand grenades on top of them. 16 were killed, now huddled in a grave in the garden, and others have since died. Darling, its true, God's truth, and the Bosch must be made to pay. It's justice. Goodness it makes me wild.

We have a big roaring fire in one room with lovely blazing logs, very civilised, but we need English weather and I need Redhead for it all to make sense.

I'm glad the other stockings arrived safely. There are two pairs, silky ones, to put in the post, but goodness how the prices have risen since we first entered Rome. There are some other odd things including panties! Can you feel me blushing?

I love your 'Cyril Fletcher' ode – send me some more please.

The girls in Rome had dainty flowery frocks and were very pretty, but Darling I've never seen anyone as lovely as you looked in your blue flowery dress when you came to see me off at Knebworth. Remember? You make me very happy.

We called in at Perugia and had a look at San Pietro again. Norman was thrilled. It is a lovely old church, though all the Perugino and Raphael canvasses have been removed for safety.

Norman loved his stay in Rome, I think. By the end he was talking about narthexes, campaniles, pietas and altar canopies quite expertly! And he is a Methodist too!

Oh Tweedle, I need to hold you in my arms tonight, with kisses for your hair, eyes and lips. God bless you my Darling. I love you, love you, from your own, Bill.

ADOLF HITLER'S LAMENT

. . . from the days when Mussolini had capitulated and Churchill was conferring with Roosevelt . . . a sort of 'camelius humpf' song. (with apologies to C. Fletcher):

'With a basinful gone to Joe Stalin,
And the oil getting low in mein lampf;
That Jack Boot I borrowed from Musso
Slipped badly and gave me worse crampf.

> *All these wretched conquered are champfing –*
> *The Franklins with Winnies are campfing –*
> *The whole situation is dampfing*
> *And I can't get a word of Mein Kampf in*
> *Now Berlin's an R.A.F. dumpf . . .*
> *Ach, Himmel! wie blau ist mein humpf!'*

13.9.44.

My Darling,

It is a lovely fresh day again up in our pine woods. After breakfast we went to see some of our men who are having a bit of a rest in an enormous and rather bashed hotel, looking out across a huge valley. Each man could have a suite to himself if he wished. In the lounge there was still a huge pile of travel literature and souvenir copies of a waltz specially composed in honour of the hotel! I'll send you a copy.

6.30 p.m. Busy afternoon rushing about finding where everybody is. 'Winkle' Watkins, one of my very dear Engineers was killed on a mine and Bill Grant was seriously wounded in a booby-trapped house. Bill got an M.C. He's been blown up dozens of times. They were both very experienced Engineers. Gosh, what a job they have. This Italian campaign has been a bloody slog from river to river, from mountain range to

Typical Sapper bridge, Appenines, Autumn 1944.

mountain range, with Jerry able to watch every movement. It is an engineer's war. We are helpless without them.

Your letter from Il Nido, West Malling, arrived today. It was about our getting married at the earliest date, even if we cannot settle down immediately. I've already written about the same time on the same subject. So my Beloved whenever I come home you'll get asked the question 'When?'. I think the 8th Army stands a good chance of coming home early, for a leave at any rate. We haven't had one for two years, and the Second Front people have been having theirs regularly. We *may* go to the Far East of course, and should be prepared for this. Oh Darling do let's get wed as soon as possible, when I come home. I'll be the proudest man in the world to change your name.

14.9.44.   Thursday,   7.0 p.m.

I called at the monastery this morning and came away with a big dixie of honey — at least 7 lbs. I would think. I wish you could have some. We had honey for tea. But best of all was the mail.

FLORENCE
17.9.44.   Sunday afternoon

My Darling,

It has taken months to get to Florence, surely the most famous and beautiful city in the world. It is ours now, and you may well imagine that it will soon be a marvellous centre for welfare and rest and recreation.

Tomorrow we hope to go and have a look round. The Ponte Vecchio is famous — a medieval bridge full of jewellers' shops, the Duomo (Cathedral) and Baptistry. There is Michaelangelo's 'David', and the Uffizi galleries are re-opening soon.

Tuesday afternoon,   3.30 p.m.

We had sandwiches for lunch, then I called to see the Boss and had to have lunch with him as well! My Sappers had a bad time yesterday and last night, so I've been trying to be of use.

Last night they were talking about beds in the Mess! The old fashioned people said you must have a double bed, a very large double bed! The moderns said two single beds of the kind that can be single in summer, and put together to be double in winter! What do you think, Darling?

Yesterday was good. We left early and went to Florence. Some of the streets are wide and modern, but the place is much more medieval than Rome, with lots of ancient houses and palaces. First we went into the Duomo. A striking exterior with a wonderful Campanile, and the world-famous Ghiberti bronze doors, full of Biblical scenes, truly 'the Gates of Paradise'. Inside was the most austere Italian church I have seen. It was rather Anglican except that the architecture was crude and square compared with our Gothic and early English lines and arches.

The Baptistry is an octagonal domed building at the west end, beautiful with the most famous gates in the world.

We have a rest camp in the city, and I met Reggie Snaith. We went round together. We spent most of the morning among the shops, but things were very dear.

The Officers' Club there is a famous peacetime hotel by the river Arno. We had a good lunch and a bottle of wine.

On the way to the cinema we climbed over the debris of demolished houses to have a look at the Ponte Vecchio, the only Arno bridge that Jerry spared. It is like the old London Bridge, with shops and houses perched on both sides!

All the Galleries are closed, so no Raphaels and Michaelangelos to view. We did see a copy of Michaelangelo's 'David'. It stands outside the Palazzio Vechio with the original inside.

Bill's 15 cwt. Van turned into a Caravan, Autumn 1944 in Italy. William Penn with Tina, their little Appenine mongrel bitch.

THE APPENINES – A SUMMARY

So winter came on, and with it the battle was joined. The armour did impossible tasks in mountaineering. When they could go no further the Armoured Regiments became Infantry. Often Jeeps could go no further, and oxen and mules were used to haul guns and supplies. As usual the Sappers did their sterling work.

It was a privilege to be with these gallant men.

OUR CARAVAN

Life was very mobile for William and myself, and in the mountains winter was closing in. No longer could we cope with an occasional billet or a bed under a bit of canvas or under the stars. Life was a strange mixture. We alternated between the luxury of a Florentine suburb, and oncoming winter in the bleakness of the High Appenines. So we decided to turn our 15 cwt. truck into a caravan. The Sappers were very helpful and provided us with materials. We took off the hoops that held up the canopy. With battens and plywood we built up the sides to give us standing room. Bunks were built in, and a door and window. Later we were even able to fit a plywood roof. To make it weatherproof we put the canvas back. We had quite a lot of storage space. Until the winter was over, and we were in Austria next Spring, this caravan formed our home, our transport and my Office.

Appenines.

13.10.44.   Friday morning.

I've just given the Sappers some Whist Drive prizes from my Comforts box, hankies, towels, cigarettes. Then I said Mattins. The New Testament lesson was from the end of Ephesians – about husbands loving their wives as their own bodies. He that loveth his wife loves himself. We've had that idea for a long time haven't we? I mean finding completion in each other. Dearest Heart, I love you.

We spent last night on the mountain top by the roadside with some of my Sappers. They're a grand and friendly lot, bless them. We had a service in a rather forlorn café. All the little community turned out, including a REME officer and

continued on p.222

BEDDING? — HELEN'S REPLY

Drawn to Pip, Clerk in Holy Orders in a/c with an Apple whose heart is solely and entirely enamoured of the aforesaid.

The simple interpretations embodied in the following humble illustrations are expressions of the author's conclusions when, being provoked by an argument of Bedlam in a Florentine Mess, she was driven to seek through Nature some answer to the problem embedded in the debate, and to find, if haply she might, some revelation of the truth through the agency of Natural Objects.

From the Preface to the Edition dated September 28th, 1944

INTRODUCTION

*I do not seek, my love, to deprecate your
Friends' ideas, but lest they cultivate your
'single' urge, I'd refer you to Nature.
The illustrations humbly penned below
are open to controversy, I know . . .
In their interpretation you may view
The Simple Truth . . . or 'read' a thing or two!
And, should you read the silly thing right through,
With Nature's pattern-form eventuallee,
Perchance you'll be persuaded to agree.
And, if you should a 'double' meaning see
I'd have you know that that's OK by me!*

1. The Old-fashion Way —

   Roses cluster in profusion.

2. Yet, even among our Forefathers, there were the 'moderns' who trained their Old Men's Beards to hide the confusion of their Lad's Love.

3. Among modern gardeners we find two schools of thought at work; both are included in the class who follow the bedding-out-in-Spring theory.

(a) In those symmetrical and aristocratic gardens where Dahlias boast a singular glory a mixture would probably cause no added joy to the sophisticated.

(b) Then we get those enthusiastic novelty gardeners who seek to culture simple plants. Yearly they bed out different plants from their home soil to adorn fresh plots. Indisputably the more tender specimens subject to this treatment are apt to wilt. For example: Love Lies Bleeding.

And, in passing, I would remind you that most plants have feelings . . . even Cabbages have usually boasted some sort of heart, at least before grubby ideas crept in.

But let us turn from the cultivated to the purely natural. Take the self-sown flowers that entwine in that . . . Blue Heaven of Love-in-the-Mist.

Finally turn to the wild flowers: Convolvulus* alias Bindweed

*con (L. conare) — to know
vol (L. volere) — to want
vul (L. vulgaris) — common
us (E. we, us) — You and I
i.e. convolvulus:

> We know we want to be Natural (follow Nature)
> Q.E.D.

N.B. For the purposes of this investigation the Wild Oat is not considered to be a recognised flower, and barely ranks with grasses even.

SO . . . if You still bid two . . . I'll double it . . . !

the place was packed. We started off with Cwm Rhondda and the building trembled as they sang. Then we had Communion, and a lot stayed.

I spent the first night in the caravan. It is lovely to be in a square-built affair after a tent. I do miss my bed though. At present my bed is hard underneath, and rather narrow, so I'll have to think up something. Perhaps a mattress from a bashed house.

Bernard, Bob Martin's successor at the 17/21st Lancers, the Padre who came with me on leave to Rome, was killed by a shell two days ago – I think he died instantly. Poor Family, he has a wife and children. Poor 17/21. They've been unlucky to lose two Padres.

The sappers have given me more wood today. This time for a bed frame. I've got some heavy duty motor inner tubes. You can cut them into strips and weave them into a mattress – very comfy indeed!

Sunday evening.

Darling Redhead,

This morning was very busy. There were services for D.Y. and Sappers.

Keith Leslie showed me his nice little black and white bitch with her litter of 5 ten-day old pups. Two of the three dogs are promised. Keith is giving me the other, but I suppose it won't be weaned for about a month. I've been wanting a dog out here for a long time. William is thrilled too.

Had a good night in the caravan last night. The elastic sprung mattress was terrific. Only snag is that it's a bit narrow.

Monday evening. We're both camping in the truck tonight. Before dinner the tent was struck, and it was all stowed away, and there is a fair amount of space. The R.Es gave me a couple of walnut windows with glass, which had been intended for the General's caravan!

Tomorrow we set off to the Confirmation by the Bishop of Portsmouth. William will probably range the town for accessories for the caravan! He's got a long list of beading, cuphooks, spring curtain rod and door handles!

Oh Tweedles! Time for bed now. Be happy, my love. I love you utterly, completely and forever.

WHAT NEXT?

In war time every person had to be in an approved occupation. Teaching was one of the reserved occupations, but it was expected that teachers would work, during the holidays, at hospitals, canteens or some regular job, apart from fire-watching duties: members of Ipswich High School Staff did firewatching duty for a week at a time during their holidays. When West Malling children were evacuated to Wales there were not enough pupils left to occupy all the regular teachers. I was the most recently appointed, and therefore the first to look for other employment. My doctor advised that, as I was very 'run down' I should try to find outdoor occupation after a period of recuperation.

So back I came to Diss Rectory, my father's encouraging company and the nourishment of Mrs. B's appetising meals, cleverly produced from rations. Whenever I came home, for weekends or holidays, I had first to ascertain whether any-one had my room, and if so, where I was to sleep. Only once was there no room at home and I was kindly bedded over the road. In October 1944, whether by chance, or by Mrs. B's caring foresight, my room was ready for me, and here during the early Autumn days I slept many hours of recuperating peace. It did not do to toss and bounce on that little bed for, beneath it, in a tall hard box, was Bill's scale model of the 100 gunship St. George, waiting for him to rig and finish . . . when . . . he came home.

CONFIRMATION IN FLORENCE

Tuesday night — very late. We're in the Regimental Rest Camp, a big house in Florence. I've a large and lovely room all to myself, with a posh bathroom next door, only no tap water!

As the SCF would say, I made a Blot this morning. I called in at his office with a car load of ordinands and confirmees on the way to confirmation, to be told that it was tomorrow! They've given us an extra day's holiday. My prize shopping today has been a bottle of Quink.

I also got an old carved plaque of Savonarola, about five inches in diameter, from a woodcarver's shop.

Now to sleep. Dearest Heart, I love, love, love you with all of me. Sleep well. God bless you my Darling.

Wednesday night 11.15 p.m. Such a happy day. Jack Oatway and I went shopping this morning. Silks were tempting. We had lunch at the Officers' Club, and dashed to Holy Trinity, one of the two Anglican churches. There were a couple of hundred candidates, the church was lofty, dim and inspiring. The Bishop of Portsmouth has a lovely voice, spoke well and roundly though not strikingly. Probably the candidates won't remember anything except the Bishop himself. Coo! what a lot of parsons' collars there were to be seen!

After tea, with Harry Hearsey, Padre R.H.A. and Stevens, a padre who used to be with 1st Brigade in Scotland and early N. African days, we went to see Deanna Durbin in *It began with Eve*. Dinner and a walk home. Tomorrow morning is first communion at 8 a.m., so we'll have to be up before 7 a.m. Sleep well, bless you. I love you awfully. Your own Bill.

15.10.44.   Sunday afternoon.

My Darling,

Apparently there is an article in one of the papers to the effect that our Division has been in action for a longer continuous stretch than any other Division in the whole war. A dubious honour, don't you think! Oh well, I suppose we're doing our whack. I certainly won't get let in for Burma!

Darling what fun it will be when we settle down and become us. Goodness you'll never know how electric the very mention of Helen is, and how I long for your presence. Tonight there is a service and Holy Communion in the Evacuation Ward of this hospital. Tomorrow we are going over the mountain for a service at 11.00. We may take the afternoon and night off, and return the next morning.

Monday evening. Feeling low tonight. Norman was killed last night – poor lad. (He was my most promising ordinand.) He was repairing the telephone cable on a much shelled bridge at Rocca San Casciano, when one landed on the bridge. The wound that caused his death was in the groin, with a severed artery. I went to fetch him this morning, and some of his many pals came down here to the cemetery. They all liked him. His ordination was not to be.

Last night we had a good service in a smallish well-lit and warm room. Quite a lot of men came, including one of the surgeons, an awfully nice Captain. The other surgeon, a Major, works in Ely in peace time. At dinner last night he told me to remind him whenever we have a service, or his Cathedral city old ladies will be cross with him!

First of the new batch of airmails began to come in today. There'll probably be news of you soon. Oh Darling, darling, you're infinitely precious. Now for dinner.

Tuesday evening. Hallo Darling, I've been out all day. Felt fed up so we crossed the mountains as a tonic. Got to Florence for the bank and officers' shop, where I bought a scarf, a pair of pyjamas of the right size, but which will shrink and be too small (no larger available!), 2 collars and 2 figure I's for Africa Star. Then lunch at the Officers' Club. Here I relieved my 'dumpiness' by buying you something jolly for our honeymoon. Think I'll keep it until I return. Hope you'll like it anyway. Gosh, I've got an awful cheek – but there was a lovely tempting stall with them all spread out for inspection.

Coming back I called in at our Echelon, and went through Norman's stuff. One or two special things and a lovely leather India paper 1928 *Prayer Book* I will be returning myself. The other things are going through Army channels. Goodness he had a lot of books, bless him. He would have made a good Parson.

Sunday has been lovely. At the top of the Pass, the highest peak has a little snow on it – beginning of winter. The hillsides covered with little deciduous trees are a wonderful blaze of colour.

Churchill talks of the war ending next Spring, or early Summer. Oh Darling we've all talked wistfully about home for Christmas, but in our heart of hearts we've known it was not possible. But here is Winnie giving a time at last. And I think we can look forward to Victory then. Be strong and happy, its only a few more months to go. I've been toying with the idea of a Summer wedding. It had better be a summery one in view of this afternoon's purchase I think! Anyway you're the depth and point and purpose of all my living.

Be happy, Darling. Think I'll make a gloat list and tick the days off until the end of the Spring, and the beginning of Summer. God bless you. Love and kisses from your very own Bill.

29.10.44.   Wednesday.

Today I'm feeling cleaner than I have done since about a fortnight before Cassino! Just across the road and down by the river is a mobile bath unit, with hot showers. Water is pumped from the river into a petrol driven geyser affair – with lots of lovely water. To begin with it's just too hot but by the time you've dashed in and out about twenty times, and got lobster coloured all over, it is just right! I think it was the same lot who had a pitch at the back of Cassino.

Dearest Heart I love you. I first tried to tell you even though it was against my better judgement – I just had to, but you seemed to be far too wonderful, and out of my reach. Even when you allowed my first kiss I couldn't believe my luck. But you've worn my ring for nearly three years now, and goodness how proud I've been of you. 'May I introduce my Wife?' What fun you will be as a wife. Roll on the day.

The greatest craze in the Mess is roulette, and the two guiding hands are 'Tusker' the dentist and Father Holman. I've managed to keep clear of all invitations so far. Too much money seems to change hands, usually to the bank.

Darling do you get cross when I keep trying to say how lovely you are? Hurrah for auburn hair and brown eyes and dimples.

Good news again tonight – great Pacific sea battles with disaster for the Japs – new British and Canadian successes in Holland. Cracking advances by Russians with Transylvania liberated and Norway entered. Darling the evil influence of Nazidom is shrinking every moment.

This evening I wandered in to see our two surgical cases – both doing well. If all goes on like this they should be O.K. They showed me some of the little bottles of penicillin – tiny bottles about a quarter as big as an ordinary size ink bottle – about half an eggcupful size – each worth about £100. Between the two of them these men were having nearly a bottle a day. Thank goodness there's no meanness about these things.

Thursday morning. William and I are marooned in the truck. He was pleased to have your Sept. 10 news of Brian. Rain started at midnight and it has rained continuously since. The mountains look full of water. The river is a raging muddy torrent, and new rivulets trickle down from gulleys. The rocky streets are running with water and quite a few houses have muddy water running from the front door! Poor dears up on the mountains in their slit trenches, with only blankets and gas capes against the elements. Gosh how lucky I am to have a truck and all my knick-knacks.

Last night I came to bed as the roulette session started. AMGOT, (the Yankee Captain) and Blood (Blood Transfusion Officer) held the bank and lost 3,000 lire between them – £15. Silly chaps. You always lose – or nearly always.

I've pulled out my Purcell and Handel music from the bottom of a tin box. Soon I'll be having a tootle. It's ages since I last played. Darling you'll have to join me in these duets. They're lovely, though you'll probably have to play the 'seconds' as they are more difficult!

Darling, be very happy. You are, aren't you? This war is nearly over now, and we've everything to work for, and to look forward to. My whole being longs for you. Your very own Bill.

1.11.44.   Dinner time.
My Darling,

I'll be asleep in two seconds tonight. We've had an unusual day. We set off in two Jeeps after breakfast bound for the mountains, the scene of fairly recent fighting. The idea was to find two laddies who had been killed over a month ago, and who were unburied. So we set off with crosses, picks and shovels, and blankets. The first few miles we wound up into the mountains along a bit of track that had been improved and used by the Infantry for Jeeps to take supplies. Goodness, what a track! Partly it was a river bed and boulders, partly queer wiggly bits on razor-edges of hills and spurs, which Jeeps alone of all motor vehicles could possibly negotiate. The track hadn't been used for a week or so, and there had been heavy rain so we had to deal with four or five baby landslides. We passed three bleak and desolate farms as we wound up into the clouds, and the view was like a map.

Just before the fourth and last farm we had to dump the Jeep and start our walk. Most of the way we followed a track and a blessed yellow telephone wire. After a four mile hike we found the first laddie, and whilst a grave was being dug a Sergeant and I walked over about two more mountains for the other laddie, but no use. We couldn't find him.

After a little service in that bleak, wild, lovely spot we picked up our picks and shovels and came back in single file following the yellow wire. We got to the Jeep about 3 p.m. where a Trooper was waiting with a brew of coffee – lovely coffee and our sandwiches.

We stopped at the second farm were we had seen puppies and lots of kiddies in the morning, and I bargained for a little black dog.

So home we came in our Jeeps, me clutching my Forestina (that's her name). She was ravenous so we gave her lots of food, and William gave her a Lysol bath in case of fleas. Now she lies on a blanket in William's room in front of a little tin of glowing peat, getting dry.

Now for dinner – goose tonight – then bed. How I'll dream of you my Darling. You're infinitely sweet and lovely.

2.11.44.   Thursday evening.

William and I and Forestina are in the truck. I can't suppose she's ever had so much food and such variety. She slept soundly last night but started to run around as soon as it got light. I tried to calm her and then got the Guard to take her for a walk! William turned up with some breakfast for her, bread and milk which she wolfed down. Having done this she slept soundly again!

Spending the night with Ambulance 'cos bridge washed away and we can only walk across on foot to the Regiment. There were two airmails from you. The Oct. 29 only took three days!

Please don't rush into things until you're awfully well, my darling. I told Carl (an old Ambulance chap whom I've known for a long time) about you and he said – coo, it's 'cos you're not there!

I always try to be humble about us because I'm really so unworthy of you, but I feel and know in my bones that God has a great work for us to do – something greater and deeper than our greatest dreams.

No, we haven't any board up with the Vicarage on yet! William has just suggested 'The Kennel' since the arrival of the Pup! Everybody seems to think that our caravan is a good achievement!

Mess 9.15 p.m. Your Sept. 28 bed rhyme caused enormous admiration and enjoyment in the mess. It really is a superb effort. Thank goodness you feel like I do! You're beautiful and lovely and all my inspiration. I love you, love you, love you. Your Bill.

17.11.44.

Harry Hearsey (Chaplain to the Royal Horse Artillery) who was wounded two or three months ago by a bit of shell through the neck came back a day or two ago. I saw him flashing by in the car this morning. He's getting quite old, over 40 I believe, but it doesn't seem to have shaken him unduly, though his wound was very severe, bless him.

My fleabag has been shedding its feathers though at present its only use is an extra mattress. Anyway I've sewn lovely big patches over the torn parts with a couple of khaki handkerchiefs.

We are now allowed to talk about the battle up to the fall of Rome, so I'll see if there is anything I can remember. The crossing of the Rapido was a difficult operation, 'cos Jerry could see every bit of the river and the bridgehead from the monastery. Quite a few bridges were put across, and most of them had smoke screens round them so Jerry couldn't see how his shells were landing. We certainly got used to digging slit trenches. The Germans dropped quite a few bombs round about during the first few nights. One afternoon we dug a lovely trench, and had to move on that night!

Highway Six ran through Cassino and then up the right side of the Liri valley. The rest of the valley was closely cultivated country with little tracks and roads everywhere. To begin with four crossings were made and four roads – Ace route, Spade, Heart and Club. As we went on each was marked and each formation and Division had its own routes – very complicated. The Hitler Line was a devil, and many good men and tanks were lost there, but Jerry had to keep falling back.

For the last stretch before Rome, the Division came right across a mountain road, barely a track in some places. The R.Es were kept busy. Once we were on a road in a tremendous column miles and miles long. We did 28 miles in 21 hours! It's lucky that Jerry seems to have so few planes, these days.

Hugh Waller and I did sneak into Rome but the Division wasn't allowed to stop. Instead it turned right with Rome only about four miles away to the west. The men will feel grieved if they aren't able to visit Rome before leaving the country.

One of the outstanding feats was the work of the French Division on the left flank at the Rapido crossing. The Moroccan Goums are as terrifying as our Ghurkas! They hopped over tremendous mountains and cleared an enormous block in about three days. Good old Goums.

This morning I collected 200 odd books for my library. I packed up 50 for the Rest Camp and the remainder are in the Truck. Dick Witney has been nagging away for weeks about these books, and now he has taken away 8! The books are the result of book drives throughout the country. Each book usually has the name and best wishes of the Borough that provided it — sometimes even the Mayor's name.

9.12.44.   Saturday night.

Darling Beloved,

Feel very precious and awfully loved when you read this, please. More than anything in the world I love you and need you. My love seems to be boundless and complete, and yet it is always growing. Your look, your manner, the colour of your hair, the shape of your hands, the things you inspire and our life together soon, are always in my thoughts. Waking, sleeping, resting, working, you form the very background and shape and texture of all of me.

My work for the Kingdom, all the dearest, deepest things in life are bound up in the wee frame that constitutes my Appleblossom.

Be patient, Darling Woman, our time will soon be. When first we meet I'll pester you about our complete Belonging together. You'll get no peace from me 'til we share and do everything together. Happy Dreams, Darling Heart. I love you, love you, eternally.

A CHRISTMAS AIRGRAPH 1944

1. *Christmastime meant Christmas fun*
    E'er your life had long begun
    Christmas stockings, Christmas tree
    Parties, presents, jollity
    Lighted windows, church bells rung
    Christmastime meant Christmas fun.

2. *Christmastime meant Christmas joy*
    When you grew to be a boy
    Hearing Who the Babe that came
    This the day that bears His Name
    Love and awe and funs alloy
    Made your Christmas pleasure joy.

3. *Christmastime meant Christmas peace*
    More than home or pleasures ease
    Christmas love that Christ began
    Youth endowed and made you man
    Yearly since — never to cease —
    Christmas brings you Christmas Peace.

4. *Christmas 1944*
    From the heat and noise of war
    Go again to Bethlehem
    Peace, Joy, Strength is there for men
    And Love, the love the world needs more
    Love for Christmas 44.

CHRISTMAS DAY 1944

My Darling,

A Blessed Blessed Day. I hope you're very very happy. Today is crisp and sunny. Late lunch is over. The Officers and Sgts. have been down with the men serving Christmas dinners.

But let's start at the beginning. Last night my service, in the mountains, was taken by another chaplain, so I was free to go to the English Church in Florence – All Saints. It was beautifully done and the church was almost full. Lessons and carols – you know, the unmilitary ones. Darling it will be such fun to have all the background of a church and parishy things. I love all the preparations for Christmas and all the wireless programmes. Until last night the background for Christmas had seemed so slight, but it was a lovely service. Lots of men came. Walter James and I stayed in for dinner at the Club. We had a bottle of wine and towards the end a Yank Pilot came along to say Happy Christmas. He was slightly merry and in a very expansive mood. We swapped stories about sweetie pies and everything else including theology (he was R.C.). He insisted that I wrote my name on the back of his Mother's picture, so that he would be sure not to forget me! He promised to write in the next two days! Then a Yank sailor came along but we came away before we got too involved.

This morning William borrowed an alarm from the people of the house and got up at 6 a.m. He had to go over to get people from another unit to the 7.45 a.m. communion. Services were in the Regimental theatre. It is not a posh place, and has suffered badly by German demolitions. A doctor came over to the Celebration, and we went back to his Ambulance unit for breakfast and service. But poor chaps, they had started Christmas too early and so nobody turned up! So I wandered round the billet to say 'Merry Christmas' and there they were drunkenly singing and waving beer bottles in the air at 8.45 a.m. Then back we came here for two very good

Derbyshire Yeomanry Christmas Day Parade.

Parade services – Two Squadrons at a time marched up through the village (Settignano) looking very smart. Fortunately there hadn't been a lot of spit and polish so everybody was in good spirits. Some of the local people came and stood outside to hear the noise. We sang five carols and they seemed to go very well, better than last year. We took a bag full of collection – paper money lire which will take a long time to count – there should be quite a few pounds for the Waifs and Strays.

The best bit of Christmas was the A Squadron Orphans' Party yesterday afternoon. 50 boys aged 5 to 7 came from one of the orphanages in best suits with little pearl buttons down the back, shining skins and well brushed hair. The Sister who brought them must have been busy for hours. First they had an enormous meal, bigger than they've had for a long time, I think. Afterwards there were Christmas stockings full of sweets. And when their joy seemed to be overflowing squeakers and whistles were passed around – then toys, bars of chocolate and oranges. It was wonderful and pathetic to see the little chaps completely overwhelmed. Staid Troopers and Sergeants were rushing round blowing trumpets and passing glasses of milk. Every few minutes some little chap would stand up and say a well prepared little speech in Itie, of course. Finally, the Sister gathered all the presents up into baskets and they all went away. I strongly suspect that the proceeds would be pooled so that the other 300 children of the Orphanage would get a share too. It was fathers missing their own children who gave this party.

Space nearly up. Oh Dearest Heart I love you, and I need you awfully. Everything makes me love you these days, and makes me feel how much I need you. God bless you, my Darling, Happy New Year. We'll be married in the year that you get this letter. Whoopee! Your Bill.

[This was the third year of Christmas letters in which I had forecast that we should be together by the next Christmas! It was my first forecast to come true!]

POST CHRISTMAS DEPRESSION!

26.12.44.   Boxing Day Evening

Last night we had a Regimental Dinner for Officers –

quite formal with very solid food – turkey, plum pudding etc. – no speeches and only one toast 'The King'.

Darling, I've been so down in the dumps for the last few days – perhaps you've seen it in the shallowness of recent letters – I don't know. I won't live with a Regiment like this in a static period of occupation again. These last few days have been a wet blanket on my spirits. It has been women and filth day after day, meal after meal. Even more depressing is the thought that this is typical of our leaders. Christmas comes along with all its depth of love and brotherhood so I get exalted, and then at the next meal it all goes flop to the ground. Oh, I can't explain it. It's just a periodic browned-offness I think. Dearest Heart there is so much to do.

Please don't write and sympathise. I need a kick in the pants, I think – or a walk with you over mountains, or better still some of your kisses. Write and tell me you love me very much. I think that's the best cure. Though I'll be alright again when you get this.

I got a letter from Mrs. Balshaw, Norman's mother, yesterday. She hadn't met Norman's girl until I asked Mrs. Balshaw to tell her about the tragedy. She used to write to Norman every day, I think, and he thought quite a lot of her. But I don't think she was awfully Christian – not of Norman's calibre. Anyway she went to see Mrs. Balshaw and said how sorry she was for her, but said nothing about herself. Later it turned out that she had just been married to someone else.

Yesterday's collection for the Waifs and Strays came to £22. I can't find the Waifs and Stray's address. The money should be paid into the Field Cashier, and on through the Army, but some of our extravagant officers want to have the ready money and to pay in a cheque. So may I send it to you and ask you to forward it please!

SUNNY ITALY!

The winter battles in the Appenines began to turn into holding operations. Battles on the Second Front and in Russia were leading the Allies into the heart of Germany. There was little chance of the enemy being able to mount an attack any more on the Third Front, in Italy. During the winter the thin line of the much diminished 5th and 8th Armies had endured the toughest fighting of the whole war. Far up in those passes, windswept, rainsoaked and snowbound, they lived under fearful conditions. Simply to have lived there would have been difficult enough, but they maintained themselves as an efficient fighting force, and more than that — an advancing Army. Yard by yard they fought themselves over mountains. Every hill was scaled and captured, and at the top of the hill they looked forward — and yet another hill stood in front.

The New Year dawned with a lessening of activity. The 6th Armoured which had been in the line longer than any other British Division, and had taken on an Infantry role, began to return to Florence to prepare for a final break out. Florence became the great Allied Base for preparation, rest, entertainment and renewal. Basil Calver was the Garrison Chaplain and responsible for the English Church which was full at all its services. Here I was joyfully to rediscover Henson Maw, my former D.Y. organist, in charge of the splendid organ. We had not met since landing in Italy as he went to be organist at the Garrison Church in Naples.

The many Chaplains had fewer services to take, but an increasing load of welfare cases. Most of the men had been away from home for over three years and the strains were beginning to take toll. Thousands of families began to break up.

Florence was surely the most beautiful city in the world, and here, in one of the cradles of culture, art and civilisation was a Mecca for entertainment of all kinds. Cinemas and hotels were taken over and well used.

I messed with C Squadron in Settignano. In due course I met a most distinguished ancient Italian widower — Grand Officiale, Luigi Pittoni in a wing of whose large house William and I found accommodation. Nothing pleased this aristocratic Anglophile more than to be able to practise his English. I was able to lend him many books.

Italian houses were built for summer coolness and in wartime especially there was little heating. William and I fetched sacks of lignite from the mines. Its heating capacity was far inferior to coal, but coaxed into a rosy glow, it warmed us, and gave hot water for baths once we mastered the boiler.

The contrast in our style of life during this winter was very marked on Christmas Day. All the available men, splendidly turned out, marched through Settignano where we had a hearty if somewhat chilly service in the local theatre. After lunch William and I set off for the mountains. Here services were held in barns and broken houses. Perhaps the most telling service was held with a group of Sappers in a barn. The end of the barn, away from the enemy, was missing. Seats were old planks held up on oil drums, and this was my most memorable Christmas service of 1944.

Settignano – Florence.

28.12.44.   Thursday.

My Darling,

Supper in my room tonight including some cold turkey and parsnips, and a mince pie. Do you like parsnips? I love them.

Last night we had our Squadron dinner to which the Colonel came. There was a most excellent brandy butter with the Christmas pud. And we had a bottle of Benedictine to finish with. Ian Dolan came by it near Perugia months ago, and has nobly kept it ever since.

In a few minutes I'm off down the road to the RASC Christmas show. It is supposed to be terrific. Tina sends her love.

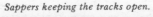

Sappers keeping the tracks open.

29.12.44.

Brr! What a cold windy night. What fun, I'll wear my lovely warm double gauntlet gloves to go up to dinner. Dearest, they came tonight, my new gloves. How nice of you. They're so warm and strong. I'll wear them a lot. Thanks very much. I love wearing and using things which have originated from the Sweetie Pie. This pen for instance. I always think of you. Oh, how sentimental.

The RASC show last night was very enterprising. They have a nine-piece band led by Cpl. Cunningham, who was a pianist to some famous broadcasting band. The band was started up by Arthur Philips (Chaplain) just before he went back to England, and has become quite famous, doing one or two broadcasts. The only snag was the coldness of the theatre.

Some more Christmas mail came in today, chiefly Christmas cards.

The S.C.F. turned up for tea. He found me, William and the Itie gardener busy with the canvas canopy on the caravan.

Next week I'll probably be going to reside at Divisional HQ, on and off. The S.C.F. is away on a nine-day course, and I've to stooge for him, send out bumph.

Oh Tweedle, Darling, I love you always. Time for dinner. God bless you. Thanks tremendously for the gloves. I'm going to put them on now. Love and kisses – Bill.

30.12.44.

This afternoon C Squadron entertained the whole 300 of the local orphanage. I got there just as the concert had ended. Joe Davies, the Sgt. Major and QM Sgt., who did all the work with a party of helpers, were sitting rather selfconsciously on a dais, being clapped by hundreds of children when I arrived!

After that the little 'tackers' marched to the big dining room – each chap stood marking time by the place at table until a Sister blew the whistle, quite regimented, poor kids! Still they were happy enough, and the Nuns seem dears.

After the orphans' party, Cliff, Doc and I came up the hill in our pet Fiat. Do you know Fiats? They're the Itie family car, and very little bigger than a toy. For the last bit up to the mess the path is very steep, and you can't get a good run at it, so Doc and I had to get out. Even so Cliff couldn't quite make it and had to sit there until we arrived to give the final push!

Tomorrow night is a great time for the Ities and New Year's Day is much more of a party day than Christmas. But I like our own way best.

31.12.44.

My Darling,

The old year, such a great year really, is on its last legs. It is such fun to think that tomorrow will be OUR year. I'll hold you in my arms and make you dizzy with kisses. I'll marry you too. Will you? Do say you will.

It is quite a few days since any air mail turned up. They say that a plane has gone down. Hope the pilot is safe. Probably all the letters just before Christmas are lost. I've a feeling that you may have made your pronouncements about marriage in them! If so, and if they have been lost you'll have to restate your case!

Tea time. Cliff Jones is asleep in a most ridiculously uncomfortable position along one settee and Doc Edwards in a reversed position on the other. Joe is making his bit of toast in front of the stove. In an hour's time I'm off to meet transport for church, and later on there will be a midnight Eucharist. Goody.

31.12.44. New Year's Eve. 11.15 p.m.

My Dear Man,

This year is ending. Surely the most momentous year of the war — Cassino — D-Day — everywhere Hitler's empire is crumbling. The second whole year without us seeing each other, my Darling, but somehow we have grown even closer. I've learnt that you can be so close to me that distance can't take you away, and being here wouldn't bring you nearer my heart . . . you lit something that is always being relit and growing all the time . . . now you are very alive in my heart. We believe that we have a great job to do and perhaps 1945 will let us start it together. But you know that the greatest thing of all is our love now.

St. Paul's Watchnight Service is on the wireless . . . there are so many things I would like to say at this great step in time but most of all it seems to be a step towards Our Time — to the time that everybody — all the US's all over the world are looking to.

> *God bless you my Love,*
> *Happy New Year*
> *I love you always,*
> *Your Helen Mary.*

New Year's Day.   Nearly 8 p.m.

Beloved Helen, Happy New Year. You know 1945 is OUR year. I'm going to make you mine. Today and tomorrow are full Regimental holidays, though William and I had to be out all day. I saw the S.C.F., and he showed me all his files, and where his blue rubber stamp lives.

When Doc gave me 200 tablets to finish off my dysentery I took 50 and then felt better, so now it has recurred and I've to take the remaining 150!

Your December 22 airmail came today. Whoopee! It is so long since any airmail came through. Last night about 100 turned up for Eucharist. It did seem a good way to see OUR year in. The bell was tolled at 12 and as we knelt at the rails a great roar and noise of 'Old Lang Syne' seemed to engulf everything.

Tuesday 10 p.m. Well I was whisked away last night to the party before much letter got written. It was Sgts. and Officers mixed — quite unusual and good fun. We drank Vino Sancto steadily from 8.30 'til 1.30, though I didn't have too much! Food was served from a buffet — good grub though you had to fight and use your elbows to get it!!! By 12 everybody was singing 'Silent Night' and all the current songs, mixed up with heart to heart talks. A bit of booze certainly opens peoples' minds and tongues!

An opera star came and sang bits, chiefly from 'Boheme', but she wasn't awfully good, and then there was more opera from A Squadron cook, an Itie who has been with the officers' mess for ages. Finally, some very indifferent dances by two scantily clad girls brought in from the local variety club, I should think. So we got home about 2.30 a.m. Today was a holiday so William and I made plans to have breakfast in bed. After about 10 a.m. he appeared with breakfast and I was finally washed and shaved by 11.30!

I had lunch at an Officers' Club with the S.C.F., after which we went to the Officers' shop. It is a new one which only opened yesterday, and consequently full of everything. I got shirts, gloves, woolly pants in case it is very cold.

THE EPIPHANY

6.1.45.

Diss has been rung over by a 'Double Norwich' peal, composed by Mr. Golding of Norwich, who was in charge, and who brought three of their Ringers with him. Bertie Harrison also rang. It could have been in honour of the Epiphany. They started three times, but managed 3¼ hours and completed the peal. It had only just been introduced to them. They did well.

You might like to have my scribble for Epiphany.

> *Surely on this happy day*
> *When long ago and far away*
> *The Wisdom of the East bowed down*
> *To give the Little Jew his Crown:*
> *We should give thanks, adopted sons*
> *And pray for all the Chosen Ones.*
> *And we within the Church's fold*
> *Should recognise, and count for gold*
> *Perception of all other kind*
> *Of His Name, and of His mind*

Mrs. B., Phyllis and I went to the pictures last night. This is the Army — yes Sir! We were too late to book when we tried on Wednesday so we had to queue, but the Manager put us in some seats whose owners hadn't turned up. What a lot the Tommies think of their girls at home. There should be some films for troops about how the women folk think of their men. You see you are very precious. By the time you come home I'm going to be very fit indeed.

Dad's lumbago is much better. He is reading a book of short stories he had for Christmas, and doesn't fall asleep in the middle! Good night My Darling, I love you, love you, Helen.

7.1.45.

I fear that you didn't get an Epiphany letter as we were up in the mountains. The journey was only possible by Jeep, so I went with a driver going to relieve another who had been at the sharp end too long.

Now for dreams . . . when we began this strange adventure future dreams had to be somewhat stifled, but now my longing to be with you is becoming daily more overpowering. All round me the men feel the same, and, sadly, so many can't cope any more.

There were two sad welfare letters waiting when I called in at D.Y. today, and four from you, my Beloved. I took a service at the workshops and they all turned out with greasy hands and straw in their hair. My face muscles were almost frozen and it took time before they were thawed out!

In A Sqn. Canteen there was a meeting with two M.Ps. About 80 men turned up to ask questions, some very good ones, but neither M.P. was very sparkling. However there were some laughs.

At Christmas the Sappers sent out a letter from me to all the wives and sweethearts. It was a letter of Christmas hope and of the need to hang on to family ties. I have had many replies, some sad, some hopeful.

15.1.45.

My Darling,

The frozen pipe is mended, and I'm feeling lovely, clean and washed. You know that feeling after a soak in a really hot bath. Today has been a bit on the warm side for my winter woollies. This afternoon I dispensed with my greatcoat.

We got quite a haul from the Welfare Department today — bundles of papers, magazines, cigarettes, scarves, two boxes of assorted knick-knacks (pipes, soap, etc.) and a large box of packet sweets from the Cuban Rotary Clubs! After lunch I took them to Frank Hartee (Q.M.) for distribution. Tina and his Wendy met for the first time. Tina is still a very nervous dog and whenever she meets another dog she rolls over to be kissed!

Now we've had dinner and the iron stove is burning strongly — only Ian, Roy, Baldy and myself are in. This armchair would hold you as well as me. It is rather like the one in my bedroom in the Rectory.

16.1.45.   Tuesday afternoon.   Middle of Welfare period.

Three laddies have rolled in so far. One had been away for five months since he had his lung pierced by an explosive bullet. The line of tanks was sprayed by non hostile aircraft.

A CHAPLAINS' COURSE IN ASSISI
run by ROBIN WOODS, S.C.F.

23.1.45.

We came to a snow clad, freezing Assisi, and glimpsed the wonderful view across the plain with S. Maria degli Angeli floating above the mist like a ball. We are housed in a medieval hotel where everyone is welcoming – even to Tina. She is the first dog to attend a course and is an instant success . . . women of the civilian staff clap when she appears. She stalked into Evensong, but I had to deter her from chewing a pile of English Hymnals.

26.1.45.

We have visited the Castle, which is the key to the defence of the plain, and St. Damian's Church and Monastery where St. Francis worshipped as a boy. It became home to St. Clare and her Sisters.

Robin's first subject was 'God, the Lord of History' and dealt with so much: A better Social Order, Education, Social Security, Health Service, Town and Country Planning, Reconstruction. Never before have we had such a chance of building the new Jerusalem.

27.1.45.

This evening's session was on the Post-war Church.

Tonight I had to tell the Mess how I fell in love! I passed your pictures round and soon everybody was opening up about their families. Dearest one, I'm so happy and I hope you are too. At the General Hospital, with Nancy who is to marry Pat, and some of her nurses, I had my first feminine tea of the war.

29.1.45.

This is the last night of the Course. Never have I enjoyed anything so much since leaving home. Delirious happiness will not come until you are my other half, but it has been a great intellectual, spiritual and social tonic. It is the sheer joy of being with men who love the things I love, who are hurt by the same evils, who have the same hopes – it has been a privilege to be part of the love and friendship of a worshipping community. Four of us, in a last outing, climbed to the Carcere, the tiny, 9th century Chapel, hollowed out of the living rock, where St. Francis spent so much time. Here he composed his Hymn to the Birds.

16.2.45.

Far East News reports a devastating air raid in the heart of Tokio by a force of planes based on ships only 300 miles away. All over the world retribution is closing in. How lovely if there could be world wide peace before our marriage, my Darling.

26.3.45.

The Germans continue to fall back. Today I took a laddie 50 miles there and 50 miles back to file a petition for Divorce. His wife had a child by another man last summer. He forgave her although she continued to be unfaithful. Then an airman came along and started to terrify the two real children of the family, so they have gone to our own man's parents. Now the wife is pregnant again with another man's child, what a mess.

The Grand old man is dead. Lloyd George has been a back number for such a long time now. I suppose he is one of the great men of the century in spite of his family life.

FRESH FIELDS

It took all autumn and winter, well into the New Year, until I was fit for any 'outdoor' job, and by the middle of February a most interesting one turned up. At Bunwell, some 8 miles north of Diss, Banyards Hall, home of Mrs. Buchanan, was the depot for a fleet of 16 Church Army Canteen vans. Their

object was to take tea, buns, cigarettes and sundry other
requirements with cheerful service, to personnel on the RAF
airfields and USAAF bases which spanned the Norfolk
countryside. I was invited to test my aptitude as a driver.
At 7.40 a.m. on Monday, February 19th, 1945, three years
and a day after our engagement, I was on Diss Station waiting to board the down train to begin a new chapter in our
expanding time of separation.

19.2.45.   Monday. Bed.

This is an interesting job. The van conked out, but I
thoroughly enjoyed today. They are vehicles too crocky to
be trusted in London any longer. So they are 'put out to
grass' on miles of country lanes. They also have to sprint
round the perimeter tracks of airfields, to reach their sale
points before a plane is on the runway! I helped John, a
discharged Army boy (about 19). He told me lots about the
job, as we drove the 20 miles to Stanton. We spent the day
on the field, picnicking at lunch-time by a wood with two
staff from another van. Then we filled up our 6 urns with hot
water at the Cookhouse. We dished out £23.10s. worth of
tea, buns, fags etc. (tea: 2d a cup; a cake 1½d; cigarettes:
(mostly Woodbines) 4d a pack of 10). That is the best John
has done so far. ... so sleepy . . . and a lovely comfy bed. I am
staying with the Easton family at The Villa, a farm near the
church. Molly (c.14) and John (9) go daily by bus to Norwich
High School and Grammar School respectively. Peter is 7 and
goes to the Village School. The eldest boy, Dick, is a boarder
at Norwich. Mrs. Easton is very nice and I feel at home already.
She is going to call me at 7.30 with a cup of tea . . . what a
spoilt girl! I have not yet seen Mr. He is a poultry farmer,
and his lorries have contract work; taking sugar beet to the
factory at South Lynn in the winter.

Good night my Beloved . . . your L.M.P.

I do feel happy. This seems to be a useful job. xxxx

22.2.45.   Saturday 8.45 a.m.

Last night we had a party at Banyards. It was quite fun.
I met Walter from Garden City, Long Island; like all these

chaps he comes from 'God's Country' . . . very interested in architecture, literature and classical music. He may come to look at the 1550 documents at Diss Church.

Diss 10 p.m. Irene dropped me at home on her way back . . . 6 *air letters . . . what a flood of love . . . bed now. God bless. xxxxxx*

27.2.45. Tuesday.

6 letters at the weekend and another today. Yesterday and today I went to Fersfield with Mrs. Moore (John's mother). Nice set of 'boys', North Country, with a good sprinkling of Scottish, so perhaps that accounts for it. We had a little Ford van and I drove home. On Friday I think I am going by myself. We should be getting a 'new' van which someone will have to fetch from London. I expect John will have it as he has furthest to go. Then I MAY get the little van.

We call at the baker in New Buckenham for our supply of cakes. The trays contain various kinds modelled on pre-war varieties . . . even 'Eccles Cakes' are represented . . . 'we used to put dried fruit in them' Mr. Goulder told me 'but we ha'er use. stoil coik crumbs now'! . . . an enterprising war effort. When we returned the empty trays on our way home he had just taken a tin of hot ginger biscuits from the oven . . . they were delicious. He was fishing about with his oven shovel for a burning loaf he couldn't locate! They are a friendly family, Pa, Ma and daughter Joan who sometimes comes on the vans. Oh yes, I'm very happy, and the boys ask me 'what's that badge?'. When I say 'Derbyshire Yeomanry' they look very impressed. Sometimes I see them eyeing Twinkle (my engagement ring) and then I feel myself swelling!

Bless you for being you and most of all for being mine.
Goodnight, God bless.

5.3.45.

I called in at home at lunchtime and there was your Feb. 23rd letter. As I stuffed it into my pocket the birds seemed to sing and the sun to shine again although I suspect it was raining all the time.

You see I had not too good a morning: no hot water at the Cookhouse instead of 3 urns full of boiling hot tea. Then, when I was just getting away half an hour late, the gear stuck, in reverse! I collared hold of a driver but he was stumped, so I trotted across to an office and found a handsome boy beside a phone, and very soon a M.T. Sgt. and a man came along in their little Austin and got me unstuck. The gear box was nearly dry. These vans are supposed to be kept in good running order. Thank goodness I was not responsible for the oil being low. I like my little bus and I like my customers. They are good lads. I would have been in a fix without these mechanics to put my bus right. When anything goes wrong with my crocky little van, I open the bonnet side up and stick my head inside and nearly always the first Service vehicle stops 'hello, what's up then?' emerging from the bonnet I brightly announce that the nearside back tyre is flat ... or whatever. With a laugh they kindly get to work.

. . . American tanks are fighting into Cologne . . . Peace Conference invitations being planned . . . things are really being made ready for the end now. All this fighting and slogging will be over soon. Then the real work will begin. Happy dreams my Beloved. God bless you dear Heart.

Appenine cemetery.

MOVING TO PESARO ON THE ADRIATIC
TO PREPARE FOR THE FINAL BATTLE

11.3.45.   Mothering Sunday.

We have been on the move today, so there haven't been any Services, but you have been very much in my heart. Everything whispers these days of our love, of our families, and the deep strong roots from whence we have sprung. God works through the Family, and I'm so happy to dream of you in the centre of our Family.

We were up and away early. We came through the hills and passed the Cemetery where Norman Balshaw and Padre Bernard are buried, so I stopped to take a few snaps. Since last winter it has become a tidy and cared-for place. We said a prayer. I borrowed a Zeiss Ikon camera and hope I got the controls organised.

The end of our journey brought us to the sea. I have a little room to myself on the second floor of quite a nice house. You will gather that we have been properly on the move.

The Odds and Ends, Doc and E.M.E. and myself have come back to R.H.Q. to live again. We enjoyed C Squadron, but we are back to dignity, and quite a little pomp and splendid meals. As you might expect R.H.Q. has brought quite a bit of furniture and a carpet.

After breakfast I discovered a very promising Church in the local Law Court. It is a very fine room with Judge's Desk and semi-circular carved stalls. These form a very good background for the Altar. Last week the place was so full that some had to be turned away. For next week the Judge's stalls will have to be removed and replaced by chairs.

Harry Hearsey and I met Mike Wilson, one of the Padres from the African days. It would seem that we may be here long enough for us to plan an Easter we've never dreamed of before.

DEPLOYMENT

12.3.45.

Mrs. Buchanan met me at Diss today and we went to the Ministry of Labour and National Service Office for my inter-

view. I was applying to be directed to work on the Church Army Canteens.

We had a nice interview and Mrs. Buchanan has a charming way with her, puts a good case for the vans, as, perhaps, only those who have to do with them know the worth of the job they do. So soon, D.V., I will be in the 'Army'.

I am rearing to go in my little Khaki VAN: a DRIVER in the Church Army with the evidence of my engagement ring that I am also, truly, a part of my Bill's very extended Khaki Parish . . . I really feel as though I am on his STAFF! Well, we both know we do nothing in our own strength, and we serve the same enabling Boss.

By licence I am qualified to drive, amongst an impressive list of vehicles, a Motor Roller! My only incumbrance is that I am also qualified to teach!

14.3.45.

My Labour Exchange interview resulted in my being allowed to continue working on the vans until the end of June, then I should return to teaching unless I volunteered for overseas service. In Norfolk I might as well carry on until the next academic year began in September . . . I thought! There are no hop-picking holidays here. There were attractions abroad (notably Bill) but enquiries showed that I would probably be stuck 'out there' when Bill had come home; that would have been absurdly tragic!

Meanwhile, through the lovely Spring days and the rest, I drove my Austin van to Snetterton where I was hailed by 'Hi Red', and serenaded in a tuneful Texan lilt 'here comes my lil' raaay o'sunshine'. When the Red Cross canteen hove in sight, giving away coffee and doughnuts, my boys lined up and announced that they were waiting for their Church Army van! The canteen had a 'stable' type back door with handle only on the outside . . . yes . . . once I was shut inside when the counter roof (van side) was slammed down so hard that it jammed. I am convinced that my imprisonment was not planned . . . unlike my urgently requested visit to the M.T. section where I did a huge trade, cleared up, shut down (from outside) settled in my driving seat mid cheerful wavers . . . goodbye Sunshine . . . The Austin was in reverse, brakes

HELEN'S CANTEENING — 1945–6

Legend:
- River
- Road
- Railway
- ★ USAAF
- ◉ RAF
- ☐ Army Camp
- ■ Small Units

Banyard's Hall – Church Army Depôt

Starston
Harleston
Tivetshall
Thorpe Abbotts
Banyard's Hall
Tibenham
Eye
Tacolneston
Bunwell
Carlton Rode
New Buckenham
Old Buckenham
DISS
swich
Bakery
Fersfield
R. Waveney
Eccles Road
Snetterton Heath
Harling Road
Roudham Hall
R. Thet
Riddlesworth Hall
Knettishall
Coney Weston
Stanton
Shepherd's Grove
Haughley
B R E C K L A N D
Danger area
Snarehill
Brettenham
Shadwell
Little Ouse
Honington
Ixworth
THETFORD
Elveden Hall
Mildenhall
Brandon
BURY St. EDMUNDS
Norwich

*off . . . why was I stationary? I opened the door and looked
ou` . . . my back wheels were spinning freely . . . jacked up!
Very soon I had a burst back tyre, so I rang those M.T. boys
and they did come bouncing along in a Jeep to mend the
offending wheel . . . in a holly hedge!*

*I went to Stanton, to Harling Road and to Pioneers,
stationed in the Servants' Quarters of Roudham Hall. At
Shadwell Court, North of A1066 near Thetford, were Indians,
many with turbans and silver bangles. They would lay a
towel on the counter, hold up two fingers and proffer a
florin, 'two sheeleen, two sheeleen' they chanted as I tumbled eighteen cakes onto the cloth which was gathered up
and spirited away. I wondered why they were whispering . . .
what were they pointing at? I asked an English Officer . . .
'perhaps it is your bangle and they wonder if you are a
Sikh!' My chromium bangle made no further appearances
there! I hoped that I had never caused distress by any of my
attire. The longest time I spent at Shadwell Court was when
my van broke down to such a degree that I had to wait for
another, bigger van to come from Bunwell and tow me to
Norwich.*

*When my usual customers were not available because of
change of duty times, I went to look for other customers.
At the check point on A1066 soldiers told me to go to the
hut in the valley . . . when I arrived the oaths nearly blew me*

Helen at an American Airbase in the Spring of 1945.

'The Flying Ginny'

back to the road . . . I was dragged from the van and into the hut as faulty bombs were exploded nearby . . . the personnel at the check point were in for a blast of further oaths on the (then) hot line!

There were quiet days on the airfields such as when the huge planes with freshly-painted bombs and swastikas (for kills) on their fusilages, showing the success of their last sorties, stood by a gap . . . an empty parking bay . . . one plane had not returned. One might look among the morning customers for Types . . . and assume their absence meant that they were in the missing plane.

OUR GENERAL

On April 8, 1945, just before the final battle each Chaplain received a letter personally signed from General Dick McCreery, the Commander of the Eighth Army:

Dear Padre,

Now that we are on the eve of final victory over the Germans, I want to take this opportunity of thanking you for the magnificent work you have done, as an Eighth Army Padre, towards this victory.

During this Italian campaign I have had many opportunities of seeing the great gallantry of the Padre, not

only on the field of battle, but during those long intervals when spirits flag. You have by your courage, endurance and humanity, done wonderful work by helping to
keep up morale, and by bringing comfort and encouragement to many soldiers.

When the end of organised enemy resistance comes,
many fighting soldiers may feel that their chief job is
finished. With the Padre, however, the reverse is true,
the more difficult task will be winning the peace.
Within the Army the Padre will play a tremendously
important part during the years immediately following
the armistice. The chief aim of this letter is to emphasise
this, and to say I want to give you all possible help. In
every unit you are one of the family, and a good C.O.
helps his Padre, and sees that his team of officers all do
the same. I want you to feel that you always have the
friendship and backing of the officers of your unit.

Work, unselfish service, and above all, God's teaching
are the essentials which will see us through the difficult
days ahead. Wherever the Eighth Army goes it must have
the respect of the civilian population. I know that I can
continue to count on your whole hearted support.

Yours sincerely,

R. L. McCreery.

W. G. Cook, C.F.
1 Derby Yeomanry.

PESARO

The Allies were relentlessly advancing into Germany and the
time came for the 8th Army to put in one last effort. The
plan was to try to trap all the opposing Germans in Italy between the Appenines and the river Po, fifty miles north.

In the middle of March 1945, the 6th Armoured Division
left Florence and the Appenines behind and assembled at
Pesaro on the Adriatic coast. It seemed queer to be looking
back on the German side of those dreaded mountains. The
three pleasant weeks at Pesaro covered Holy week and Easter.
There were plenty of troops and Padres, so a very traditional

Holy week was planned. The Church was packed out for Palm Sunday. Each day there were services of Holy Communion and Devotions, morning and evening. Maundy Thursday was observed with traditional rites. Good Friday had a morning service, a Three Hours Devotion (how many times I wonder has this been possible in a theatre of war?), and a service in the evening. The hall was packed out for all the services. Pesaro was covered with Holy week posters of a woodcut of a ruined town and a cemetery, surmounted by the three crosses.

Pat, one of our officers, came along with the necessary details of himself and of Nancy the nurse, who were to be married in Assisi on Easter Eve. Pat seemed very happy, and had even had a haircut! We got to Assisi about 6.15 p.m. to find it just as peaceful as ever. Pat and Nancy, a couple of her nursing friends, Doc Edwards, Pat's best man, Padre Lee the Hospital Chaplain, Reggie and Joe with a couple of others were waiting for dinner. We had a good one and enjoyed Spumanti. We all sat talking until five minutes to twelve when Nancy and her two nurses went back to the Hospital.

Reggie and I shared a room in the hotel. At 10.00 a.m. Padre Lee and I went to the Patients' Dining Hall, which was beautifully decorated with banks of flowers. There was an altar with two red velvet cushions before it. About 50 nurses, 30 officers and quite a few men came. It was only my second wedding during my war service. Nancy was very pretty and looked well in her uniform, and Pat was handsome, so they made a good couple. I married them and Padre Lee took the prayers. After that there was a reception in the Nurses Home – good food and a most wonderful 3 tier wedding cake, made by the Sgt. Cook.

The Doctor Colonel, who gave Nancy away, made a speech. He said it wouldn't be long, and then he proceeded to drag in Burns, Shakespeare and all the poets! I hope they will be happy bless them.

Looking back on such a marriage it seemed to be such a rush. Shortly Pat had to be back with his Regiment for the final battle. The question of wartime marriage occupied a great deal of thought and correspondence between Helen and myself. I don't really think there is a ready and complete answer.

On Easter Day about 70 came to the 8.00 a.m. Communion. A similar number came at 9.00 a.m. At 10 a.m. we started to move the altar, pots of flowers and all the other trappings over to the lovely Rossini concert hall. It was packed out at 11 a.m. We had the grand piano and the violins and cellos of the Rossini orchestra. It took the strings a bit of time to get used to congregational singing, and I don't suppose they've ever done such a thing before! Afterwards another 70 stayed for Communion.

As soon as lunch was over we had to go back to the hall to collect all the things and bring them into our church again, so that all was shipshape for the evening. Easter Alleluias continued in the Evening and more Communion followed. Could any Army preparing for final battle have ever kept such a happy Easter?

2.4.45.   Holy Saturday.

Three lovely letters from you and the sweetest little angel; her little legs are bent to balance her head, just like a child praying.

I'm glad you have Reggie [later, Bill's Best Man] *to introduce to his new flock and to keep you company. Yesterday's Three Hours was a great Service. 2–5 p.m. in St. Mary's Diss . . . our time is not 'God's time', as they say, and Dad says it is more convenient than through the dinner hour.*

3.4.45.   Easter Day.

I got well roused at 6.20 a.m. by your alarm, so I got to Church for 7. All the 'boys' say I ought to be having a holiday, and ask with concern if I went to Church this morning. They can swear snow black, but they have a certain reverence which is all the more striking because of the contrast.

I was offered the post of Kinder Garten Mistress at The Entry School, yesterday, but I told Miss Pike that I was not to go back to teaching for three months, and she wanted someone permanent . . . so I dare not agree to go!

Time to fill up urns at the Cookhouse. Nancy Noble is coming on Wednesday to stay for a week and come round on the van. What fun . . . she can clean the van and get the urns ready while I write to you! We will be making plans for THE DAY. If we hear your leave is imminent we will have a shopping get-together. We can't get ready too early or we might be sweltering in mid-Summer or shivering in thins in winter, and coupons can't be un-spent. Roll on THE DAY. Joyful Easter love.xxx

5.4.45.

Nancy arrived last night. She had quite a welcome from the load Irene had collected in the shooting brake . . . she and I and four Yanks! Today we had a good day on the van at Old Buckenham and Snetterton.

7.4.45.

Nancy and I biked to Diss last night. Dad and the Burling-hams had been at Fen Cottage since Wednesday and got very stuck on the railway trying to get home yesterday.

Three letters for me at home. How lovely that there were all Pat and Nancy's Army and nursing pals to make a fuss of them. Oh my Bill you do need a bit of parish practise, don't you.

Your letters are so very like you and going to be such good company for me to pull out and read at odd moments during the day. I soon know big chunks of them by heart.

10.4.45.   Low Sunday.

Nancy and I had a good day on the van after we collected a spare wheel from a garage.

Monday. We went to see the Colonel on a depot which is attached to my Base to see if we might call there. So we can go in the morning and hope to meet some new customers. Today our usuals had had inoculations and were feeling 'lousy'. Oh goodness what a time this is with the new offensive of The Eighth to add to all the excitement over the rush forward across Germany.

No cigarettes to sell today, so the £8 we took was all for tea and buns, a few boot laces and bars of soap.

Mr. and Mrs. Easton are out so I am housekeeper. Peggy

(Mr. E's brother's wife) was here with baby Margaret. We talk to each other about our men, and how we met and all those things that one must share with someone every so often just because of the joy of it all.

Friday. 11 a.m. waiting for level crossing gates to open. Sad about Roosevelt dying . . . here we go . . . love, your L.M.P.

THE LAST BATTLE

During the following week we moved up into Cesena, the Divisional concentration area.

At Cesena the 6th Armoured Division was placed perhaps to fulfil its proper role of bursting through a narrow gap, for the first time in Italy. We were ready to go through the 78th and 56th Division if they could fight through the Argenta Gap, or due west through the Poles and Indians if that should prove the better way.

9.4.45.

Pat and Nancy came back from their Honeymoon in Rome, last night. Poor Darlings, what a change! They had a wonderful few days, but now is their sad parting. This morning they had breakfast together in army mess tins cooked by some of Pat's Tank crew. Soon Pat will be leading his Troop for what we hope will be the last push. When this is over they will be together again.

While we were in Assisi, William went to Perugia to spend the night with his Sapper friends. He twisted an ankle coming downstairs. The Doctor thinks he had broken something, though he insisted on driving back that afternoon.

11.4.45.

We're on the move at last and I expect there will be news on the wireless. In the Mess we drank to the Colonel's D.S.O., and to Pat Radford's M.C.

A first copy of Henry V in technicolor has been flown out and is showing twice a day. The sound was good but the colour was rather blurred. Perhaps you have seen it?

13.4.45.

I am getting quite argumentative in Mess these days! Somebody said 'let's have a sensible argument tonight! So I kicked off about Education, and then suggested that in 50 years time there would be a 20-hour working week. Machinery will be so efficient that we will be able to produce everything in that number of hours, and to have the rest of the time to live a fuller life. It started a serious discussion. I was able to drag in the thought that it must always be people that matter.

To-day's news has been mostly of the passing of President Roosevelt. What a Leader, and what a rock-like Champion of Democracy he has been. What a friend he was in our need, when we stood alone.

Sweet dreams, my Darling. I love you.

14.4.45.

Summer is really here and it is lovely to feel the sand between one's toes. This bit of beach is so overcrowded that we are going to try a bit further North. The Regiment has four petrol-driven motor boats and a host of Jerry dinghies! We are all in good heart and I love you very much. Soon I'll be saying it personally. Roll on the day! my Darling Brown Eyes. Most vehicles seem to have a girl's name painted on them. The other day I saw a Jeep with 'Brown Eyes' painted under the windscreen. Goody!

17.4.45.

I had the help of a 'K.P.' all afternoon. I think it means Kitchen Personnel . . . a little man from the Cookhouse had the day off and was all dressed up in his posh clothes to come round the Base with me, when I arrived at his Cookhouse to fill up the urns at dinner time. He was very helpful. I have a list of people who want to come and help me on their days off! It is a great help to have someone to wash up and turn the urn tap, though I'm not really happy to think that they spend their free time working for me, but they do seem to enjoy it. I think perhaps I cheer them up. I don't feel shy, and they aren't 'dreadful Yanks', they really are good stuff when you get to know their ways. Nancy was

*awfully struck by the way that they look after each other
and all pal up together. Their friendship is sincere and goes
right through rank. Of course they have no class distinction
'back home' and I think that makes more difference between
their outlook and ours than we often realise. This job has
made me aware that I am an awful snob. I mean it did feel
odd to find the G.Is. slapping Majors on the back!*

23.4.45.   Thursday.

*5 p.m. Six letters from you! Dick came to help me today,
and we were very busy, having to fill up an extra urn for the
RASC; there are lots of ATS there now.*

*Mr. and Mrs. and Molly are out, so Dick and I put Peter to
bed. I told the turnip story and Dick and John both sat on the
bed to listen; How Peter's eyes lit up . . . and what a smile
when the turnip eventually came up! He is a pet but could
do with a younger brother or sister so that he would be a bit
older . . . when we have a family perhaps we should just keep
on so that the youngest wouldn't be the youngest for long.
It is a lovely evening; perfect for a walk across the cowslip
field (very good district for cowslips) and under the lilac
hedge. It smells so lovely. Oh to have my Pip in England now
that April's here.*

God bless you, my Beloved.

On April 16 I went into the local Super-Naafi, something
new to me, and ended up in a voice recording department.
For 1/9, I could have sent 150 words on a tiny recorded disc.
My friend Joe sailed in and made one for his twins' birthday.
The room was full of soldiers. I got tongue tied at the thought
and feeling that I would be unable to send my heart in that
sort of a way, I returned to my airmail forms. Helen might
also have been shy to play in public what I would have
wanted to say!

The next day was to be Sunday, but I feared there would
be no services. Instead it would be reverting to active service
conditions when every day could be a Sunday. The following
Wednesday there were services and Communions in the morning and evening. The next day we moved to a farm just south

of Argenta. The battle had been raging for a week, and our break out was to be through the Argenta Gap. The 78th (Battleaxe) Division had broken through, and now the Derbyshire Yeomanry were out in front. We were all very fit and rearing to go. The weather was good. In an airmail letter to Helen I wrote 'Here is blood and hate and destruction – thankfully fleeting and transient things compared with our own love which is eternal'.

There was a bridge on the Reno still useable, and the next water obstacle was the Fossa Cembalino where the crossing was held up by three German Tiger tanks with 88 mm. guns. Finally the Airforce moved in to bomb them, and as they withdrew the crossing was made. The crossing was made by driving a Churchill Ark tank down into the water on top of bundles of sticks. The tracks were opened out and the tanks began to cross. Quoting from the D.Y. Regimental Scrap Book, Colonel Sir Ian Walker wrote 'The General of the 6th Armoured Division told me some time afterwards that the crossing of that bridge by the whole Regiment left more impression on his mind than any other incident in the whole campaign'. There were literally not more than two inches to spare on either side, with terrifically steep banks down on to the boards and again up on the other side, and if one single driver had made the semblance of a mistake nothing could have crossed afterwards. But no driver did, and 72 tanks crossed that bridge.

Now the Regiment was out in front on the way to Ferrara, and on the first day the bag was 225 prisoners. Our men were to face minefields, anti-tank guns, small arms fire, bazookas and tanks but there were no casualties. The river west of Ferrara had an unblown bridge, and so they fanned out towards the river Po, the final objective. Here they were halted 4000 yards away by the General as there were no infantry up in support.

It was surely a sign that the Germans were cracking as on April 20 I went into a farm house to talk to the people, to find that the Germans had taken their food and all the oxen had been driven off for towing guns and vehicles to save petrol. I picked up a Nazi flag, with some sort of Young Fascist banner highly embroidered and tasselled.

Having got to the river Po we dug ourselves into a go-ahead little village. The foe had only just moved out the previous evening. There was a Quartermaster's store to be ransacked in our farm. I don't seem to remember what we took, except to say that we left piles of guns, ammunition and other war equipment severely alone.

Three young men wearing Italian colours on armbands, a partisan sign, came through the camp. I always encouraged partisans with a cigarette and a greeting, so they stopped to speak, and then 20 kids came in too. One young man had been abducted from Florence by the Germans because his uncle was English!

We were still south of the river Po and the Allied Air Force had prided itself that it had knocked out every bridge long before. Paul Clark reported that his troop was on the flood bank. The advance had been spectacular, and for once the Engineers were well behind with their bridging equipment. The next day a New Zealand officer and two of his men crossed in an assault boat. They were followed that night by a strong New Zealand force who formed the bridgehead. The Po is as broad as the Rhine. The enemy were few, and so others crossed, Grenadiers in their DUKWs (Ducks) and swimming Sherman tanks. Soon the Sappers made a raft capable of taking a tank or two lorries at a time. I still have a couple of R.A.F. aerial photographs showing the bend in the river where the first crossing was made.

FIRST NEWS OF NAZI EXTERMINATION CAMPS
29.4.45.

Darling Brown Eyes,

We're rather lazy 'cos its a bit difficult to find any Jerries to deal with at the moment, and there are so many of us to deal with them now! Anyway it will all be over soon, and how glad we'll be. The news from Germany is good, and all the rumours of offers of unconditional surrender are signs of the times, aren't they?

William told me to look out of the wagon window as I was shaving this morning, and there were the Alps — far away and snow covered. The first time the atmospheric conditions have been right for us to see them. After breakfast they had gone again.

Two airmails, April 24, came in last night — the first airmail we've had since crossing the Po a few days ago.

5.45 p.m. News of Mussolini's death. Perhaps it's just as well like that. The 8th Army weekend paper *The Crusader* is devoted to atrocity pictures and reports of articles signed by British MPs, who have made rounds of the various concentration camps. Darling, what ARE we to believe, or do about it? It IS true. Or IS it? If it IS true, this awful Nazism is a much more terrible scourge than we have ever imagined. The German foe here has been a very professional one though he has been utterly ruthless in suppressing any opposition — BUT THIS. I remember writing to you my last letter before we set sail in November 1942 saying that I was glad and proud to be in at the killing of the Nazi cancer. But now events are unbelievable. How much more worthwhile it has been, all this sweat and death, than we ever imagined.

Let us hope that this terrible tangle can be sorted out. We must try to get the right perspective and use justice before we can bring love into our reconstruction. That's right, isn't it? Oh Helen Darling it is all such a muddle.

Three evenings ago five Russian slave workers managed to escape from the Jerries as they retreated. Most of them had been prisoners for two years doing work in the north of Italy, digging defences, working on the land, etc. One was a laddie of 18 who was taken from Russia as the Germans retreated. There was a deep underlying hatred in their hearts. Berlin had just been encircled, and it reminded them of Rostov, Leningrad and Moscow. We gave them food and talked with them in Italian.

Brown Eyes, our love must produce something strong and constructive in this crazy mazy topsy turvy world. How I love you, Darling Woman.

30.4.45.

We were expecting to rest for a few days when we suddenly received orders to continue. Once again we are in a farm, large and clean. Everybody seems very prosperous and well fed. By the farm entrance there is a bakery with most welcome fresh bread smells.

Here I paint a picture of 'Josser', one of our most irrepressible Yeomen! He was a fitter, who had worked at Rolls Royce in Derby. Josser is 'good going' as Helen's Father would say. He cares for nobody, is never awed by pomp and dignity. He's always got a chortle and a laugh. He's got a mouth of round English oaths which always come out, except when he talks to me! He was confirmed after the Tunisian campaign, and never misses a service. He always stays behind to shift seats or collect hymn books. A rough diamond with a heart of gold. He has a wonderful Missis, who is a very fine Christian.

Cor, he's just been commiserating with a duck who has lost her eggs! Though he didn't tell her that four of her eggs are being boiled for lunch.

3.5.45.

This morning we see the foothills of the Alps, and here and there in breaks in the clouds are snow covered peaks. The B.B.C. said today that we are in Udine, so now you know where we are. I had a lovely haircut and shampoo this morning.

Goody, there was some mail today. Your April 25 and 27 airmails.

JERRY CHASING!

May Day 1945.

Darling Helen,

Still the great chase goes on. Everywhere are Italian flags, cheering crowds, and groups of partisans nosing out isolated Jerries from odd places. Every day great batches of tired dishevelled Jerries go straggling down the side of the road with hardly any one guarding them. Sometimes the guard is a grinning Ghurka, sometimes South African, sometimes our own people, marching with the prisoners, or riding on a horse, or crawling along in a Jeep. If they are lucky, the prisoners are whisked away down the road in lorries. There may be pockets of fanatics who will go on fighting here and there, but in the main they seem to have had it, thank God.

Here the countryside is quite unspoiled and unharmed by war. Occasionally there is a burned out vehicle, and every few yards the roads are lined with air raid trenches that the Jerries could dive into on the approach of our aircraft.

The houses here have glass in the windows, electric light that still works and running water. Instead of the dreary picture of great electricity pylons and overhead wires sprawling drunkenly over everything, with water and power stations blown up, there is no damage here.

Last night as we came along a very good straight tree-lined road, we were told that Himmler had asked for unconditional surrender from the Three Powers. We didn't go wild. Something seemed to snap inside, and we dared to begin to think about peace. The people on the roads had heard it too, and they shouted 'Viva la Pace' and threw flowers. But when the 9 p.m. news came along there was no mention of peace.

Oh, Tweedle. Anyway the peace is brewing up and I don't think it will be more than a day or two now. Oh my Darling when it does come I'll be writing about the trousseau you'll have to be thinking about soon.

Dearest I love you – your brown eyes, your nice hair and everything about you. Soon I'll have a chance to tell you these things in looks and kisses. Now for the post. Be happy my Darling. Love and kisses from your very adoring Bill.

4.5.45.

My Darling,

Continued good news of the occupying of Germany. Silly ass Doenitz to keep on fighting. 14th Army are doing well. Gosh they would be front page news if it were not for the Western war so near at hand. In a few minutes we're off to Udine. The shops hadn't opened yesterday, and I noticed all the barbers at work, so I'll try to get a cut.

9.15 p.m. Good news again. Surrender of all Jerries north of 21 Army Group and link up of Americans between Austria and Italy through the Brenner Pass. Brr! How cold it is. I believe this very cold spell is all over Europe. Last night the temperature was 2° above freezing, they said.

5.5.45.

My Darling,

Your April 29 came in today. I hope these letters of mine

are going to your new address alright. Tweedle, about your trousseau preparations. My darling, of course it would be silly and impossible to buy clothes and only start wearing them on marriage. Clothes will be in short supply for years, and one must buy sensible things for the future. But do go an extra splosh when you buy a few things – buy the best and loveliest you can and I'll send you the money. I'd love to, please.

Darling if it is still Spring now, I hope to ask you to marry me before the Autumn, though Autumn at the very latest.

When the war finishes in the West and we begin to see the various plans and policies working themselves out, we'll make such lovely plans ourselves. All I know is that the war is nearly over, and that soon afterwards I ought to come home on leave. What a lot of kisses you are in for!

7.25 p.m. Nearly dinner time. Darling I'm lovely and warm now. I donned a thin vest and a thick Yankee long sleeved pullover this evening. Will you be very fussy about my wearing my thick woollies at the right time, I wonder, and not going out with wet hair after a hot bath, like Mother?

My Darling lass, you've such lovely lips and they do need to be kissed. Soon, soon – oh roll on the day. I'll even put up with a slow joggly ride in reconstructed railways across Europe to come to you. Now for dinner. God bless you my Sweet. Love and kisses from Bill.

7.5.45. Rogation Sunday.

Hello Darling,

Today has been quite warm. After tea we had such a nice service at RHQ in an upper room. Quite a few stayed to Communion. There are some really good chaps at this Head-quarters. They will form a solid backbone when I start my Church and Church Council going in some static camp some-where.

After lunch I spent a couple of hours reducing a Jerry parachute into its component panels, eight of them. Four are white and four are pink. The material of this particular chute is quite nice and bits of each panel are big enough, I think, to be a possibility for dresses or undies. The material is quite silky. The pink dye is not good, so I would wash a sample bit before you decide to do anything with it. The white is quite nice. I've packed them up and will try to send them off tomorrow. I'll send Mother a white and a pink one. The silk ropes in another parcel would make nice pyjie or dressing gown girdles.

They say that Winnie is to make an important announcement sometime this week. Oh why don't the stupid Germans give in without any further fuss.

Early to bed tonight. Oh Helen Darling I love you – love, love, love you terribly. Soon, soon will be our day, and cor, you won't half get kissed! Love and kisses from your very own, Bill.

VICTORY EVE

7.5.45.   Afternoon and Evening.

Whoopee Darling,

Admiral Doenitz has just said that it is useless to continue the struggle, so its all over now. Hope Winnie makes the statement in Parliament this afternoon. Oh my Darling to think of it all being over after all these years. Now on with the Great Day.

We came away from our village east of Udine this morning and are climbing up into the Alps. Darling, it is good to be in the mountains again, and what mountains too. We are heading to Trevisio, the last Italian town, and across the Austrian frontier to Villach and Klagenfurt.

This is a wonderful spot. A flat triangle of land, with a village at one end, and a church halfway up a small hill, with a monastery at the top, white in the sun, flying an Italian flag. The road goes to the right and that way the frontier is twenty miles off. What fun it will be to see the shops and road signs in German.

When the road is repaired we shall move on. Let's hope there are not too long delays, by too many demolitions. I'm anxious to see Austria. The sun is hot and there is a wonderful breeze, and the air is like champagne.

Now for a rejoicing letter home. Be happy my love – you Darling, Darling Helen. You'll soon be in for lots and lots of kisses. Love from your own Bill.

VICTORY DAY

8.5.45.   7.45 a.m.

My Darling,

Its time – VICTORY. Here is our General's message of congratulation. Six years of war are really over. God be praised.

 SPECIAL ORDER OF THE DAY
by
Major General H. Murray, D.S.O.
Commanding 6th British Armoured Division

The campaign in ITALY is over. The final battle lasted twenty four days and resulted in the capitulation of all German forces in ITALY unconditionally. This campaign, at a blow, completely destroyed an Army Group and caused the capture or destruction, of about a million Germans.

It is difficult for me to express in words the admiration I feel for the magnificent job which you have all done to make the victory possible.

The attack by 26th Armoured Brigade and the Derbyshire Yeomanry between April 18th and April 23rd broke the German line on a twenty mile front south of the PO, and paved the way to final victory.

The operations flowed with a smoothness and despatch which spoke volumes for the excellent and untiring work done by the Services to keep pace with this remarkable battle.

Seldom in a campaign of the magnitude of the ITALIAN campaign has one formation contributed in such great measure to final victory.

Our fighting qualities and our outstanding team-work have made this possible. It is indeed a privilege to command you.

Well done indeed, the 6th Armoured Division!

We were up at 5 a.m. this morning and in a few minutes we are going on northwards. The air in this valley is wonderful. I slept like a top last night.

Down the road goes the long procession of people getting back to their homes – Italian soldiers stealing back from fighting, with the Todt Labour Corps, and men torn from home to work in Germany, trudging along painfully with boxes, bundles and cases on their backs, with a blanket rolled tightly into a horseshoe sausage. There were even a few women.

Winnie is to tell us that the war is over at 3 p.m. and the King is going to speak at 9 p.m. Oh Darling the only way to celebrate this peace is in the family. There is a strange lack of desire to go wild and whoopee here.

1.30 p.m. Spam sandwiches for lunch. We have drawn up on lovely springy turf with the mountains all around. Trevisio, the frontier town, is only just round the corner and then for Austria. The houses are exactly as I imagined mountain houses, tall pitched roofs, masses of wood, with overlapping wooden tiles.

There are daisies and dandelions, forget-me-nots, cowslips and a little blue flower that I haven't seen before.

Helen Darling, will you marry me soon? I've a hunch that I'll be able to ask you before September. Just to think of holding you in my arms again after all this long time. What a wonderful inspiration you have been.

Alps full of hugs and all the kisses you want, short of having real ones. Oh Darling I do love you. Just round the corner from here is a great block of jagged snow clad peaks that are the beginning of Yugoslavia. The three frontiers are all fairly close together. Be very happy my love. Your very own Bill.

7 p.m. and nearly dinner time. About 3.15 p.m. we crossed the frontier into Austria and have now come into a grassy patch in the suburbs of the second town on our route. This part of Austria is lovely. Everywhere is fresh and green with spreading big trees – Oaks, chestnuts, and the whole lot. The towns, houses, and whole countryside is so very much cleaner than Italy.

I haven't seen a single Nazi salute, and the people seem genuinely pleased to see us. There was waving as we came along, and even flower throwing. We got a lovely bit of purple lilac.

There is a funny mixture here, British troops going forward, Jerry troops in all sorts of transport, carts and lots of their own wagons going all over the place, and freed slave labourers trudging home. We've seen at least two trainloads going back to Italy with Italian flags flying. There are released New Zealanders in the streets. In the last town one of our men saw his brother-in-law who had just been liberated! There are Dutch, Poles and French, the whole world seems to be here in miniature.

The truck is parked by a little fence at the end of somebody's garden. The woman and her four little boys came and looked at us. But it was so difficult to say anything. The mother had learned a bit of Itie at school, but knew less than I did. William is already making a good vocabulary. He is amazingly quick at languages.

9.5.45.

V.E. II Day.   Wednesday.   Ascension Eve.

What fun it will be when these days really mean something again! today we've been rushing round the parish. The wireless says that we are in Klagenfurt so I suppose that is where we must be!

Pat Sylvester is sitting in his Scout car next to mine, and everybody is queuing up to have his money changed into Austrian currency — 40 schillings to the pound, I believe.

I saw the S.C.F., who is a long way from here, and collected 1750 copies of the Thanksgiving Service, which will be held when we get really static again. They have the coloured signs of all the Corps and Divisions that have ever been in the 8th Army.

Bunwell.

8.5.45.   V.E.   Most Memorable Day.

Darling Man, congratulations to everyone and most of all THANKS BE! . . . for this tremendously whoopee and deeply moving event — Unconditional Surrender. Oh Bill, my dear, dear Man, all your sweating and aching and working and waiting has won through. Now we need to engage a lower gear with our patience, to wait a wee while longer and then . . . How wonderful it all is! It means freedom for multitudes and so many people will no longer have to fight and butcher and waste; you are nearer being home and into your new style parish life. I can't write sense, but I live for US.

We have just had a Service of Thanksgiving, but the big bust-your-lungs Service is tomorrow at 11 a.m. – all denominations. Tonight they will light a 12 ton bonfire on Denmark Green. Oh yes, people are feeling 'whoopee'. But maybe there are some others who, like me, feel that the rejoicings of this day will only be complete when we find our homes in our Beloved's arms. If you were here the sheer joy and relief would almost seem too much! But there is a teeny ache no V-day can fill . . . it is your place.

H.M. the King is speaking. I guess you are listening. Soon we will share all the things we've been fighting to secure. There certainly is much hard work ahead, but any efforts will be a joy to make if we can make them together.

Last night was Club Night. Rather hard work after a day on the Van . . . everyone told me that I seemed as if my thoughts were far away, so I was able to share you with lots of people. I listened to Winnie after morning work and then biked home. We have tomorrow off . . . to celebrate! Now we can look forward to the near future with hopes of all our dreams coming true.

Diss.

9.5.45. V.E. 0001 hrs. Wednesday a.m.

PEACE in Europe at last – Marvellous dreams tonight . . . mostly plans.

We went to see the Bonfire . . . a huge blaze. The whole sky was brilliantly lit by coloured flares they were sending up from airfields all around . . . peacetime spares . . .?! All the kids were so thrilled because they hadn't seen anything like it before. Thank goodness our family will be able to have these treats.

Wednesday 6.15 p.m. Very warm, lazy day. We had a good Service this morning, but things seem flat this afternoon. Perhaps it is that when there are great things to celebrate there is no Bill to rejoice with.

13.5.45.

. . . Billy, I'm in such a muddle these days – all about this Victory business. I never know what to write to you. I ought to just overflow on to paper and be bouncy about it, *but somehow I feel kind of stumped. It's been coming so long and now it seems almost unbelievable and anyway we will celebrate so very extra much on V, Everything Day.*

This dreadful war was all because we didn't have the essential awareness we humans need of how precious everyone is, and how we need to accept and respect each other ... yes ... and love.

15.5.45.

What do you think I've done? ... gone out riding from some stables about 5 miles away. They gave me Sheila the old grey mare and she kept me on quite happily, we even cantered and galloped and still I was on top of my mount! They thought I must have ridden before. When I rode back to The Villa, after supper at Banyards, my bike saddle seemed unusually hard. [It grew to feel harder every day for a time while my bruised seat paid for its ride.]

Tibenham boys seem likely to go soon. I hope Johnny goes home and finds his girl and they decide to get married then and there. He needs that I'm sure; and don't we all need our Beloveds. It has got to the stage when things are getting a frightful strain. But soon you will be home ... do we wonder, too, whether we will find all the things that matter in each other. We must have changed, with all we've been through, but we have kept in chatting touch. I believe we will soon be one.

Bunwell.

18.5.45.   Friday 8 p.m.

Tomorrow I'm going to look at a table in Wallace King's. Iris rang up about it. We alert each other about things that appear in shops; we buy two items when we have a find ... she produced teapot stands and I found dustpans last week, in Woolworths. We share them for our bottom drawers.

WOOOOCH! Molly is trying to play the piano while Vera Lynn sings on the wireless ... about the 'bluebirds over the white cliffs of Dover, Darling, when you come home to me'. I don't know about the birds being blue, when YOU come home ... I would think it will be a golden day!

POST WAR REFLECTIONS

AN ARMY CHAPLAIN

Sadly I was to hear a prominent Churchman who rose to high office, ordained after the war, say that the influence of the Army Chaplain had been minimal as far as he had been concerned, as a combatant soldier. It is true that he had been a prisoner of war at the hands of the Japs. A Chaplain's experience in the Far East must have been a very difficult one.

In the final days before the First Army went overseas the battle experience of any returning soldier was eagerly seized upon. One day the Officers of the 6th Armoured Division were invited to a large cinema to hear about the experiences of a Padre newly returned from the Desert. He told about his experience of desert warfare, and answered questions. At the end he made a religious affirmation. He said 'I believe that in the desert, and under the stars, the men of the 8th Army are a brotherhood and they are coming to see the nearness of God'. The Eighth Army was richly blessed in having a succession of fine Christian Commanders.

Out of the early failures and catastrophes of the War the Eighth Army was forged. Initially there were no guidelines for a Chaplain; he worked out his own role. Gradually he became an integral part of a close knit family. When a Chaplain had shown his worth by humble service, he earned his place and was backed by his men through thick and thin. By his inner life of prayer, his services, and his personality, he came to share every aspect of the life of the Army.

By 1944 the Chaplains' Department had crystallised its experience into a forty-page handbook entitled *The Experience in the Field of the Eighth Army Brotherhood of Chaplains. The Chaplains of the Grand Assault.* The booklet goes into detail about the rôle, opportunities and duties of the Army Chaplain as well as the procedures for the burial of a soldier.

Death comes to all of us but in wartime, apart from actual warfare, there seem to be so many extra hazards. Exercises in England were often a source, and I well remember men being killed by being run over by a tank as they slept in the early hours in a roadside ditch.

In Tunisia, I established a cemetery, for there were many casualties. In Italy many were killed during the crossing of the river Liri as the advance was made over and around Monte Cassino. Here I started another cemetery. Presumably both these were quite temporary resting places, but burials had to take place often in the area where the men had been killed.

The Derbyshire Yeomanry, as the eyes and ears of the Division, lost 180 officers and men in Africa and Italy. My Engineers were always to the fore, laying or clearing mines, bridging rivers and restoring roads. They made it possible for the passage of tracks and wheels on mountain roads which had been blown away. They lost 100 men and 213 were wounded.

After the North African campaign was over, I went with several Derbyshire Yeomanry Troop leaders to find and give proper burial to solitary desert casualties. The map references were given as accurately as possible, for them to be collected later on by the Graves Commision.

At one time in the African campaign where supplies were short, we were ordered to sew up casualties for burial in old blankets, but I think wherever possible we buried them in one of their own.

A soldier wears two identity discs round his neck; one is round and reddish, the other is octagonal and green. At a burial one disc is buried with the soldier. The other accompanies the man's possessions, the burial report and map reference. to the nearest Echelon. It is, I suppose, from here that details of death are eventually supplied to the War Office whence comes the official telegram. It was always my aim to be the first to pass on the news to the family, and to give as many details as I could of the circumstances, and place of burial.

I still have a number of replies from bereaved families and I cannot but still be struck by the incredible fortitude of nearly all the replies.

One sad letter dated 4.9.44 from a coal merchant's widow in Linconshire was very bitter. 'What could we not have done if my husband had been spared, but the Government drag our men from their homes, and they don't care if they never return.' Here is a chance of a further letter and an attempt to link her up with her local Methodist Minister again. He has already said truly 'there are a lot of things happening in this world that you or I will never understand'.

A letter of May 1943 at the end of the African campaign, where the husband was a Sergeant in the Coldstream Guards, must be a real testimony to the acceptance of the call of duty. He was killed in the battle for Longstop Hill. 'Your kind letter and thought I am writing to thank you for. My dear husband was one of thousands who fought and gave his life in a great cause, and I feel certain God does not forget such people. I have two children, one 5½ and my son 4 years and 4 months, thank God my little ones have been spared me – it is something to know my husband has been buried. Thank you for having been so good as to have written.'

A widow writing after the African campaign: 'Please excuse my writing to you, but as it is through you only I've been informed of my dear Husband's death, I should like to have some details of his death, either through you or his friends. I dare say all were strangers more or less to him as he had only just joined up with his new Regiment. I'd feel more satisfied if I could have some details, anything of his personal belongings I should like to be returned to me, but I dare say it is impossible. I can hardly believe that he has been killed in action, but to know that by you he has been buried is one comfort to me. So please forgive me writing to you, it's so hard to bear such a loss. A letter from any of his friends will be most acceptable.'

Later on I received an airmail letter from the same widow: 'Dear Chaplain, Many thanks for your letter giving me further details of my husband's death. I'm grateful for all, more than I can describe on paper. "Yes" it was the "Hampshire Regiment" he belonged to, and also I should like to come in touch with some of his friends. It's a terrible feeling that we had to be parted so far away from one another. May you have strength and courage to carry on with the good work. Wishing you the very best.'

Here is a letter from Sheffield: 'Dear Padre, I feel I must write and thank you for your very kind letter, concerning my husband's passing. Although it has been a bitter blow to me, I know that we shall meet again some day. I shall always be grateful to you for writing to me, and I know my husband would be grateful to you if he knew. God bless and keep you always.'

On 18.1.43, the first officer from the Derbyshire Yeomanry killed in North Africa was Lt. John Donne. He was a descendant of John Donne, the Elizabethan poet and Dean of St. Pauls. Lt. Donne had been married at Bressingham Church, near Diss, to Mollie Peck in 1942, just before embarkation.

Probably the last Yeomanry officer to die of wounds in Africa during the last push on Tunis was Lt. Charlie Blucher. He was wounded on May 7 and died in hospital on May 22, 1943. Originally in B Squadron, he had commanded R.H.Q. Troop and at his own request he had taken over a fighting Troop once again, this time in A Squadron. In a way it was fitting that a direct descendant of the great General Blucher who helped the British so much at Waterloo, should have done the same in North Africa in his last battle.

FAITHFULNESS AND LONELINESS

The 8th Army in the desert was the first to come up against the grim statistic that family ties and faithfulness come under a strain, and often snap, after two years of separation. Certainly the statistic applied to many of my own men. Letters were written, help sought of local clergy back at home and the Soldiers, Sailors and Airmen's Families Association was used in all sorts of ways, to try to keep homes together.

I can think of a Schoolmaster Trooper, happily married for years, with a lovely wife and family. He was a fine Christian and an artist. One day towards the end of the Italian Campaign he received a letter from his wife. She could bear the strain of separation no longer, and had found another soldier quartered in England. After many letters and much sadness we were able to get him a priority posting back home in February 1946, a number of months before his proper release. Such was the quality of their foundations that penitence and forgiveness were possible, and their marriage was reborn. I still treasure a lovely water colour that he painted of the village of Niederwöltz in Austria in August 1945. He gave it to me as a thanksgiving for all that we had suffered and shared together.

An Officer's wife was my home link with families. Many were the visits we both made, many were the letters we wrote. It is very sad to report that at the end of the war the grim statistic caught up with her. She wrote that it was an ironic comment on fate that after she and I had done so much to try to keep families together, she had found some-one else with whom she was going to live. I may have the letter somewhere, and do not remember whether her man was from Australia or New Zealand.

9

Austrian Occupation

10.5.45.

May 1 and 3 airmails and two lovely pictures. Sweetest Helen, I'm so lucky and I'm terribly proud of you.

I wrote to John Derby (Bishop) to ask him please to say when he would ask for me from the Army. I said I'd been engaged for over 3 years, and in the Army for four and a half including two and a half abroad, through two campaigns. I felt I'd done my whack. I also told him I intended to get married if I had a leave, and I rubbed in how much we longed to settle down. It was quite a straight letter really, 'cos I said that I thought some more of the younger clergy back at home ought to be prepared to come abroad and do a bit of chaplaining for a change, especially as the war is over. So we'll see what reply it brings!

After breakfast we had a good Ascension Day service with B Squadron and Communion afterwards. Meanwhile RHQ had been moving to a site a few miles out of Klagenfurt. William is sleeping in the truck and we've pitched the tent for the first time this year.

I'm sitting in the shade of the tent looking down on to the Wörther See. Across the lake is the famous White Horse Inn, and beyond, the snow capped mountains of Yugoslavia.

Evening. You would love it here for a holiday. There are wild strawberries in flower, and banks of magnolias. We have two rooms in the house, quite a nice Austrian house with lots of gables. One large room with a polished floor, square dumpy settees and chairs for a sitting room, a wood panelled dining room with a 3-sided ecclesiastical sideboard in one corner.

This morning everybody was told that there was a no-fraternisation order. I don't know what to think about it. Perhaps it is right and just if it is only for a limited period, but if it is a permanent thing I'm sure I won't fit in. These soldiers are super at making friends and making people like us. And if this is to be a complete barrier we are eternally throwing away our chances of new friendship. Not that I will take any notice of the order. It doesn't apply anyway, to me.

Late evening. After dinner we sat on the verandah looking across the lake, but I came in for the 9 p.m. news. We must try to take a real and prayerful interest in the men who are bashing the Japs in the Far East.

The lake is so calm and placid. The distant snowy peaks are disappearing for the night.

Oh Tweedle. I've been writing letters most of the afternoon except for my swim and I think you've had some of the scribble. Poor lass, you do get a conglomeration – never mind, we'll change our letter currency to kisses very soon. And now for bed. Love and kisses you Darling Woman. Your Bill.

11.5.45.   Friday.

Beloved,

Mail comes through pretty well again now. Your May 5 and 6 letters came today – you're a Darling Happiness. I'm glad the combs arrived so quickly. I bought them at a village called Vigarano, just south of the Po, before we crossed it.

After breakfast we took sandwiches, and I visited all the R.Es, save one Squadron which was on the move. This particular Squadron had a catastrophe a couple of days ago. They were shoring up a stone pier of a blown bridge, preparatory to putting a Bailey over it, when the whole pier collapsed killing 23. What a tragedy. The R.Es have had very heavy casualties all through this war. They've been heroes. But in this last push they've had hardly any, and now this happens to them after the war is over.

Darling, for scenery, Austria is best of all in my travels. Oh we must try to visit some of these places, especially Austria.

One of my R.E. Squadrons is next to the Headquarters of the Todt organisation, so there were plenty of 'pickings'. They got over a million pounds worth of Italian lire – German printed, and not backed by them, but still valid. However, it was thought best to burn it all. So for three hours last night they burned lire notes!

Space up. God bless you my Beloved Heart. I'll be seeing you soon. Your own Bill.

12.5.45.   Saturday Teatime.

My Darling,

This is a lovely part of the world. After breakfast we went round the other side of the lake after the Sappers, and over there it is even more of a fairyland than here.

After Tea. It is very hot and I'm sleepy and having difficulty in concentrating. My Darling, you are very lovely and beautiful. I long to hold you in my arms. I dream of the brown eyes more and more these days; you are constantly in my mind. It won't be very long before we are US.

7.45 p.m. Quarter of an hour to dinner. It is a postcard scene from this balcony. The lake in the setting sun, calm and placid with streaks on the surface made by a few rowing boats. Away in the distance there is a tiny white sail.

Oh, I do feel so fit! After tea I prepared for tomorrow's services, and then went on with my parachute unpicking. I have a white one, all except 3 panels which I gave to the Doc. So altogether I've red, green and white parachute stuff for my altar frontals and hangings. I'm even toying with the idea of having a pair or two of pyjamas made up of the same stuff.

I wonder whether the parcels of red and white that I sent you will arrive safely. Hope they don't try to charge you tax. Please do say if the stuff is any good, and whether you would like me to send you a few more panels of the colours I still have.

And now it's dinner time. Be happy my love. Sweet dreams and God bless. Love and kisses from your very own Bill.

17.5.45.

My Darling,

The weather has picked up again now and is very hot. So here we are in the shade of a tree for an hour or two until it is time for us to go off for 4.30 p.m. service at the R.Es.

This morning we had a long wander round the countryside finding odd Troops of the D.Y. I found Frank Powell for the first time since Victory, I think. He was just the same as ever, calm, smiling, imperturbable. You'll like Frank Powell, D Squadron S.S.M., one of my Ordinands.

Ronnie Watson, Frank's Troop Officer, was busy with a local family, breaking a lot of the fraternisation rules! He came back with a bag of lovely apples.

7.30 p.m. Oh, boo! I've finished with this camping life, I think! At the R.Es. this afternoon an awful thundercloud burst, and, of course, my poor old tent was a leaky old thing. So I had to camp in the truck again. Anyway I'm going to get billets in houses henceforth.

Roy and Freddie Wragg were out in motor boats on the lake when the storm came.

There were some nice little kids at the house where I had the service. Mother and Father were thrilled because we had a Celebration in their house. The mother has a brother who is a Priest.

Darling Helen Appleblossom I love you very much with all of me. You are a Darling Sweetie, and such an inspiration. Lots and lots of love and kisses from you very own Bill.

AUSTRIAN SPRING

22.5.45.

The Colonel came back from a recce today. It looks as though we'll be rather scattered again. Darling it seems as though I'm never going to get a compact parish in the Army! And everybody and everything keeps changing all the time –

more and more I live for the future. Oh yes, life is good now, but nothing to when we are 'us', and can do our life's work. Every day is a day nearer to marriage, and then on to our own home together. It doesn't really matter when the leave is. Earlier will suit our longings. Later will mean a shorter time until our final reunion. And it will be a terrible thing to have to part after our marriage. But it *is* a good prospect is it not? Darling I love you – I'm longing for you to become Mrs. Cook.

23.5.45.

Darling Brown Eyes,

The first Post War Elections are looming. It looks as if the socialists will win, but it seems hard to think of Winnie not being P.M. anymore.

After breakfast I called at the Sappers HQ to fix up the Victory Thanksgiving Service. I spent a long time trying to get a ceremonial S.S. Dagger. One of the men has four. I offered him my Luger gun and my NAAFI liquor supply, but all to no purpose. However, they are trying to get me one.

Plans are afoot for us to move to our permanent Regimental area. Eddie Clark (our 2nd I/C) has found us a super little lake called the Klopeiner See a little further east. It consists chiefly of one enormous wooden hotel belonging to a Viennese Bank, with a fringe of little chalets round about. I am to have a house of my own and I will set up a Church in it. The Sappers are making me the riddel posts to hold up the curtains at the back of the altar. We move at the weekend.

24.5.45.

There was asparagus and new potatoes and lots of cherries last night, all from the Po Valley. Our late Colonel Peter was given a flash German car as our farewell gift to him, and he sent this up as a present. The Po Valley is very fertile and much earlier than in Austria.

26.5.45.

This evening I took Bill Harvey round for a tour. He's a new officer and new to everything. We went into Klagenfurt to collect the sewing for my Church. The Altar frontal has a white parachute silk cross, with a strip of yellow ribbon down the middle. After an ironing they look very well.

The Sappers have finished the woodwork. We had a cup of tea before going to the hall. They had filled it with chairs. The altar looked nice and we are ready for the service.

RHQ had a fishing competition this evening, to see who could catch most in two hours. Many were using the hooks and rods I bought them this morning. Sgt. Ken Smedley won both prizes for largest fish and the largest number.

Phil and the Colonel went into a boot shop this afternoon. The Colonel bought a pair of great tough climbing boots, covered with nails, for 3/- and Phil got a pair of very soft leather boots for 4/6.

3.6.45.

My Darling,

R.S.M. Patterson helped me to find a lovely site among the pine trees for our Regimental Service. We've never had such a large congregation before. My altar was central, with hangings and the Sappers cross and candlesticks. The piano had been manhandled through the trees. I felt it was a good service. The Colonel read the lesson. The service sheets had the emblems of all the 42 Brigades, Divisions and Corps of the 8th Army set out in full colour round the border . . . all the units that have belonged to the 8th Army during these last six years. Most recent additions included Free French, Jewish, Greek and Italian . . . a mighty mixture. As we remembered

The altar at the Derbyshire Yeomanry Victory Thanksgiving Service at Klopeiner See, Austria.

fallen comrades we finished with a prayer for the Peace-makers.

This seemed very apt, my dearest One. We have all so much to do Your Bill.

10.6.45.

My Dear One,

The Sappers have such a heavy job of reconstruction, roads, bridges and buildings, that I have had to hold the Thanks-giving Service with each Squadron individually. This morning I held the last, at St. Veit, and the Colonel read the lesson. Last night's rain made it too wet to be out of doors, so they swept one end of a large barn. Afterwards we had a cup of tea. This Colonel has been a bit sticky and proper, but in the Mess today he called me by my Christian name! There is always a first time, isn't there?

How I love you my Sweet. Your very own Bill.

CANTEENING PROBLEMS FOR HELEN

Bunwell, Norwich.

10.6.45.

My Darling,

Last night Mrs. B brought Irene in the car and picked me up and off we went. It turned out to be an Officers' Party instead of a G.I. dance. Well, I suppose it was a good thing to

The congregation at the Derbyshire Yeomanry Victory Thanksgiving Service at Klopeiner See, Austria.

go and see what these are like, but goodness I really think my estimate of Yanks was a bit too high!!

They seem nearly all to have the same idea – booze, and find a girl who will dance a bit and then go off to their barracks and complete the evening. It's a beastly idea. One chap asked me to go to his barracks, and when I refused and wouldn't let him kiss me he was very surprised. When I told him about my 'boy across the water' he began to tell me about his girl back home. He soon palmed me off on a drunken pal, and got hold of another girl to try again. I told the next chap I didn't care if he stayed or went, so off he went. Crumbs what a do. I suppose some of your Regimental do's savour a little of this, but Billy, its hopeless, with these Yanks there doesn't seem to be any other idea of 'fun', other than booze and sex. No wonder they get a bad name. Gosh, it is a shame for Officers to let down their lot like that. Of course there are other and better types, but they probably wouldn't be there.

The King has just been on the wireless to say that Civil Defence is now over. Our island home breathes freely again, but there is a huge task to be done in the Far East, and at home, and yet another kind of job to be accomplished on the Continent. Darling – oh dear, don't let me fuss and be greedy, but isn't there some job for me, with you? I'd love to come on the Continent.

I enclose some lines about how many more letters! – but I'm not really tired of writing . . . yet!

The apple boughs are tipped with fragrant bloom,
And full rich yellow burn the gorse and broom,
And bees at pollen-kissing buzz this May
Against the fruiting day, which is not long:
Good pen, flow smoothly while I write this song.

The blue Spring skies are flecked with wisps of white,
And sweetly sings the nightingale at night,
And little birds carol the light away
Against their nesting day, which is not long:
Good pen, flow smoothly, till I end my song.

The surging sea is tamed to Summer tide
And laps caresses on the row-boats' side,
As they float out in their new-tarred array
Against the crabbing day, which is not long:
Good pen, flow smoothly, while I write my song.

Clear evening noises tell the gardener's toil,
Where now he digs and rakes and plants the soil,
Which soon his patient working will repay
With a fulflowering day; . . . our wait seems long.
Good pen, flow smoothly, till I end my song.

Now parted lovers, in the cool of night
Sit by the fire more of their love to write
E're their good pens are pocketed away
Against their meeting day, and wedding song:
Good pen, write smoothly, help us both along . . .
                                    till letters end. Anon.

NEWS

Bunwell.

4.6.45.

I rang up home from the Buckenham phone box at dinner time and was told that Iris has a SON born this morning at the Entry Nursing Home. Dad sounded a very proud Grandad. He is very special, being Baby Richard's only grandparent. I'm so glad her baby is safely here.

This is a week of parties, mostly before personnel go home. At the Hospital it was touching to see men discard their crutches to try to dance. The staff were miserable by comparison, the men just sitting and looking at rows of girls, and not dancing or talking. It warmed up a bit towards the end. When will we be able to put up the Banns? They are valid for three months, aren't they? When . . . oh . . . WHEN! Dad is so looking forward to your being a son to him.

6.6.45.

My Dear Bill,

Hosts of letters . . . jolly good news in them too . . . you may count on your LEAVE now, surely . . .

. . . I've been home this evening to see the babe. He is very like Dad. Iris is very well and very happy, and pleased with the way everything is being done. All the evacuees have gone back to London now. Much love my Darling, come soon. God bless you. Your L.M.P.

ONLY TROOPERS

7.6.45.

We've had a hot day on the roads again, visiting the Sappers. The great thrill was to visit the men's Rest Hotel. About 70 men go there at a time. It perches on a cliff over the lake, with lovely terraces, and boats and bathing down below. Two men share a large bedroom, with pile carpets and telephones and pink silk lamp shades. You know the kind. At lunch time, when I called in, it was their first meal on their opening day. There they sat at little tables, with a band playing in one corner, printed menus, waiters in livery, rows of forks and knives disappearing into the distance on either side of their plates!

When I got back to D.Y. one of our cocky, young, and not very experienced Officers turned up his nose and said, 'Oh, Troopers, it's wasted on them'. I nearly floored him. These Sappers have been the heroes in this long Italian slog, making victory possible.

I was very cross at such a stupid class-ridden statement. God forgive him.

HOME FRONT

17.6.45.   Bed, Saturday.

Today was a very busy day as it is the 'day off' for the Vans. Two are to go out, one to each of the two English Bases we serve. I went to Fersfield and tried to get round everyone, and to do the work of two Vans. I missed out quite a lot I'm afraid, but I took £16, so a lot must have been served. When I got home there were three letters, and three Roman silver coins. We'll be able to rejoice in lots of wet days, now that we have so many things to sort out. But if It's Mondays that are wet, there will have to be quite a number of kisses to make up for the thought of washday on Tuesday or of wet linen round the house!

YANKEE DOODLE DO'S AND DOINGS IN NORFOLK

Sometimes we were invited to local Bases for 'A Hop'; On the whole these were quite fun, and people talked about wives and sweethearts at home – in their 'God's Country' – but, sadly, many thought of dancing and a few, or many drinks, as only the prelude to a trip to their quarters . . . I fear my failure to co-operate in this turned away many a work-worn hopeful. These generous men were able to lavish gifts of nylons, and other luxuries ordinarily unobtainable, on girls; making them vulnerable to further attentions.

Once I was shown over a Liberator Bomber. The hundreds of levers, switches and instruments on control panels made the mind boggle. It seemed incredible that men could cope with operating these giant machines, for such long stretches, in hazardous conditions. Little wonder members of these air crews needed contrasting, relaxing off-duty times; but how nice some of us found it when they came to terms with standards of our culture, and behaved in ways more conventionally acceptable to us.

When these liberated sons and nephews of Uncle Sam came to join us in our war effort, they flooded East Anglia from their bases, seeping into our village pubs, halls and homes, in their free time. Together with their genuine friendliness, they brought their easy-going approach to personal relationships, sometimes behaving in ways which shocked our village folk . . . Yet how enchanting could be some of the attractions, imported with them, from the New World; it may well be that Norfolk nightingales were primed into song by the 'Glen Miller Sound' gently thudding from, and adding a measure of its own magic to, a 'Dairence' on the Base.

FIRST PEACE TIME LEAVE – VENICE
2.7.45.

The border controls had not yet been set up, so we merely left Austria having booked a room for a week in the Palazzo al Mare, Venice. It was an interesting return from the invigorating atmosphere and crisp efficiency of Austria to the dear old, lovely, smiling, inefficiency of Italy. We could feel the change of temperature and atmosphere as we came through the Alpine Pass.

VENICE – PALAZZO AL MARE

3.7.45.

I embarked on a Z Craft, a big creaky flat boat used for invasions in sterner times, and we waddled round Venice, past the end of the Grand Canal, San Marco pier, and across to the Lido. The Lido is a mixture of islands, all full of hotels taken over as rest camps by all the Allies. Palazzo al Mare is the biggest, and for Allied Officers. Food is splendid. There are lifts and ballrooms, and women soldiers are partners at meals and dances. Don't worry, I can't dance!

After lunch I boarded a Duck (DUWK) and went to St. Mark's Square, the one open space. First was a visit to St. Mark's Cathedral, a copy of S. Sophia in Constantinople. Cruciform, with 5 domes, it is full of mosaics, some from the thirteenth century. I suppose the greatest treasure is a gold and enamel jewelled reredos. We had to do with pictures as it is still in the Vatican for safety. There is a military half-hourly ferry to the Lido. A couple of smiling young Gondoliers assured me that the last ferry had gone. It took them half an hour in their Gondola, with a nice Yankee Sgt. Of course the Army boat got there ten minutes before! Still it was fun.

4.7.45.

There's a girl selling silky things in the hall of the Hotel. I made her produce all her stock, and lots of shy men gathered round and started to buy! No! I didn't buy anything, but I got some good ideas!

I met Reggie Snaith who has been down to the Florence area buying Vino for the mess! So we went sightseeing together. First to the top of the Campanile. The view was fascinating, but difficult to take in the whole scene. Then we did the Doge's Palace, his home, his public and state apartments and, of course, his prisons. The state halls gleam with colour from Veronese, Titian and Tintoretto. For it's time it was an enlightened state, and had world wide influence and connections. Most exciting were the four bronze horses which should stand over the principal facade of the Cathedral. They came from Nero's Arch in Rome, via Constantinople. Napoleon pinched them, and later had to give them up.

Then Reggie and I sprawled on the leathery cushions of a very posh gondola with a sharp prow, and a couple of gondoliers took us round the Grand Canal, Main Street of Venice. As we passed the Palaces the Gondoliers named them. Salviati's is the most famous of the glass shops. We stopped off and were amazed by the range of styles and the colours. The glass is indescribably expensive, £7 or £8 for a tiny pot, but they are lovely.

Finally I walked some 300 yards across the island to see Reggie off to his hotel near St. Mark's Square. The lights were blazing in all the hotels, and all the posts marking the channels in the Lagoon were lit up. Dark shapes of Gondolas and larger craft sped by looking most romantic. And everywhere the Allied Armies are on holiday. There were drunks and girls and crowds and lights. Oh My Darling all this is making such a mess of the family! These chaps need to go home. So do I! Darling Helen how I long for you, and only you. I'm yours entirely, and this time of keeping faith will make our Usness all the more precious.

6.7.45.

This morning I sunned on the Lido writing letters, and after lunch returned to window shopping. Near the Cathedral is a small glassmaking shop where they turn out little pieces as you watch — beads, mosaic pictures, and little animals. I walked from St. Mark's to the Rialto. It must be about a straight mile, but what a wiggle it turned out. You need to go by a compass bearing, and progress by means of right angle zigs round blocks and across canals. Yes, Venice is romantic, but I wouldn't like to live here, not even in a Grand Canal Palace! No greenery, no terra firma, and it's all so enclosed.

7.7.45.

Into Salviati's glass shop again. I'm narrowing my choice down for a major 'buy'. A nice tall old man, who spoke English perfectly, showed us round. He was wearing a little golden Union Jack with R.I. on it. When I asked him about it he said he used to be with Thomas Cook and Sons in Naples, and that Edward VII sent it to him for services rendered on many occasions.

8.7.45.

This morning at Salviati's I got my glass; a huge carafe with a big twisty handle, tall and chiselled and six tall dainty and ever-so-thin glasses. I do hope you'll love them, and that I can get them home safely. I also hope you won't ask me how much they cost!

9.0 p.m. After Dinner. I met a Padre from Bologna area after tea, and we strolled along the Lido front before dinner. Can there be a better set-up in Europe? It does me good to see this great centre of fascist luxury and magnificence being used by the chaps who have had to tear down this Fascist Dictatorship.

I struck a wonderful Gondolier this morning, Piero Grossi. His family goes back to 1400 in Venice. Canny old rascal really – just after the cash! While I was at the glass place he polished up his brasswork and put up his little flag of St. Mark, in my honour, he said. Only two rooms of the Palace of Fine Arts are open. I was glued for a long time to Tintoretto's canvas of the washing of Christ's feet by the Magdalene in Simon's house. Nearby is the English church where I plan to go tomorrow. The sea is rolling in and the lights are up now. The last people are finishing supper, and soon the band will be starting up for dancing. There are too many of these flash women here eating our rations! They seem the sort who probably went for meals with Jerry a little while ago. Perhaps it's time I went back to my men and reality!

8.7.45.

I prefer Austrian weather to his hot sultry kind. I walked along the beach for 8.0 a.m. Celebration and then on to a ferry for St. George's 11.15 mattins. I had time before that to go in to St. Mark's Cathedral. It was fairly full and I find it hard to express my feelings. High mass was at the High Altar, with lots of Priests and Acolytes, and a congregation shut in behind the gates. The organ was playing and a lovely choir singing. Elsewhere were milling crowds, at the altars on either side. People seem to pop in for a few minutes. A man wandered round continuously among the crowds with a money box. In the nave the scene was like any week day with guides taking people round. It seemed that one just needed to be there.

9.7.45.   Monday evening.

How long and unreal this marvellous holiday seems to have been. Last evening I got a ferry and wandered among the Venetian crowds in the sunset. The quais where Marco Polo and his adventurers used to tie up their galleys are now thronged with mine-sweepers and all sorts of Naval craft. How surprised Marco would be! This morning I took a really good look at St. Mark's. It simply glitters with mosaics. The giants hit the bell on the Cathedral Clock tower.

I must be up early tomorrow to return to Austria. Such a lot will have happened to the Regiment, I think. It has been fun to have lived in Venice, but how I wish you were here. The Military women in this hotel are chiefly American Nurses, and I think they have had to be a hard boiled lot! There are lots of pretty girls, and I think they are very much in demand, mostly by the Yanks who are in a majority here. But My Beloved there's no one like you, and I do believe that we shall soon be together again. Dearest Heart I love you utterly.

A VOTE AND A VEHICLE

Diss.

7.7.45.

Busy day yesterday and I came back via Diss where I registered my vote in the Election. Afterwards I called for petrol at Carleton Rode, and Mr. Cook had an autocycle out for sale. He said he would put it in the shed while I thought over whether to buy it for £27.10s. Dad came over today and we bought it. I came home on it and it came very well. Things cost such a lot . . . but it would be easy to sell . . . It does 100 miles to a gallon, and has a permit for two gallons a month; it has a full tank so this month I could do 300 miles! . . . your Helen.

P.S. I really am grown up now: I became an Aunt last month, had a vote on Thursday and now am the proud possessor of a Popper and a petrol ration book!

AUSTRIA, KLOPEINER SEE

10.7.45.   Past bedtime.

My Darling,

I've been sitting up in bed going through the family part of the huge mail awaiting our return from Venice tonight. About five of yours, some from home and Jay, and dozens of electioneering addresses for the West Derbyshire and University Seats. Tomorrow I shall do my voting, and I hope it will be in time. The thing seems to be to vote Tory in Derbyshire, and Communist in University – or vice versa!

We got back in time for tea for William at 6.0 p.m. How much cooler and more refreshing it is in Austria. It is 200 miles, and we took 7 hours.

Colonel Sir Ian said goodbye to the Regiment yesterday. It was unexpectedly sudden, and I missed his farewell party, so I must write to him. Eddie Clarke who was Ian's Estate Agent, is now the Colonel. He must be quite a low demobilisation number, and I think that the active days of the Regiment are numbered. I must go into Klagenfurt tomorrow to see the Boss about my own future. I think I'd sooner stay with this Regular Division, of which I am now one of the senior members, than to cling to a disintegrating Regiment!

14.7.45.

I had such a nice letter from my Mother today about our getting married on our leave. I had to ask your Dad before I could ask them at home. Everybody seems to be pleased, so I hope you are still happy my Darling.

I wandered round the camp this morning. I saw a couple of men who urgently want to go home. One seemed to have a very good case, and I will do my best to get him home. His wife has been pinched by a Flight Sgt. Helen Darling, this separation of families is playing ducks and drakes with people's hearts. I hope the leave numbers increase when they get the railways going, or else I'll write to a Bishop or start a revolution or something.

'Individual Fraternisation' is now allowed in Austria! What an expression! I suppose it means no parties yet. We've got our chance to do a bit of bridge-building with our former enemies, though I fear it will be the girls everyone will be after. Troopers Prince and Ruby were doing half an hour on pianos on Radio Klagenfurt this evening, and Pat Trollope, our D.Y. officer, was doing the announcements. He sounded very much at ease, and so professional.

MAKING THE MOST OF PEACE

18.7.45.

A fellow Chaplain, writing from Vienna, remarks on what a good time the Armies of Occupation are having. But of course it is true. Our rations are good and our billets are the best. Leave centres are set up in famous places, and there are many sporting facilities. There is ski-ing and wood-cutting in Cortina, and racing with German horses.

The Chaplains set up Schools of Education and Retreat Centres in lovely and peaceful places. A Padre's time can be filled in with many useful things. Church Services are now static, and scattered over a wide area. Hospitals too are often far away, and the Padre is the only link. There is little new equipment coming through, and the great problem is to keep a vehicle on the road. There are countless welfare problems, and welfare cases. Sometimes a Chaplain can get a man a home posting, or a leave, in dire necessity.

The Derbyshire Yeomanry are happily stationed round their own diminutive Lake, the Klopeiner See.

MY FIRST RETREAT – AT DOBRIACH

The day before I set out for Dobriach my Church Chalet had been burgled, and my case of clerical robes and communion set had been taken. I stayed at the Transit Hotel, and vainly tried to get some more things at the Officers' Shop.

Next day we came to Dobriach. The village is about half a mile from the lake, and all the big houses and Gasthouses are wholly taken over as a School of Education. The lake is nice, but not as attractive as the Wörther See.

There are about a dozen Chaplains here. We keep silence till after tomorrow morning, and then can talk for the rest of the time . . . Now for Evening Address and Compline. The Retreat is being taken by Canon Pat Carnegie, Wakefield Diocesan Missioner.

Patrick wrote a most flattering but reassuring letter to Helen:

Dear Miss Appleton,

I am a peripatetic Parson out here on a mission to the Chaplains, and in the course of my wanderings I came across your Bill, who attended a retreat which I held at Dobriach, July 18 to 21. He was very insistent that I should write to you and tell you how I found him. I found him to be delightful, and thought him one of the most charming young men I had met for a long time. It is most refreshing to meet someone who is so enthusiastic about being in love, and takes it for granted that everyone around him will share his enthusiasm! He tells me that you two hope to get married when he gets leave in November. I gather that he thinks himself to be the luckiest man in the world, and I am quite sure that you think yourself the luckiest girl. That is as it should be. May I as a staid married man of over 17 years standing (and very happily married) wish you every joy and blessing when you start your great adventure. Bill seems wonderfully fit, and other Chaplains have told me what an excellent work he is doing. Incidentally I owe your young man a debt, for he has collected some cartridge cases and other souvenirs for my two small sons (5 and 3), the elder of whom will regard me as a complete failure unless I return with the foresaid cases. He is not particularly bloodthirsty minded and will probably use them to play at blowlamps or petrol pumps!

May God bless you both.

Patrick Carnegie.

When I returned to camp all my Priestly robes had been returned. I think that the thief had a conscience about stealing such things. The only item that was taken was a standard Nazi wide black leather belt which I had been using as a cassock belt. It served me right I suppose!

Bunwell.

25.7.45.

My Darling, I have been trying so hard to find words to

*express our deep need of each other . . . it is impossible.
Life is only a secondary existence until we are US!*

*Our lives are spent in travelling round,
answering calls of each new day;
but when the evening shadows creep
and things of daylight fall away . . .*

*Deep in your lonely heart is found
the ache to be found in mine,
for the cry of our unbegotten child
whom distance keeps from time.*

*We tasted the sweets of life-to-come;
we dwelt on the verge of things to be;
war-parted love with a dreamland home
and a letter-link over miles of sea.*

*For how much longer must we write
paper love songs with an inky pen?
when can our dreams begin to live
and I be home in your arms again?*

*Now to sleep and be ready for what tomorrow brings.
Love and kisses. xx your Helen xx*

MATCHLESS EIGHTH ARMY BREAKS UP

On 29th July 1945 Lt. Gen. Sir Richard McCreery announced
the official end of the Eighth Army.

From the many messages received by the Army Commander I quote two:

1. From Field Marshall Sir Harold Alexander:

   After four years of matchless battle record the famous
   Eighth British Army passes from the pages of the Army
   List into as honoured a place as any of the great military
   Battles of the past. No Army in this War — and probably
   never before — has advanced so far in so short a time,
   and fought as many battles, every one of which has been
   a Victory, from El Alamein to Austria — 3000 miles in
   30 months. Proud indeed may the Soldier be who in
   years to come is able to say 'I fought with the Eighth
   Army'.

2. From Field Marshall Sir Bernard Montgomery:

I feel I would like to send a message to my old Comrades of many Battles. The Immortal March of the Eighth Army from the gates of Cairo along the North African Shores to Tunisia, through Sicily and Italy, carried this ever-victorious Army to final Victory in Europe. It was a great part which was played out with an unfailing spirit, and it will long shine in history. I am proud to recall that I commanded the Eighth Army through the time of it's most famous Victories. I shall never forget the comradeship of those days, and the splendid spirit that existed in what I used to call the great family of the Eighth Army.

This family is now scattered all over the world, but the spirit will remain for all time, and will be a shining example for future generations of the British Commonwealth.

25.7.45.

This morning I spent with B and C Squadrons up on the Yugo-slav frontier, then lunch with A Squadron. It looks as though the Regiment will continue in being for some little time. A Regular Army Major, Noel Wall, has just come from the 7th Hussars to be 2 I/C. At A Squadron this morning, Cliff Jones took me up to the frontier where his Squadron is on guard. The Sappers have built a huge road block. Our men guard one side and the Red Starred Tito men the other. I went through the barrier to look down into the valley and to talk to the Tito guard. I gave him a cigarette. They look a lot of country bumpkins bless them. He has his rifle, on his side. We had our armoured cars, new, brightly painted and gleaming in the sun. We have changed from Sherman tanks to armoured cars again. It was such a contrast.

Darling I'm beginning to dream of OUR time as something near, and real, and practical, after all these years of waiting. It's difficult to imagine what your kisses will be like, except to know that they will be lovelier and more wonderful than my wildest dreams.

27.7.45.

William had a sweet letter from Mrs. Burlingham today — all about growing chrysanthemums for decorating the church on THE DAY! Darling what are you going to wear for your wedding? How do you want me to be dressed? As a soldier or in a cassock? I'll have to write to ask mother to chase away any moths that may have collected in my best service dress! I've just finished Jordan's *Tunis Diary, an account of North Africa* — quite good. The publisher Collins, White Circle, paper back at 9d. Will you please look out for it? After dinner we sat looking across the lake into the sunset. There are lights twinkling and fish rising and all the magic noises of a lovely evening. A flock of rooks came cawing over.

Phil has been doing a reconnaissance 100 miles to the north. There are no troops there — hence no AMGOT (Allied Military Government of Occupied Territories). So on Wednesday Jack and I are hoping to have a look round there and to buy some leather. I'm after some pigskin to make a suitcase. There is supposed to be shoe leather too. I'll try for some and if you'll send me your shoe size I'll try to get a pair made for you. Send a tracing of your foot.

29.7.45.

My Darling,

Now that the Russians are withdrawing a little further north we are to leave our Klopeiner See, to go into the wilds. This morning at Div. H.Q. I got a set of motoring maps, four for the whole of Austria. Then we went north on Route 116 from Klagenfurt, a very good road. We turned off the main road west, along our narrow valley where the Regiment is to live. It reminds one of a bit of wild Yorkshire Upland from a Bronte story. There is only one little town of any size, Murau, where A Sdn. hopes to be. Some of B Sdn. are away at Ulm. The rest will be at Stadtl, a few miles east. They will be on the edge of the British zone, and the Yanks take over from there. Murau is more or less in the middle of the area, so I'll probably live there. The houses are timber and will be very snug.

Darling, I'm hoping to hear some news of my leave in a couple of days.

4.8.45.

These chalets are really quite fun. The furniture is simple and made of pine. Very clean! I've had a couple of skins made up into two pairs of lederhosen. I thought that your Papa might like a pair. Though I think it's quite unusual I've also had a pair of dainty ones made for you! They are all pretty with leather bibs, and ornaments and buttons carved out of stag horn.

10

Marriage
August 23rd, 1945

———————◆▰▰▰▱◆———————

Beloved, I'm coming home in the MIDDLE OF AUGUST —
Really, honestly, truly. I can hardly believe that our long
wait is nearly over! How long has it been? A thousand years?
Or merely fifty? I think it must be 3½ years. But Dearest
Heart, its true, and HERE I COME!

WEDDING PLANS

Bunwell.

4.8.45.

My Darling Billy,

*How very thrilling all this! August 18th. Do you really
mean AUGUST THE EIGHTEENTH? Oh, I wish I could
fully realise that it is really true . . . it is so terrific, and so
strange, that there may not be time for you to answer a letter
from me! Everything seems to be waking up and it all seems
new, and yet it has a mellowness about it. I've got such a
surging feeling right from the depths. All our dreams and
plans are going to come to life, and everything is going to be
so happy, so very happy. It's been a long time, but not too
long. Only I need you so much, and I just ache for the
twentysomethingth . . .*

PLANS

5.8.45.   Sunday.

Too late for Banns . . . I have written to cancel the reading of Banns at the Earl Sterndale end, and Dad will get us a licence. Your Pa and Ma are planning to come to Fen Cottage on August 20th. I hope they will, and we are trying to persuade your Pa to get the Sunday off, so that they will be here for more than four days. If they are here when you come home we won't need to go to Derbyshire first. WE could go there after our UStime.

Mrs. B. will do a lot of cooking, but supplies will be a bit taxed. It might be best to get a cake from a baker. I think they must be allowed ingredients without points.

If we had the Marriage Service at 2.30 p.m. we could catch the 4.40 train with ease and stay the night in London, and go North next day. Miss Kingsford has offered her flat in Ealing.

My little Godchild, Cara, is about six and her Mother would make her a dress in a pattern of her choice if I send some material. Nancy is in London on holiday, so I will try to get a day off and meet her there for our very-long-planned shopping date. She will help me choose things. I tell you all this in a dictatorial way, because there is no choice but for me to make plans and tell you which have become facts when we meet! Yes MEET, soon. It is all so thrilling. Practice taking me in your arms tonight and get used to that kink you have to get in your back in order to reach down to me!

Dearest Love God bless you. Good journey. Your own Helen.

The Best Man had to be alerted. Fortunately he had come on leave before being posted in England. I learned that Bill would be able to send a telegram when he reached Calais, telling us when he would arrive at Victoria Station.

Mrs. Buchanan arranged for me to lay down my responsibilities with the canteens. All the Staff gave us a box of six lovely, plain silver teaspoons as a wedding present. After I had packed belongings at the Villa and dropped the bulk of them at home, I started to apply myself to final preparations for our WEDDING.

On a trip to Norwich I found a dress of écru crêpe; the long skirt was slightly dropped to trail behind. I also ordered a bouquet of the traditionally fashionable cascading type. This was an act of faith . . . and hope, as we would need to collect it, somehow, together with the dress which, inevitably had to be adjusted to fit little me.

The going-away dress that Nancy and I had found in London was blue, and had a dark brown belt. The outfit was completed by nigger brown gloves and a pillbox hat.

'Mummy Cara' made her little daughter a long dress and sun bonnet from the blue muslin we sent.

During these busy days I found myself with an added dimension, after making the attempt to squeeze letter-writing time into every day/night, for three and a half years . . . Each time it occurred to me that it was TOO LATE to write! HE would BE HERE before I could write again . . . a whoosh of excitement flushed over me.

Mrs. B. was her unflappable self and did not turn a hair at the prospect of having a host of family and friends to feed and bed, after the multitude of evacuees, and people of many nationalities accommodated in the Rectory during the last four and a half years.

HERE COMES THE BRIDEGROOM

7.8.45.

It's nearly three years since our farewell Kiss at Ipswich Railway Station. Tomorrow week I should be on the way home. What arrangements can be made? I'll try to keep you posted from this end. But poor Darling, I'm afraid you will have to make all the arrangements. Reggie has promised to be my Best Man. I will write with the good news. You'll like Reggie. I will meet you at a Boat Train at Victoria, and will be able to let you know which. Whoopee! How I have longed for your lips and to hold you in my arms, and to see the exact colour of your hair. It's all too deep for words. How empty these last years would have been without you.

12.8.45.

Monday evening. When I got in your nice reassuring letter

302 - KHAKI PARISH

was waiting. It's good to know that my folk will already be in Diss. If there is time would you please ask them to bring my best Service Dress. I'll bring my old one, just in case!

Our Doc has a sick wife. He is due for a leave in a week or two, so I suggested to the Colonel that he should be allowed to come home earlier, and he's coming home with me.

Kenneth and I gave our A.M.G.O.T. Captain our monthly bottle of whisky yesterday in exchange for some shoe leather. Tonight we went to the village shoemaker who measured us up for pairs of shoes.

This morning I gave the Ordination File to the S.C.F. He made a little speech about the Wedding, and wished me luck. We've had so many Bosses that I don't imagine that any of them realises what your love has meant to me over these long years! This may be the last letter that will arrive! I keep on thinking about how busy you must be, my Darling. I love you eternally. Your Bill.

TOTAL VICTORY

14.8.45.

Darling Brown Eyes,

I've been finding out about the leave and marriage legalities today. I am to get 130 clothing coupons of which 100 are supposed to be spent on things military! Then we shall be given coupons for 300 miles of motoring. My monthly pay is now £30.13. I am entitled to a Mediterranean allowance of £6.6.0 a month, and you bring in £5.12.0 a month to our total. You are also entitled to first class travel on all journeys of over 30 miles. How wonderful to dream and know that you will be in my arms in another week. I'll keep on scribbling letters, though I may arrive first! It's just second nature now.

Tea Time. Surely this afternoon's news is the best we've had. Darling you too will have heard of today's surrender of the sub-human Japs. This really has brought in a new perspective. I'm on the way home to make you mine. Nazidom has been exterminated, but as long as these evil Japs have gone on fighting many men might have to go to the Far East. I shudder to think what the casualties might have been if it had been necessary to invade Japan. But now, my Beloved I'm on my way, and I know that our leave can never be long enough. But at the end of our final stint here there will be life together forever. No more fighting. No more need to kill or be killed. Darling Sweetheart this will colour all our leave, and the final military months. God be praised, V.E. and now V.J. I love you so much.

L.I.A.P. (Leave in addition to Python.)

Python was an ingenious hope whereby soldiers would be sent home on leave in turn, if it was at all possible. A python presumably goes on swallowing his tail. In May 1945 Europe was in ruins. The railways were smashed and few bridges had not been bombed. How to get us home? That was the burning question.

The 8th Army came up with L.I.A.P. By the middle of the summer men in the early release groups (of longest service) were beginning to go home on demobilisation. But by far the largest movement was for the long-awaited leave. Five of the 8th Army Divisions set up transit camps across Europe. A fleet of army lorries was converted for passenger carrying by being fitted up with benches looking outwards. Two hundred miles a day were driven for five days. The beginning of the enterprise started at Villach, and the camp was named 'El Alamein'. The first day's drive was through the Brenner Pass to the next camp at Innsbruck. Here was a magnificent Schloss looking down upon the town. After a good evening meal, bed and breakfast, we went through Augsburg to Ulm on the left bank of the Danube. Ulm had been badly bombed, and in the middle of the ruins stood out the great spire of the Cathedral which miraculously had been spared. From Ulm the road led through Stuttgart, Karlsruhr and Heidelberg to Mainz. From Mainz on the Rhine the road led to Trier where we crossed from Germany into Luxembourg. The next point was in France in Sedan. Our final journey was across northern France to the huge Calais Transit Camp.

By the middle of August 1945, it was estimated that out of a total force of 1000 men the Derbyshire Yeomanry had 400 men either on leave, or beginning to be demobilised.

I still possess the long battered brown envelope containing detailed instructions for leave, from H.Q. Squadron, 6th Armoured Division. On one side I have added all my Austrian schillings to turn them into Italian lire. Anyway my money seems to be worth £35.18.0. On the other side I have worked out a permutation of telegrams to keep Helen informed of my movements.

MISSION ACCOMPLISHED!

Helen received my telegram to say that I would be leaving Austria on August 15th, 1945.

So I spent a night in the Transit Camp at Villach. I might have had to remain in a queue for several days, but no! My holiday documents were in order, and our party made 200 miles across Europe each day. Among my luggage was a watch for Helen, the result of hours of window-shopping in Padua. Previously, in Florence also after long search and much cogitation, I had found my wedding present. It was a large silver cross studded with amethysts. She wore it for our wedding, and often wears it today for special occasions. It is as large as a Bishop's pectoral cross, and much grander!

In my hand luggage I had a stout wooden box containing a very large cut glass water jug and six very fragile goblets, the ones from Mr. Salviati's shop on the Grand Canal in Venice. On the day we reached Calais I was in time to see our luggage being thrown out of the lorry. Miraculously the glass survived intact.

Helen was waiting for me at Victoria on August 20th at 1.30 p.m.

What would our meeting be like after three and a half years of separation? Would reality live up to our expectations? Would the hopes and dreams built out of daily prayers, and many thousands of love letters, be larger than life? Would we even recognise one another? I think we needn't have tormented ourselves with any of these speculations. In the middle of hissing steam engines, and scurrying crowds, and piles of luggage, she was in my arms, and more wonderful than my wildest dreams.

HAPPY DAYS

Admiral Taylor hoisted the Union Jack at the Manor House across the road, in honour of total Victory. Every time I answered our front door bell, and saw the Colours wave aloft, I felt like cheering. I was hoping the Telegraph Boy would soon pedal up on his red Post Office bicycle with news that Bill had got to Calais and would meet me next day in London.

Friends were generous with offers of accommodation. Bill's parents came on the twentieth, in accordance with their holiday plan. As we gathered together, we realised that Family and Bride were awaiting the arrival of the Bridegroom!

JOURNEY'S END

On Monday evening THE TELEGRAM arrived

I was to meet Bill at Victoria Station next day; the Boat Train was due at 1.30.

Family history does not relate whether I slept that night. Next morning I was on the London train . . . wondering if I would recognise him. Would I know it was him? Of course I would know . . . I was glad that I knew my way about the Underground. What a tantalising age of waiting . . . is that Bill?? oh no . . . quite a relief! – there – surely . . . THERE HE COMES with loads of baggage . . . Oh BILL . . . his arms were round me. The hardships and endurance of years fell away and I was H O M E.

In this sort of situation we might do with a Fairy God-mother to wave her wand and hold all in suspense . . . a moment two could enjoy for a long, long time . . . and it is gone so quickly . . . a moment slipped into the treasurehouse of our special memories.

But the first kiss, after long separation, puts the seal on all that is to come. We could spare Victoria no more of our togethertime. We must gather up the baggage and go forward in the press of passengers trying to realise each other's presence. We seemed to be walking on air, little checked by misty reality.

We were on the L.N.E.R. behind a pounding steam engine

speeding us towards Diss and Marriage. Bill would see his People again, after so many years, and meet others whom he had only got to know through many letters, including Iris and the Baby . . . Here comes the tunnel – When we parted on Ipswich Station, three years ago, the tunnel's darkness had drawn him in . . . closing an era – now we popped out into the light from welcoming Suffolk skies.

OUR WEDDING
Bride Recalls

Our Fathers were to marry us, so it was the arm of my brother, my other lifelong friend, that steered me, followed by our little bridesmaid, under St. Mary's Tower. It was 2.30 in the afternoon on Thursday, August 23rd, 1945. There were many people who had come at such short notice. Above the box pews we saw the backs of relatives and friends, some in uniform; Richard's carrycot was hidden in a pew. Suddenly the church seemed filled with all our friends who could not come – from schools, and airfields and from Bill's ubiquitous Parish; I also sensed that Mother, Granty and many friends we can no longer see, were very close. There are two, smart, khaki backs with encircling Sam Browns; two chaplains, whose khaki parishes are disintegrating a thousand miles away; one is soon to become a father, the other, even sooner MY HUSBAND.

The organ plays; I grip Jay's arm and, behind my bouquet of roses and trailing fern, carefully descend the steps. Our robed Fathers greet us and lead us in that dream-walk between loving friends towards that dearest of backs. Little Cara holds her posy firmly and patters demurely after us, looking enchanting in her blue puffed-sleeve dress and bonnet . . . up . . . the long, long Nave.

> *HERE WE ARE . . . WE ARE US*
>
> *I am deep in his eyes, he in my brown eyes.*
> *'to have, hold love cherish' – whatever –*
> *all that we are, all that we have we pledge, each to other,*
> *within the Love of God.*
> *It is my Mother's ring that Bill slips on my finger.*

We kneel as Dad covers our joined hands with his Stole; he confers a Blessing and, in the Name of the Holy Trinity pronounces us MAN and WIFE.

Surely, to us, this is the most meaningful title we could have, in common with many of the fortunate ones who have come through this dreadful war.

At last we are US . . . our thankful hearts soar in prayer. 'Love Divine . . . Joy of Heaven . . . come down . . . changed from glory into glory till in Heaven we take our place . . .'

We sign the register; I sign my maiden name away . . . this gives rise to gentle teasing about 'the Apple' being 'Cook-ed'!

As we come, arm in arm, from the Vestry, light from the Altar candles shines on my wedding ring and Twinkle sparkles, as if to claim that it has served us well! So we begin Our Future, walking (or is it really floating?) together down the

US AT LAST!

Nave among our happy friends. Bill's Ribbons, the Amethysts and all the gleaming jewels on my Florentine Cross declare the devotion of my truly loved and loving Husband.

The joyful ring of Bertie's handbells draws us out to sunshine and photographs.

Being a warm Summer day, more photographs were taken in the garden. Among the flowers we noticed 'Uncle Charlie's' chrysanthemum plants. They promised to be lovely by November; he had originally expected to produce them for our wedding at that time! We wandered in and out of the house, enjoying the company of as many friends as we could talk with. Before we had to disperse — some to return to their units — we crowded into the drawing room to admire and enjoy the wedding cake, complete with white icing, a silver shoe and sprig of white heather, a cake such as we had not seen for years . . . it tasted 'real' too! It was such a happy time . . . everything was special. Mr. Fairs proposed a toast and Bill replied; Canon Chapman wore his tail coat, adding fitting dignity to our informal family celebration. It was wonderful to think how many people had done so much and how many had come so far, at such short notice. It was also amazing that, even in this hospitable house, we had had a Baptism tea and two Wedding Receptions in one week, on rations! I hope that someone made a speech about the real king pin of it all . . . our Mrs. B.

Happy day.

Bridegroom Recalls

The Rectory was a busy place on our Wedding Day. I remember that Reggie and I booked the large bathroom for 11 a.m. While he shaved, I bathed. Soon we were polishing our Sam Brown's. All leave-going Personnel had been supplied with campaign ribbons, and mine had been sewn on the previous evening. Reggie and I eyed one another up and down to see whether we would do.

Soon two seasoned Chaplains were occupying the Bridegroom's pew in St. Mary's Church, feeling just as nervous as any of the Bridegrooms we ourselves had married! The Bridal March was being played, and we edged ourselves into position. Glancing round I saw our two Fathers leading the Bride on her brother's arm, followed by a sweet and composed little bridesmaid, up the aisle. Four years of hopes and longings flooded over me as Helen stood by my side. Surely my Sweetie Pie was the most beautiful Bride there ever can have been. After a fleeting calculation as to how many years it has taken to come to this moment I got lost in the peaceful love in her brown eyes, and humbly knew that it has all been well. So we make our vows, and kneel for God's Blessing, and we are on the way to the Vestry to sign the Registers. The Wedding March heralds us down the long aisle, and as we pass through the South Porch our friend and Verger Bertie Harrison plays a peal on a stand of hand-bells. In the evening after our departure Bertie managed a Tower peal in our honour. This was no mean feat for those days.

The Reception was a happy gathering in the Rectory Drawing Room, for those who had been able to come at such short notice. Gilbert Fairs, the Grammar School Head Master proposed our health, and I tried truly to say that She was my pearl of great price. But my heart was too full for many words. At the right stage Helen disappeared. She shed her dainty wedding dress to emerge in a smashing going-away outfit. The family came to see us off on the London train, and we took our Best Man with us! He and Joan were expecting their first baby very soon. So our honeymoon really began when we had put Reggie into a taxi for the train back to Cheshire! For a present I had saved Reggie a large and very special Calabash pipe with an amber stem. It was the favourite of the hundreds of pipes I had bought for the Regiment from the Philippeville pipe factory in Algeria, two years before.

We spent our first night in a family flat in Ealing and then took the train to the Lakes, where we had two weeks at Glen Rothay Cottage at Rydal Water. Most days we were up on the fells. One day a bus dropped us at a whitewashed inn at High Whitestones, on the road to Keswick. We walked the fourteen miles over the Dodd's, Helvellyn, Fairfield and down Nab Scar to our starting point.

Our month sped by with visits to my home in the Peak District and to Helen's home in Diss. All the time our loving relationship grew and deepened and was more wonderful than I had ever dreamed.

Soon there was our farewell kiss at Diss station, to be followed by the longest eight months of our lives! But it had been a beautiful summer. An engaged state was hard to bear in over three years of separation, but I found that eight months of separation after a blissful marriage was infinitely harder. And yet we had proved that our wait and trust had been so worthwhile. We were now one. We had a permanence and understanding and a stability that nothing could shake. I did not know at the time that I was destined to be a soldier for a further eight months, and not in Austria but in Padua, in Northern Italy.

But what a change there was in our relationship. It was no longer a dream of hopes unfulfilled. We were now Husband and Wife.

A ROCKET FROM OUR COLONEL!

13.9.45.   Strathspey, Scotland.

My Dear Padre,

What do you mean by getting married without even telling me or sending me an invitation! I saw it in our local paper yesterday and hasten to send you my very best wishes for your future happiness. I am so far from shops here and I send you a cheque with which I hope you and 'Sweetie Pie' will buy something you may need for your new Home.

With every good wish to you both.

    Yours very sincerely,
      Ian Walker.

11

Italy

I went home from the crispness of an Austrian Village to be married, and returned to a warm autumn back in Italy. Here I was to stay until my demob.

The D.Y. were in the throes of moving into the Padua area, and R.H.Q. was to be in a charming house in the village of Montegalda. War had left the northern and central villages of Italy in a sort of chequer board. Our village had remained staunchly Catholic, and the next firmly Communist.

One day the Bishop came to visit the village and there was real fêting and rejoicing. There was bunting and a large banner across the entrance to the village proclaiming 'Welcome to our Bishop'.

Bill at Villa Roi Montegalda, Vicenza.

The Sappers, as usual, had been in the vanguard of the move, and so I still had my same Parish. There were centres at Padua, Vicenza, Camisano and all the main towns had Garrison Churches as well. So once again I settled down to a regular programme. There would be four Services on a Sunday morning, and an informal and well-attended Service in the Toc H Canteen in Padua in the evening.

MY WIFE'S FIRST LETTER

Diss Rectory.

20.9.45.

My Darling Husband,

You are such a beloved man and you always think of so many things to make me specially happy. Thank you for such a lovely letter you left for me with Iris. Beloved it has been such a precious time of being together . . . all part of our early loving, our writings and our future life together. I didn't think that a man could complete any woman's life as you seem to be doing. It is still hard to realise that the wonderful You really belongs with little me. Reason could never find an answer to the wonder of it, and the truth of it will always make me happy. I found three people who had been to see some one off to Greece, so I ran a bus service for forlorn women, from the station to Diss. But I think we were all happy at heart because we had folk to love very much. I did shed 3½ tears when I read your letter, but we are one and all is very well. The old propaganda question 'Is your journey really necessary?', used when transport was needed for urgent wartime use, occured to me!!

But travel safely and be happy. God bless you my dear, dear Man. I love you with all my heart. Your Brown-eyed Wife.

22.9.45.

Darling Husband,

Lots of news today, so let's begin by saying that you are the most important of everything in my world, and that I love you utterly.

Just before dinner the phone rang . . . it was William Penn. He arrived home last night, so he may have passed you in the Channel! They must have speeded leave up. He is obviously very proud of his son. The Penns will be coming here, but later.

The nurse came to weigh Richard. He has doubled his birth weight in four months. Iris thinks it is too much. She knows her data well. I have found a bank in the garden where I can lie and prop my paper when I write. Time flies when I am writing to you, but otherwise it is just a weeny bit slow at ticking over at present! Iris called me this morning with your letter, posted in London, thank you Darling. Love and kisses from your very much-in-love Wife.

25.9.45.

My Darling,

You should be at Innsbruck by my calculations. It does help so much to have had you here; it was like finding you all over again, finding you just the same . . . only lots more so. I didn't think you really could be like that, because dream pictures tend to get so desperately, wildly wonderful, but you were more so than my dreams. There is still a lot to dream about. This USness really is a big adventure — a tremendous experience. Now I am your wife, with peaceful, belonging feelings . . . God bless you my darling half . . . your own Helen Mary Brown Eyes.

MY HUSBAND'S FIRST LETTER

Villa Roi, Montegalda, Vicenza, Italy.

26.9.45.

Beloved Wife,

I'm sure you have been following my journey back to Austria, but at the Brenner Pass we were diverted back to Italy. Please note above address! The Regiment lives at Montegalda, having a charming house, Villa Roi, for our Regimental Mess.

There has been such a warm welcome back from all my friends, high and low. I've even ceased to be self conscious about my wedding ring. Dearest Heart, after all these years of waiting and writing and longing you are my very own wife and I am your most loving and adoring husband. What a joy it has all been . . . so many people did so much to make it the happiest of weddings. My memories are all full of such deep peace and thankfulness. I think our letters will have some savouring of our happy memories, as well as the now more urgent looking forwards, for we are made for each other and life cannot be complete until we can live as the good Lord intended.

Group 20 Release is now taking place . . . it can't be too long to my Group 28's turn!

Good night my Beloved Wife. Thank you for everything. I love you always and for ever. Your Bill.

1.10.45.   Monday.

You seem glad to be at the end of your journey – good to be among the chaps again. I have been back on the job – doing John's Stanton round in his van. I hadn't driven it before, but found it an easy one to manage. Mrs. Buchanan wants me to go back for the full week later on.

i love you too deep for words . . . Darling Man.

Helen and fellow Canteen drivers.

Diss.

3.10.45.

It was fun to go back to my old pals yesterday. Most of the old gang had left Snetterton, but there were still a few there — very browned off — waiting to go home. One boy, who has been away from home over three years, is being posted to Germany again! Everyone was very nice and made little speeches about you, and asked where you were, and hoped you would soon be back again. The first day was rather heavy; it is always tiring to do a thing for the first time, but I enjoyed yesterday a lot. I think it would be best to go back for five days a week. I do enjoy it and it seems to be useful work. It would certainly make the days full until you come home. Happy days, my Darling. Your own Wife.

Diss Rectory.

12.10.45.

My Darling Husband,

Joan came over in the shooting brake and took me to Banyards to have official photos taken with the other drivers. The 10 vans were all drawn up on the meadow like a taxi rank. At the signal everyone climbed into a van and stuck her head out of a window and grinned at the dicky bird. Then we got out and lolled against the bonnets while another 'shot' was taken. Irene brought me home, and we picked up a laddy and gave him a lift to Diss. He was going home to London from Burma — he landed in Southampton and had to report to somewhere up here, before he could go home! We gave him tea before he went to catch the 7.14 train. He saw your picture said what nice Padres he had met, then said a tragic thing: 'I would never have thought you were a Parson's wife. But I would never have insulted you by saying you looked like one, even if you did'!!! So I said 'Oh he isn't such a bad chap you know.' But, Darling, isn't it awful? It's not the first time I have had people in who were thinking 'what a nice house' and seen their surprise when they found it was a Rectory. They expect churchy people to be so dull and miserable. What queer things we need to bounce people out of thinking, my Beloved.

Condensed love space, but lots of it. xxx L.M.P.

11.10.45.   Bed time.

Darling Brown Eyes,

Three weeks ago to-night you left my arms. Those dear, dear eyes and all your loveliness have begun to be wonderful memories. I sought to get back into the groove of Army life, looking forward to our final togetherness. But how hard it is to settle down again. We are different now . . . man and wife indissolubly bound together. Life will always be just an existence now, until we are together for good.

This evening Luigi, our Interpreter, and I went to the Padua Officers' Club for dinner. Apparently it is the place where the revolutionaries planned the unification of Italy, when Padua was in Austria . . . a famous café!

Sweet, lovely Wife, all my three year dreams and longings are as nothing compared with your loveliness. Your Bill.

UNSOLICITED TESTIMONIAL!

A fortnight after my return as a married man my great friend Harry Hearsey wrote to me from Vienna. He had been a much-loved Chaplain to the 12th Royal Horse Artillery. His Regiment had been disbanded early after the war, so he was posted to Vienna. On Oct. 17th he wrote from H.Q. British Troops in Austria:

My Dear Bill,

My sincere congratulations to you on your marriage. May you both be very happy together. I shall look forward to meeting your wife, as I have already heard of her attractiveness and charm from two Derbyshire Yeomanry types who were on the same leave party as myself. They told me what a long march you had stolen on them when the Regiment was stationed in Diss, and how you captured the Prize before they had any chances. They were full of her praises! So I guess how happy you must be, and I expect you are just counting the days till you can go back to home and BEAUTY again.

Do please accept the enclosed cheque with my love and good wishes. I wish I could have thought of a more original present.

I hope we meet again soon. Harry.

RAPALLO SCHOOL OF RELIGION
22.10.45.

My Beloved Wife,

I've just got back to Padua, after my jaunt to Rapallo on the Italian Riviera.

It was a 'high spot' to have an encounter with a big, burly, soft-hearted, Africaner Chaplain, with Veldtprediker (Chaplain) on his shoulders, called Mike Horn. His English was broken, and he seemed to find it curious that I should spend so much time writing letters to you! So I spared him a bit of my airmail and this is what he wrote: 'Dear Mrs. Cook, It is a real privilege to meet your husband out here. Our Conference is something big and creative. I'm glad to be in this with your husband. He is looking fine – even without his Better Half. Perhaps one day the Cooks and the Horns will meet, in this new move to build a better Britain and a better South Africa. Yours, Mike.' Will this happen, my Darling? Let's pray that it will.

We have had a good Conference and much talk about our Ordination Candidates whom we have been encouraging over the years. Our men will have to face these rather frightening new Selection Boards. We have met to study and pray as much as we have been able, but these six years have not been very conducive to being academic. I can see many of them whom I would welcome as my own Parish Priest.

Always you fill my heart. I love you more and more. God bless you, my lovely Brown-Eyed Wife. Your very own Bill.

AMERICAN THANKSGIVING DAY

Dear Husband,

Yes, we have been celebrating! When we called at the Cook House and dumped our urns to be re-filled, we were led into a side room, seated at a table and proffered a portion of Thanksgiving dinner! The item that surprised me most was the yellow bread with sultanas – we don't usually get fed by the K.P., but it was kind of them to include us in their celebrations . . . and some meal!

I was quite relieved, as I had given someone a rocket one day, when we found the sink full of floating eggs – surplus to

*requirement at the last meal . . . I suggested that they boiled
them hard and used their contents! We never see a whole
score of eggs these days. So many things have changed for the
better, though; I still stop, and listen . . . at the first sound of
a plane above — and thankfully remember that there are no
more 'enemy aircraft', with their deep, undulating drone, in
our skies.*

*When I saw Snetterton Flying Fortresses, or other big
bombers from our local airfields, spiralling upwards, high
above, mustering round their own gaudy-painted 'Assembly
Ship', steering into formation and winging eastwards in day-
time, towards alert enemy fire-power; or heard them in the
night, and knew they were on another sortie out across the
North Sea and over darkened Europe — I felt a lift of pride
and hope and a weight of sadness for the necessity of such a
mission. With an arrow prayer of commendation one saw
them off . . . something of oneself went with them. When you
see your chaps off you tend to follow them I am told!!*

*Before so very long will come the day when everyone sees
everyone else off and you all come home. Roll on that day!*

*Do you know, Billy, they lost so many men from Snetter-
ton (1,898 Missing), they have made a Memorial Chapel in
Quidenham Church to men of the 96th Bomb Group. Their
Surgeon had the idea; Reginald Bell designed the window with
an airman, in flying kit, looking up to Christ; four Squadron
emblems and two 8th Air Force badges above, with an eagle,
bomb in beak, in the top light, and beneath, the fields of
Norfolk and the church spire (a homing landmark). The US
Flag and Group Flag flank the altar where cross and candlesticks and 'drapes' contribute to this 'part of America in
England'. On Army Airforce Day (Aug. 1st) this year they
held a Memorial Service when their Chaplain said . . . 'each
day when the rising sun lights this window and brightens the
altar we shall know that our buddies are surrounded by the
mercies of a loving God, and sustained unto eternal life by
His Son, our Saviour Jesus Christ'.*

*They told me all this, and showed me the citation. The
men gave the funds for the chapel. It is nice when memorials
fit in well. This one is a lovely tribute.*

Here is a happy story — Lady Moe, a little black donkey

roams round the base . . . she knows when to call for food at likely places, between her grassy meals. I wonder if you ever met her! She came, in August '43, from near Bône. The men got her on a shuttle raid . . . they flew over Regensburg – dropped their bombs and flew on to Tunisia. While the plane was re-stocked they bargained with an Arab for Lady Moe! They adapted an oxygen mask and wrapped her in a blanket, and on they came via Bordeaux, to land her safe at Snetterton . . . surely the only donkey to have flown a mission!! Some mascot! Bless you, my Love . . . Mrs. C.

Bunwell.

21.11.45.

Darling Husband,

There were lots of letters at home today when I looked in, and 4 envelopes of stockings! I had two other pairs (the first ones you sent off) last week. They are real silk and beautiful. 9½ is the best size for most people.

I do hope that your ordinands do well. It must be an awfully difficult thing to try to help people in these matters, and such a great responsibility for those whose duty it is to direct the studies and selection of candidates. There is so much that a Layman can do in the Church, and often more that certain men can do as Laymen than as Clergy. For those who have had Latin and Greek as part of their diet at school this must be of great value in the academic side of the traditional clergy training systems. But to bar people from the ministry because they have not gone through traditional channels

Lady Moe.

seems questionable. These days the emphasis in general education is training in living, and the clergy training should really be to help the men to train, and assist their flock in living the Christian life. To me it would seem that a few months spent in the Holy Land, and in studying the Bible on the spot so to speak, would give so much of the background that as an initiated unscholastic Laywoman I always imagine your clergy (hark at the mère member of the congregation!) get from a study of Greek. I mean you get a more exact meaning of the Bible phrases if you can translate them yourself, than if you have an English translation, because there are certain phrases in Greek, as in other languages which don't convey quite the same meaning in other languages. But surely there is so much more in the English translation which often goes wrongly interpreted in thought because of lack of background knowledge.

Darling if you do go to Palestine, and find the experience throws light on your knowledge, don't you think it will count for more than your detailed academic studies? Its hard to say what I mean when I don't know anything about it! But I think you will find that many men get depressed by all the emphasis on academic background (judging by Dad's reports from interviews at the Selection Board's 'Panel' at Cuddesdon).

Do you realise that you are in a position to help these recruits? If you do think that the emphasis on qualifications considered necessary for ordination is in the wrong place, you've got a great chance, Billy, haven't you? You've got 'ordinands' in your charge, and you've got Dad to tackle from the other end of the subject, as a member of a Selection Board. Perhaps I'm being nosy, but it does seem to me that a lot is out of date in the system, and there are many things new which want bringing out of the treasure house, as well as things old. Faith seems to be the chief qualification for a job in any sphere of life. You'll get a long way as a cook if you go on sound theories and stick to them, and its the principles of the thing that people will pick up from you. The same with a priest. We had lots of fine chaps preaching at school — chaps like old Woods (a real scholar), I can't remember a word he ever said, but I can remember the exact way he said it, and I can see him pick up his specs, and put them down again, and then come to the front of the platform and say some simple thought in a way that just passed on the spirit of what he believed. You could catch something that was really of the Spirit. He was a great scholar, but it was his personal faith that got his message across.

Not every good Christian is called to be a Priest, but is every potential priest necessarily called to be a classical scholar? Oh its rather a subject for this time of night!! This is the time for your arms and dreams and sleeps close to your heart.

I wish I knew more about this. I think I'll have to ask Dad about it at the weekend. Your Helen.

THE BOMB

3.11.45.   Padua.

My Darling,

Another Saturday afternoon without you. It is always a time of Service preparation. I've had in my room all week the Monday issue of the *Eighth Army News.* The front page has a picture of President Truman and banner headlines 'Truman plans talks on Atom Bomb'. I can still remember the good news of the defeat of Japan on the eve of our Wedding. Is there a thought of the bomb and the use of power for to-morrow's sermon? Roosevelt saw the significance of the bomb, but it was Truman who had to make the decision to drop it. He sees clearly the need to keep a tight grip on the secrets of the bomb. How Jerry would have loved to have found the key first! He is seeking to lay down a number of points that Roosevelt had conceived about controlling this new situation for mankind. He intends to call a meeting with England and Canada to see what can be done.

It was a relief to us all when the bomb put Japan out of the war. Some of us wondered whether such a fiendish invention should have been used a second time, before seeing whether the first bomb would do the trick.

With Hitler astride Europe, the Japs had become lords of Asia. Their treatment of prisoners was without trace of humanity . . . sub-human. Whilst fierce battles raged all over the Pacific the Japs were slowly being driven back to where they belonged. Undoubtedly the bomb saved the lives of countless prisoners, rotting in barbarous prison camps. Bombing of their own mainland towns was beginning to give them a taste of their own medicine, but an invasion of Japan would have cost millions of Allied lives.

But Darling we cannot think of this bomb as just one of the contributions to victory; it is strange, new, awesome, and has changed human history . . . the whole direction of the world.

So tomorrow we shall have to try to think about what has happened, and how this power should be used. One day Truman will no longer be able to lock up this monster like a genie in a bottle.

We fought this war to win the peace, but how can this peace be ensured? The clock can never be put back. The world will never be the same again. The bomb is here to stay. Man's skill has overtaken his humanity. May we be given grace and power and wisdom to handle this awesome monster. A new age is dawning, and we know so little about it.

Dearest Heart, We've fought for a brave new world. All around seem to be new signs of suspicion and, on top of it all, this terrible weapon. Let us pray that we will all see the warning.

I love you eternally, bomb or no bomb. Your Bill.

LUIGI

Luigi, our Italian Interpreter, and a very popular member of the Mess, has returned after a few days leave. He was a student at the beginning of war. His mother is a Countess. It was interesting to be with him as he sat down with a large sheet of paper and solemnly made an analysis of his girl friends! He gave points for each feature of each girl. He intended to propose to the girl who came out with the most points!

Luigi Lastrucci has had a most distinguished war with the Partisans. He has been decorated many times, and has had hair-raising adventures. Yet he never talks about his experiences.

LEAVE TRANSPORT
2.12.45.

Col. Noel has just been talking about his leave. He came back by train with some railway people. They told him that there are six trains a day through Switzerland and that we have to pay the Swiss Government £6000 for each train every day for going through their tiny bit. Apparently they tow us through on one of their electric engines, and also provide a guard or something. So no wonder that we are looking for an alternative route through Austria. I don't suppose we have to pay the other countries anything at all. The Swiss have certainly behaved very properly in this war, and done a lot of good work, but they have made a lot of money as well.

5.12.45.   Wednesday.

My Darling,

It is fun going round this Thetford area. Yesterday I went half way to Mildenhall to a Palace of a place, Elveden Hall, where R.A.F. are stationed. Soon I'm off to Harling, but first I am to have lunch with the S.M. at Riddlesworth.

6.12.45.

I do enjoy my lunch at the Sergeants' mess. There is a Staff Sgt. and a Sergeant Major and Jerry — a great character, 'Serge ordinaire'! The Mess Sgt. always has lots to say about the job, as that is about the only time they all meet. They were pleased when I asked if I should bring my 'irons'; they know about you as Joe from Banyards told them all he has learned of my life history (from my friends), when he arranged for me to serve at Riddlesworth Camp, and stay to lunch. I think Sergeants are good people; they don't have to be apart like Officers, and they can have privileges and do lots for their men.

OUR LAST CHRISTMAS APART
20.12.45.

My Darling, Happy, Happy Christmas !! xx

Thank you for the latest batch of letters. I would love to

have seen you as Mary in the Nativity Play. I can picture the setting . . . the light oak screen lit up, against curtains, with the actors on a stage in front . . . as you say, it is good to feel so many people use their skills in a project like this.

We've got a busy Christmas planned, and William seems to have to spend as much time keeping our wagon on the road as they do with your canteens!

Charles Ridley, my College friend and former S.C.F., comes from a military family. He volunteered for the Far East, but has got only to India. He has just sent the Divisional Christmas Card. The seasonal greetings are alright, but a really epic drawing of the assault crossing of the River Senio by the 8th Indian Division on April 19th, 1945, of which he is now the senior Chaplain, is not very seasonal! It was however the beginning of the last battle for Italy.

This should arrive for Christmas. How different our three warring Christmasses have been. Now it is a peacetime one and we do our best here to make it a reality. Before the Christmas morning rush we shall have a Midnight Service in Padua and I feel that I shall be nearest to you there.

Dearest One, a Happy Christmas with all Joy and Love in your heart. Please give my love to all the family.

Your loving Husband, Bill.

24.12.45.   Christmas Eve.

We had such a well attended and happy service of Lessons and Carols in the wonderful Sappers Canteen. It has thermal springs to keep it very warm, and decorations were up to peacetime standard. It was a completely happy gathering. Then a mad rush to be back for the tail end of the D.Y. Officers' Cocktail party at Montegalda. The people of the House were very much in evidence. We had a warm and crowded midnight Communion at Toc H Canteen in Padua. This was surely the 'high spot'.

Christmas Day

Happy Christmas Beloved,

William has been super this Christmas, so very thoughtful and obliging. We didn't get back to our beds until 1.30 a.m., but he was up at 6.0 a.m. He lit the fire and took all the batmen tea, woke me up at 6.30 and all the Officers too. Holy Communion at Montegalda was well attended, and full of joy. Our long-planned Carol Service at B Squadron for the Regiment was a bit of an anti-climax. Why, Oh why, do I always seem to fall for a big bleak cold place for the main D.Y. Service? A small crowded place is always better than a large barn.

Our new Regular Colonel, Noel Wall, is a good Leader and a fine Christian. He inspired so many to come to early service. It would have been much easier down the years to have had him as my Colonel. We got to Toc H Canteen in Padua fifteen minutes late, but everyone was patiently waiting. There were beautiful decorations. Paul Jones, the Manager, and Mrs. Fasolo had done wonders. Mrs. Fasolo is a very distinguished English Lady, who has maintained her witness through Nazi days, like so many other English Ladies. She reminds me so much of the old ladies of Florence. When Italy capitulated the Nazis took over administration and one old lady was called in for questioning. In her laced-up boots, and with her brolly folded, she stormed past the Fascist lackeys into the Nazi inner sanctum . . . She said 'Young man these Fascist dolts haven't been able to cower me, and you certainly won't. You know where I live, and I shan't run away. Good morning young man!' With her brolly whirling in the air she stumped out to the astonishment and disbelief of everyone concerned! It was a lovely fellowship and so many different units were represented.

In pouring rain we splashed back to camp in time for William's well-earned Christmas Dinner, turkey, pork and all the trimmings. The Officers had a cold Buffet. Too much food! This was at 3.30, so we agreed on 5.45 for tea, in order to have a couple of hours sleep. I think I deserved mine most!

Colonel Noel has done so much to build up a really good spirit here. He makes me feel an essential and important part of the Unit.

Tea time produced a huge Christmas cake with lots of silky sugar and almond icing, complete with D.Y. badge in red and gold. There were so many visitors, including all the Sergeant's, that there was little cake left, even though it was two feet across! Christmas blessings and love, Bill.

26.12.45.   Boxing Day.

The Sergeants came in to cocktails at 11.15 and did not depart until 3.0 p.m. H.Q. Squadron has a Dance in the Village Hall. The local Priest has forbidden the girls to go. Two Squadron Officers are trying to get me to clock on to make it more respectable, but I won't get dragged into politics! I've spent so many hours in this war trying to sort out problems of unfaithfulness, that I agree with the Priest's anxiety.

It is a good thing that my Parish is large and wide, and that I am not too closely tied to one lot. I suppose it's the post war Army getting back to normality, but in many ways this has been a very boozy Christmas. Drink is so cheap and easy to get, and I will not go through a whole boozy session. Roll on April, my Darling.

Our Second Armoured Brigade lost its last Chaplain, and the S.C.F. asked if I would like to go to the Queen's Bays, or the Ninth Lancers. But they are all new. I'll stay with my Sappers and the R.A.S.C. when the Derbyshire Yeomanry depart.

30.12.45.

We do so enjoy our time with the Sappers. Johnny Boyd, M.C., has made me promise to go and stay for a week when the D.Y. depart. They live so far away and I don't see much of them. Both Johnny and his second in command, John Church, have such a good influence on the Unit. They have moved to a very pleasant villa on a gentle slope outside Verona.

After dinner we went to the Officers' Club, and then to the cinema.

Home.

17.12.45.   Sunday.

My Darling,

When we got back from church we put pieces of holly over the pictures, and out, once more, came your 1941 crackers. We have some silver strips, the kind they used in the war to reflect their radar and confuse the enemy. They make into bunches and sparkle brightly.

Dad's present is a new coal bucket – rather dull, but I know the bottoms are out of all our coal receptacles. Mrs. B. may be able to have a set of undies, if Dad's coupons will run to it! Mary says they are giving us saucepans and napkin rings; we will soon be using them. Bach's Christmas Oratorio is on at present . . . all the men have their eyes closed, but I expect they will comment on it afterwards as if they have heard every note!

Here's to our Christmas. We have never yet had a Christmas together. Roll on next year! . . . Your Helenwife.

Christmas Eve.

Darling,

There is a hush of expectation after the bustle of Church decoration, tying up parcels and touching up house trimmings and vacuuming up bits that dropped – it is late, so late that it is almost Christmas Day. The Italians have just marched past, on their way to Midnight Mass in the Corn Hall, I presume. Perhaps you are listening to the bells pealing in Christmas Day. Dear Heart how close you are, and yet what a draught there is in the house. Next year you will suffer my pudding!

Christmas Day.   8.15 a.m.

My Darling,

A happy Christmas to you. Bob and I went to Church at 7 a.m. so as to stay with Richard, while his parents went at 8 a.m. We are putting presents round the tree that Uncle Charlie made from yew branches . . . with cotton wool and sparkly silver it looks good. Dear Heart be happy. God bless you.

2.40 p.m. The King's broadcast is very good . . . people speaking from the other side of the world sound so clear. A young wife in Canada who has a home of her own hopes that next year we will have our own home, and will be as happy as they are! Iris is giving Richard his Christmas dinner of sprouts and egg. Then we will be giving each other presents. Here are my Christmas 'Thinks'. Dearest, love to you. Your Helen.

GLORIA

Not Christmas trees, cribs, lights nor bells
so much as winter stable smells
transport me to that Christmas Day
long ago and far away . . .
there, in the oil lamp's hazy smoke
to kneel, and share with local folk
the miracle of human birth . . .
to grasp the fact of God on earth . . .
why did God send His only Son?
. . . to tell us all our lives are one?
then every being on this earth
should feel the impact of His birth!
the world should not be ruled by fears
after 2,000 A.D. years.
a village maiden, mother, wife
gave us a Son: He gives us Life!
and each of us is here to prove
the leavening power of Jesus' love.
— as angels in excelsis sing
may we all do our loving thing
to celebrate our Saviour's birth
and bring Him glory here on earth

Boxing Day.   St. Stephen.

We had a lazy morning after our happy, busy Christmas Day. This afternoon we went to Thrandeston. Uncle and Aunt had twenty people to feed and entertain last night. They find lonely folk to give them Christmas cheer. The washing-up was just finished!

We are invited to Dr. Vincent's for a dancing evening on Saturday. I have made the hard decision to cut off the tail of my wedding dress! Canteen in the morning.

30.12.45.

Nancy came yesterday so we were soon being welcomed over the road, by Mrs. Vincent. We enjoyed the dancing, and the punch! and came home about 1.30 a.m.

OUR YEAR

New Year's Day, '46

A happy new year my Sweetheart. How I love you, and long for you my Darling. Thank you for being you, and for being my Wife. Thank you for all the Christmas Letters. It was lovely to hear so much about Christmas. I suppose that it was only natural that you would be on duty some of the time. Thank you for your sweet poem. It's lovely.

At Verona we talked about past glories, including Two Gentlemen, and Romeo and Juliet. We all agreed how fortunate we have been. There isn't a famous place in all Italy, north of Pompeii, that we haven't visited, except, I think Turin. We've had the best places, and we'll never live like this again. I fear that on a Parson's pay we aren't very likely to do all these places, my Darling! But how these heroes of mine deserve all these marvellous experiences. They've been half way to Hell and back, and they make me feel very humble to be part of them.

And now they are beginning to trickle home. Soon they (and I) will be in Civvy Street, and knowing that a whole lifetime lies in the past, and occasionally, at some reunion the past will dimly come alive. But Dearest Heart, I wouldn't want it otherwise. Our new life together is waiting for us, and what glory it will be. The past is over and we have so many things to do together in the time that our Loving Lord has in store for us. I know it in my bones, and I believe in all my heart that you know it too, my very own Darling Wife. So here's to OUR YEAR and OUR LIFE together, my Beloved. God keep you eternally.

1.1.46. New Year's Day.   *Bunwell.*

Dear Husband,

Nancy and I were family-sitting and heard the service on the wireless. At midnight the five bells of Bunwell rang out in the frosty air . . . we drank our toast, in the glass of port we had been left, after Big Ben had struck. Here's to a happy, happy year and plenty more!

This morning, at Coney Weston, we had a warm-up by the

*stove in the Sergeants' Mess and I mended Staff Sgt's gloves.
We chatted to those of a formidable array of sergeants who
were not snoozing off the effects of last night, I should
imagine. But it was a cosy, snoozy atmosphere. Plenty of
'Happy New Year's' on the van today.*

3.1.46.

*Dad and Hum (Jay's friend) brought us home after work
. . . we had tea and went to Diss Picture House to see* David
Copperfield *. . . home to a very good duck dinner . . . then
port! THEN time to unpack the most exciting parcel. What
an extremely beautiful coffee set. Each item is whole, thanks
to your expert packing. You are a Beloved and you do have
such good taste, and oh dear me, how I love You. After
tomorrow's round I'll have a chance to re-read all your
Christmas letters . . .*

17.1.46.

Darling Beloved,

Little Brown Eyes, you are infinitely precious and you
make every moment charged and bright with your love.
I'm trying to say Happy Birthday, but our love is deeper than
words. Next year I'll say it with kisses.

Only Roy Hodder and I are in to lunch, so we had a wee
table in front of the stove and a mashing afterwards. Only the
servants get that privilege normally as it's supposed to be
infra dig for Officers!

This morning I collected a couple of hundred books from
R.H.Q., the ones we liberated from the notorious Officers'
P.O.W. Camp further south. I'll keep the serious ones, history,
biography etc. separately. All the covers have either been
slashed or removed. It is interesting to see the Senior British
Officers' names written on the front. Some have Gen. Carton
de Wiart, V.C., who was captured when his plane crashed in
the desert, and Col. David Stirling, D.S.O., who commanded
the Long Range Desert Group.

But now it's Happy Birthday! and many, many more,
with me there to hug you. Feel tremendously loved and
precious, please. You supply all my joy and inspiration,

and you bring happiness to so many other people too. We know that all things are working together for good. Soon you can claim your home in my arms again. I'm keeping them warm for you.

God bless you. Special Birthday love and kisses from your very own Bill. xxx

FAREWELL TO 1st DERBYSHIRE YEOMANRY

19.1.46.   H.Q.R.A.S.C.

My Darling,

It is time to end another Military Chapter. I shall miss my Regiment, even though it has changed almost beyond recognition. As I should only be with them for a couple of months I do not think that the upset will be worth it to move to Egypt. So here's to being the Officer who has served with the 6th British Armoured Division from its inception. Can there be anyone else?

William and I moved into a most comfy mess at H.Q. R.A.S.C. this morning. We dine in a huge and rather cold dining room with a long refectory table. Next door is a smaller room with a lovely fire and carpets and cosy chairs.

This evening I was off to D.Y. to say Goodbye to them at Padua Railway station, as they entrain for Trieste, and ship to the Canal Zone. But now they are off tomorrow morning instead. I have services in Padua then, so I'm off to say Goodbye tonight. Sweet dreams. Love Bill.

23.1.46.

Everywhere was white this morning. I got up early to be at Padua Railway station at 8.30 a.m. to see the D.Y. Rear Party off. There they stood in the bombed station with their kit in the snow. Never mind they'll soon be in sand and sun! It was a sad parting after 6 years.

9.2.46.

Cpl. Ford came to see me this afternoon. He is Group 26 and in love with a nice girl in Florence. The D.Y. left him behind, and he is staying on in the Army here for a month or two until his permission comes through to marry. This is one of the few mixed marriages I am really happy about. An old Yeoman, he has been the Regimental Butcher all the time. He will be taking his wife back to Derby so we shall probably see them in the future. There will be lots of nice people to meet if we end up in the Derby or Ashbourne areas.

15.2.46.

I'm sorting out the Divisional Ordination candidates file. During the war I must have been in touch with about fifteen possible ordinands, and some of us have done quite a lot of study. Now so many have gone off with their units, and to demobilisation, that very few of the original ones are left. How I miss them, I hope and pray that their dreams of ordination will come true. L/Cpl. Ball, who came from Germany with the 4th Tank Regiment is a nice Methodist ordinand. I am planning to get them all together for a Quiet Day in a week or two.

CHURCH ARMY WELFARE

10.2.46.

There are so many Camps full of assorted personnel from various theatres of war, in Norfolk now. Our Canteens try to serve them, by way of welcome, until they get Naafi ones set up. We also get a variety of odd calls to make.

When I have time I spend it with the men at Riddlesworth. Some of them are in a poor way. They show signs of shock; they deserve to come home free and whole, after all that they have been through. We do what we can to help boost morale. We made paper chains to brighten their room. In Thetford I bought a broom handle and suggested they sawed it into draught-size pieces and darken half, to make a set, to go with a board that was lying about. I organised some girls for a dance/party – planned over Mess lunch with the Sergeants. I think all this comes under 'welfare' in your 'Parish'. You do a vast mileage, I know, and my little van clocks up over 100 miles some days. It added miles extra when we went to an operating airfield, as it is such a long way round the perimeter track, to call at the parking bays, or hangars. Meantime, happy, busy days. All my Love, Helen.

UPS AND DOWNS . . . WITH BROLLEYS

14.2.46.   *Diss Rectory.*

The News discloses release for Group 28 in April and May . . . about eight weeks. Is there any delay for Officers? I bet every 'red' hair on my head that you are scribbling to tell me that there is no delay; I hope so. It is high time Bp. John took us very seriously and found you a Parish – in Derbyshire this time! What sort of a holiday do you need when you get back? Time at home with your people, of course, but as well . . . time in an ordinary home to get used to living in England again and managing with our allowances!

The men in the Church Hall Canteen sadden me. There are a number who have been prisoners, and come back wounded to find that the homes they dreamed of are not homes at all. One has a sister, with four illegitimate children, in his house. These disillusioned men come every day, and spend all afternoon and evening in the Canteen. It is sad. There are very many home-coming problems. The G.I. brides are causing storms because so many have been deserted.

Thank you for my FOLDING umbrella! We are fathoming how to put it up; at first I could open it by running into the wind! But now I can almost open it to order.

I think Dad would like to come to stay with us in the Autumn and do odd jobs – he dropped a good hint to that effect. It seems a bit early to have one's in-laws, but we will see if we get stuck with any of the inconveniences he delights in obviating! We all keep fit on our activities . . . Your L.M.P.

PRIORITY, UTILITY, ECONOMY

18.2.46.

I have filled up the priority docket form for furniture. It required the address of our home, so I spun a yarn on the page for 'Other Remarks' about 28 Group and a Vicarage with a spare room for parochial visitors!

20.2.46.

Our Priority Dockets came to-day! We get 2 blankets, 3 sheets, 15 square yards of furnishing material and some lino/

carpet felt and 17 Units: a wardrobe takes 10 or 12, a table 8 etc., so it does not allow for many items. Utility carpets are not rationed, so, when we know where we are going, and the size of rooms, we can order some floor covering. Surely this is the first documented evidence that we fortunate people are to have a Home of Our Own. I get a luxurious feeling that we are on the verge of seeing our dreams materialise!!

Warmest love, your own Helen.

A WEDDING TRIP
22.2.46.

Darling, one of our chaplains, Wilf Preece, is going to Rome to marry Barbara, a Y.M.C.A. worker in Naples, and I am going to represent the Division, armed with a pair of tiny engraved salt cellars as a gift from our Chaplains.

We came south yesterday, to Florence, for the first time since the war ended. Much of the countryside has been cleared, but some scars will remain for a long time. The old Commander was overjoyed to see us. We had our old wing for the night, and dinner with him. Such stories to swap and much interest in our wedding pictures. After a late breakfast we went into Florence. The shops are fuller than ever. We lunched at the Officers' Club, now American run, then I spent the afternoon in the Pitti Palace where nearly all the world's treasures seem to be. The Ponte Vecchio has been tidied up. I saw the della Robbias in the Foundling Hospital, Michael-angelo's David, and his carvings in the Medici Chapel of the Church of San Lorenzo.

I do look forward to bringing you to these places and showing you the treasures hereabouts. There is so much to see. We are glad to have this break and be able to call here again on our way back.

3.3.46.   Sunday Evening.

We came to Rome on Friday and I spent yesterday morning in the Vatican Museum. The Codex Siniaticus was open at the beginning of St. Luke and I could read it easily.

To-day we worshipped at the English Church and spent the rest of the day on our feet . . . Roman Rome, Modern Rome, Museums, ancient churches and basilicas.

4.3.46.   Wedding.

It has been a lovely wedding. The Bride had lots of Y.M.C.A. and C.V.W.W. supporters, and Wilf had a few Padres. He was married in uniform and she had a lovely white silk dress with a long train, from England. Darling, I was very moved by the whole atmosphere. It took me back so vividly to our Great Day, six months ago. You were so radiantly lovely.

5.3.46.

I popped into St. Peter's to salute Michaelangelo's lovely Pieta. We came north on the coastal Route 1, a surprisingly good road. We did 300 miles and it got dark as we came through Empoli to Florence, and a good meal.

PADUA UNIVERSITY
12.3.46.

Doc. Philips and I, and six more Doctors, were taken round the University this afternoon. Padua dates from 1222 on actual foundation, and it is known that there was an educational centre there before that! Padua beat Bologna by a couple of years. We went round the main Block, new buildings containing the crests of famous students. Some of the lecturers were from all nations. Two were Galileo and Harvey. There is Galileo's lecture desk, a very primitive erection of bare boards. The doctors went into raptures when they read the names of famous Medievalists like Fallopius and his tubes.

ANOTHER WEDDING
25.3.46.

My Darling,

Our wedding has got me into good wedding form I think! William and I have got a pass into Austria to marry Ian Manning D.Y. to Gretl, a Yugoslav girl. William is to be Best Man.

Hotel Moser, Klagenfurt.
26.3.46.

This morning William and I went to find Ian and Gretl in

Volkermarkt. She is small, blonde and unpainted. Her parents are good, clean, honest folk. We had a wedding rehearsal.

In the evening we had dinner at the hotel before going to see Smetana's *Bartered Bride*.

27.3.46.

I've just written to Ian's parents in Derby to tell them they will love their new daughter. William and Ian were both very nervous and hadn't had any breakfast. The wedding went smoothly and Gretl made her promises charmingly. The reception was at our old haunt at the Klopeiner See . . . soup, huge steaks and dumplings, and fruit and fresh cream. So back to Padua. With all my love. Bill, Husband.

Diss Rectory.

1.4.46.

The sun seemed so high when I woke that I put on my old patchwork gown and slipped down to see the time . . . and on the floor lay two, fat, Austrian letters . . . the freshness of the landscape, the cold of the clear mountain streams, all come out vividly in your letters. Darling, we were made for the mountains; to me the oldness and the freshness of mountain country are especially stirring. I often go to mountains in my mind; some hymns and canticles lead me there. Mother was very fond of Psalm 121 'I will lift up my eyes unto the hills' . . . it says a lot that one feels the hills knew long before we did.

Diss Rectory.

14.4.46.   Palm Sunday.

Herewith a little card to tell you thoughts that lie too deep for words. I hope you will find great, new inspiration this Easter. The whole of human life seems to be dealt with in the events we commemorate during Holy Week; all things connected with life in the world seem to be taken up and sanctified, so that every particle of earthly existence matters and is significant. There is nothing that can happen to us that Christ has not experienced in some way, and there is nothing that is inadequate to be used by Him.

The Ministers asked if they might invite their flocks to
come to Church for united services in the evenings this week.
So Dad will 'kick off', setting the theme, and the others will
lead each service in turn. God give you great joy. Special love.
See you SOON! Your own Wife.

19.4.46. Good Friday.

Just a few lines before lunch on this very busy day. I am
trying to lay meals and help Mrs. B., chauffeur the Chapmans
to Church, and we have the Three Hours 2–5 p.m., Stainer's
Crucifixion at 7.30 p.m. and Dorothy Sayers' 'The Man Born
to be King' on the wireless. Mr. Wright was rather poorly this
morning, but very cheerful. I go each morning, to light his
fire and clean up. He told me of an entry in the old church
accounts, of a sum of money and a length of cloth given to a
widow, because she had lost her husband and her pig – her
all, I suppose! Your loving wife.

THE R.A.S.C. MESS, PADUA

16.4.46.

Today is Padua's liberation day, and a holiday. Flags fly
from all the windows. But memories are short, and only the
Officers' Club flies British and American flags. Palm Sunday
and Monday letters came today.

There's a feeling among the Chaplains that we need time to
become civilians again, to read and study, to worship, to get
our homes together, and to love our wives!

Some of us are going out to the Firework Display. Basil,
one of the R.A.S.C. Officers has swum into my life. He has so
many gifts and he has come to meet Christ after a long journey.

R.A.S.C. Officers are very down. They are in short supply
and their release may be deferred. Greg has a Devon holiday
booked for June. Harry has arranged his job. Now this delay.
Poor Harry is moping, Greg shed a few tears, and will get
roaringly drunk, I fear. This stupid Army. Nothing has changed
since the war in the manpower situation. These pootling Brass
Hats, with all the figures, should have seen this long ago. Oh
its all been worth it. I've learned so much, but I need to be a
civvy again! Aren't I getting Bolshie?

EASTER

21.4.46.

Easter Day, a lovely sunny, fresh one. Some of the Fellow-ship boys had brought boughs of 'green', in a cart from the Heywood, and decked pillars, and put pots of daffodils and cherry blossom on top of the screen! Window ledges were full of cowslips, smelling very sweet. There were 81 communicants at 7 a.m., 115 at 8 o'clock, and another 40 after Matins. Canon C. always talks of you and says 'what a splendid man' you are. I know, but it gladdens me when others give evidence that they do too!

24.4.46.   Wednesday.

Today Dad was busy trying to arrange for the couple to move in to help Mr. Wright, while I was lighting his fire and tidying up. Then we got ready for the wedding of Kathleen Chapman.

We all sat in the Chancel for the lovely Service (reminiscent of our own!). The Bridegroom is a Chaplain who served with Wingate, and all over, was here when we were married, and remembers the D.Y. landing in North Africa; he is going to the Guards in Berlin; a static khaki Parish! Kathleen wore white with a beautiful veil most becomingly arranged; her Bridesmaids were in cherry red! They had a three-tier cake! The happy pair drove off trailing a clatter of tins on long strings.

Well, my 'Splendid Man' it is all I can do to keep from exploding with joy at the nearness of the YOU. I got so excited that I told them at Banyards that you would be here in a few minutes!!

Fen Cottage.

26.4.46.   Friday.

It has been a warm, sunny day, so we went down to the sea. Bomb-disposal people are digging over an expansive enclosed area, trying to find lost mines. It looks a colossal undertaking. Square concrete tank-trap blocks still stand in their staggered double line, making a barrier along the back-shore, below sand dunes. Most of the tangle of barbed-wire has been *peeled back or carted away; but the iron fence of tubular frames is mostly intact, with fearsome-looking bars pointing sea-ward, like the stake-spike fence driven in by Henry V's archers against the charge of enemy horsemen. Oh, the time when your Parents went 'for a little stroll' . . . and were discovered sitting on the fore-shore sheltering behind the huge, black, umbrella; trusted protection from the vicious wind . . . between them and us a notice on the defences warned: DANGER – UNEXPLODED MINES – KEEP AWAY.*

Perhaps that brolly had more inbuilt protection than we realised!!! Today we sat on the shore, by the boats, and got covered with 'tar'! I do keep thinking how wonderful it will be to have you home for always and no parting pending. I DO like being your Mrs. Bless you.

A LAST JOYFUL ARMY EXPERIENCE – ASOLO

In the middle of April I took William to Villach for his demobilisation. He had to wait for three days for his train, and wrote his first civilian letter which began Dr (Dear) Bill! Truly he is gone, but after six years I must know him far better than his Missis does, and now there is no army rank!

Bill writing at Asolo.

22.4.46.

After the Easter services I came to beautiful peaceful Asolo
to have a quiet break at the Chaplains' Centre. Lent this year
has been a preparation for Easter New Life, and in the New
Life in Jesus a preparation for our new life together, my
Beloved. Easter Victory, New Life, our life together. What a
wholeness! Glory be!

After dinner fellow Chaplain Jack Stevens and I wandered
round this ancient and attractive little town in the foothills
of the Alps. It's so like Assisi; stone built. Some buildings
have been converted into pubs and houses, and there is a level
sand bowling alley in a refectory. Italy is so closely cultivated
and peopled, but here in the Alpine foothills is peace, and
there are so many places to walk. My last six years have mostly
been in giving myself. In battle or peace so much has depended
on my skill in communicating. But here is just a chance to be.
We worship, and talk, and walk, and drink cups of tea.

Asolo was 800 years old when Rome was born. Napoleon
spent a little time here. Here was stronghold for the enemies
of Venice.

Eleanora Duse, the Italian Sarah Bernhardt, lived here, and
Gabriel D'Annunzio loved her here. Her souvenirs fill the
house. Her patron and friend married into the Guinness
family, and so Lord Iveagh owns the house which he has lent
to be a Chaplains' Centre.

Robert Browning lived in Casa Roberto Browning, and a
street is named after him. He wrote *Pippa Passes*, as he told
the story of a mill girl who passed his window every day to
work at the Mill in Positano. Pippa died in 1924, having lived
by signing autographs with Browning's pen. She sold the
manuscript to an American for £4.

12

Together

27.4.46.   Saturday.

All is ready for tomorrow's round of services. The thought came to me that I've only got THREE MORE MILITARY SUNDAYS LEFT! Whoopee!

This morning I collected my Officer's Release Book. It's a complicated document. There are bits to be sent to so many people, and a medical history for my medical examination. We go from Villach through Germany, and take 48 hours.

6.30 p.m. Good Old Derby County. They've won the cup at last, after a long gruelling extra time with Charlton Athletic. There will be a joyful crowd of supporters wending their way back to St. Pancras now!

28.4.46.

Sunday afternoon nearly teatime. I stopped off for lunch at 8 Field Squadron R.E., and came home to find your letters and one from my mother. Sir Ian has invited us very warmly to go to Ilam cum Blore cum Okeover. When he moves to Okeover from Osmaston I would be his private chaplain. Mother, in her letter says she has seen drinking water being carried in buckets to the Vicarage! The house is very old fashioned too! I feel honoured, but I don't think it is for us, my Darling!

5.5.46.   Sunday 3.00 p.m.

I'm preaching at Padua Garrison Church this evening, and it COULD be my last Army Service. Next weekend Basil and I may go for a prayerful and peaceful weekend. I think he will make a real commitment, and this could well be the end of my military endeavours.

Basil and I used the R.A.S.C. Launch to tour some of the outer islands of Venice yesterday. We went to Murano, where the famous glass is made, a mile from the city, but it was closed. Then we spent a couple of hours on the Island of San Lazzaro, a centre of Armenian Culture. The monks welcomed us so kindly. It was full of treasures. They gave me a glossy book of their history, a copy of their Liturgy and several theological works. The English translation was very quaint. Armenia was over-run by the Turks a few centuries ago, and the Venetians gave them the Island to be a monastery and centre of Armenian Culture. Down the years the monks have doubled the size of their island.

8.5.46.   V.E. Day Anniversary

What a long time ago it seems. It's an Army fiesta, late breakfast, and all the other holiday laziness. I think it must be an Itie one too, because I was wakened early by the excitement of lorry loads of little girls going off on a picnic. Each wagon contained a very demure nun, who was doing her best to stop the girls from falling overboard.

9.5.46.

Dearest Heart, I love you. Our time is rushing towards us now. Robin Woods, now Deputy Assistant Chaplain General, turned up at lunch to say Goodbye. But I was saying Goodbye to 8th Field Squadron R.E. We've shared so much sorrow and excitement. They have been among my special heroes. Anyway Robin returned for tea, and we had a lovely time swapping Sweetie Pie news. Henrietta will not come out because there's another baby in September. So Robin is going home instead.

I AM COMING HOME IN THE MIDDLE OF NEXT WEEK!

10.5.46.

I bought young Nephew Richard a jolly and well made Teddy Bear in Padua, with a squeaky chest, this afternoon. Then I realised that Teddies may be frowned upon in Froebelian circles as harbingers of dust and germs! Or isn't that correct? Anyway he's a nice Teddy, and I'd like to have one myself!

This morning I went all round the Fourth Tank Regiment saying Goodbye. They are a Regular Regiment, and have been so friendly and easy to get on with.

AT ASOLO AGAIN!

11.5.46.

Sweetheart the nightingales are singing in droves to greet us back to Asolo again! Basil and my new Driver, John Prosser, and I came from Padua after my final Army Services. We took the canopies off the cab and the wagon because it was so hot.

At Citadella we stopped to look at the ageless brick walls – large and castellated, with a barbican. When we got here we were welcomed so warmly. It was lovely. There is an R.A.F. Group here for the weekend.

After tea we strolled round the town, and to the ruined castle on the hill top.

We've just been listening to Beethoven's 7th, and now to bed.

12.5.46.

Good morning my Darling. Matins is at 11.0 so here's an hour in the lovely garden for a letter. There's a tinkling of a piano from a nearby house, otherwise everything is quiet except for the nightingales and the chirping of the cicadas.

I'm leaving Italy with a deep sorrow in my heart about our religious divisions. Down these years I've told you about our complete separation from the Roman Church. Even in the most desperate conditions we've had nothing to share. We might be a completely different species altogether. The Waldensian Pastor from Venice spent last night here, and today he is going on to an isolated congregation in the hills to the north. The Waldensians were the first reformers to break with Rome in the 12th century. They have been actively persecuted ever since, and have kept going by fleeing up into the mountains' valleys north of Turin. Basil met the Pastor and he was tremendously impressed with him. The Pastor speaks good English. He has been in prison three times at the hands of the Roman Church. I believe that the Banco del Santo Spirito does some shady things in trying to buy up Waldensian property when it comes on the market. I wonder sometimes whether there is any difference between Fascism and the R.C. methods of utter suppression of all opposition. We've been fighting for freedom, but here is a Church that brooks no opposition. And yet through it all these Protestant Pastors keep their heads, and their charity and God always provides for their needs, when things seem desperate and impossible.

But let us look to the future. One day, who knows, we shall all be seen to be serving the same Loving Lord.

And now for US my Beloved. Our time is coming along very quickly. How thankful I feel to God for all His great gifts and goodness — for my home, my Calling, for safety in this war and all its experiences, for eyes to see the beauty of this wonderful world, and most especially for You my Darling. I only hope that I can make you half as happy as you make me. All my happiness will be in serving you.

There are only two days in Italy now! The Bishop of Derby's letter was awaiting our return. Here is his offer of Bonsall. I only seem to have heard of it as being somewhere near to Matlock. The stipend is £349 per annum. Can we manage on this Dear? There are about 1200 people in the Parish, a beautiful Church and quite a large Rectory. But he does point out that there will be only one Church to care for, and that is good, especially for a first Incumbency. Perhaps this is the place, but I'm not impatient. I just need you my Darling. We need time for us to BE, to LOVE, and to PRAY in peace.

13.5.46.

My last but one Dinner at R.A.S.C., 6th Armoured Division. This morning I took piles of baggage to the Military Forwarding Officer at Mestre. I potter around saying Farewells, and seeing the odd laddie, but I really feel that I have finished my active Soldiering now. One more whole day and two more nights in Italy, and then the trek homewards. How I love you.

You'll have some real kisses in a very few minutes. Your own completely in love. Bill.

GETTING ON WITH SIGNING OFF AND WINDING UP

We returned from our short but refreshing holiday at Fen Cottage to find letters from Bill telling us that he expected to be back in England by May 20th. It was like another leave-coming, only there was no wedding to be arranged, and no-one else needed to be summoned. He was coming to find us and we all knew when! In less than three weeks he would be here. I had better wind up my activities and sign off at the five Canteens at which I helped. These were: W.V.S. at the Church Hall, the Red Cross Club, Sunday nights at the Corn Hall, the British Restaurant and the Church Army Canteen. The British Restaurant, on Park Road, was thriving; there a two-course meal could be enjoyed, at five pence (5d) a portion. Meals were prepared in connection with evolving plans to provide school meals in the villages. When I sat by the door taking ten pences, I heard a mother restrain her eager daughter who had risen to take her plate for a second helping of pudding; 'Sit you down, Queenie, they h'unt done their befores le' alone a'ers!' I was familiar with the word 'afters'; I have myself been called a 'puddivore', but it had never occurred to me, yet, I suppose it is reasonable to assume, that 'Afters' must, of necessity, come after 'Befores'. Conversely 'Befores' precede 'Afters'. I am sure that Queenie did have a further five pennyworth of pudding . . . in due course!

The closing of the Banyards Church Army Depot might have been specially timed to fit in with Bill's home-coming. He was one of the many returning to Civvy Street, and those in East Anglia who were still in Service were mostly being catered for by the Naafi. The week before Bill came home we wound up Banyards Church Army activity. No personal round of mine remained for another Driver to take over, and this eased my parting with the faltering vans in which I had travelled so far, suffering so many mechanical indignities which we had endured together!

During the war a further eleven million acres of land had been taken over for military use, in East Anglia, to add to the tracts of land already covered by regular airfields and Army ranges. I was grateful for the friendship we enjoyed with personnel from many nations; for a better understanding of them, a sharing in their sadness and their gladness and for the fun we enjoyed together. Had I been a mechanic I might have conveyed my van more promptly to calling-points, but then, how much good will and how many good turns I would not have received! I was very aware that the friendly hospitality I enjoyed at Banyards and with the Easton Family helped me to do a job in which, as fully as possible, with my Husband far away, I felt fulfilled.

We had a party when the Firm closed down. Mrs. Buchanan, our Leader, was in the habit of giving a party because there were 'people who could come – and would enjoy it'. But this was, in its way, a party to end the line of former parties.

I do not know when vans first functioned from their Banyards Depot; how many gallons of tea were brewed, dozens of cakes consumed or thousands of cigarettes were counted out, in tens or fives, nor how much cheer and warm friendship was generated over our mobile counters. No doubt we had brought comfort to countless people in service and we had enjoyed our deployment. We had continued to serve for a year after the war ended. Although we had much for which to be thankful it was with mixed feelings that we celebrated the Depot's demise. But celebrate we did – not with cups of tea – but with a toast to our King and Country, our Allies, the C.A. and our Customers . . . Our sentiment being to 'take a cup of kindness yet for the sake of old Lang Syne' . . . not forgetting old Uncle Sam.

LAST LINES

I wrote to Bill on May 10th, and the letter came back! He had left Padua, but this letter had raced him here. My post-ultimate Letter was to tell my Husband that I really could *not think of anything but being in his arms, and everything else was in relation to him being near.*

So Bill was on his way home and no more letters would be needed. No longer must I snatch moments in each busy day to put on any paper I could procure, words that would convey my love and my need of my Beloved; and even more, wonderful moments in which to read Bill's flood of mail about . . . whatever of his doings it was safe to tell, but always of his truly amazing love for little me.

Bill was coming back to Diss Rectory, scene of our other meetings. He would find me, as at first, with my Father and the Burlinghams. We now recognised Mrs. B., our Housekeeper, who had coped with hundreds of comers in wartime, to be our truly wonderful Homekeeper.

Bill sent a telegram before leaving Villach on May 18th. It was received in Norwich on May 19th and delivered to Diss Rectory on Monday 20th, and it declared that he would meet me in Diss that DAY!!

Bill had entered fully into his life as Chaplain, seizing every opportunity in his fulfilling role. His Khaki parish, with all its comradeship, had finally dispersed and was a warm and vivid memory; he would find village or town life very strange — we would be US at last and for ever and wherever; we savoured the adventure of his coming deployment, looking forward to our dreams being fulfilled, most probably in undreamed of ways!

So he came, and his coming brought JOY . . . Hand in hand we put ourselves into the hands of God.

RELEASE

15.5.46.   Alamein Camp, Villach, Austria.

My Darling,

This is my 365th letter to you since our marriage 8 months ago.

My beat-up and faithful wagon just got me here this afternoon. The Office was closed and I won't know how long I may have to wait for a train. I shall find out at 11.0 a.m. tomorrow, but I think I must go the next day. It was lovely to walk through the woods this evening. Austria is enchanting now.

I AM GOING HOME FOR GOOD. MISSION ACCOM-
PLISHED AS WELL AS I HAVE BEEN ABLE. The 8th Army
is now disbanded. I was the last remaining Officer in the 6th
Armoured Division. My D.Y. are in Egypt and my Sappers
are scattered. Friendships and loyalties are going to be
memories, and soon we'll be laundered through Demobilisation. All our past glories, sorrows, hopes, pains and achieve-
ments will be shadows. It is now just history, but Sweetest
Darling, this is the very moment I've been DREAMING
ABOUT FOR SO LONG. Beloved, HERE I COME. Your
adoring husband, Bill.

———◆◆———

Helen got my telegram to say that I was at Aldershot. She
was washing her hair, but by the time the Liverpool St. train
reached Diss she was waiting for me on the station.

There are no more letters to look into. A story of setting
out to war as an act of faith in a darkening world was changed
by meeting the Girl of my dreams. Now we were reunited and
we set out together into the glory of the life and Ministry
that, under God, we both believed lay ahead.

GOING HOME!
Bill Cook, Major John Boyd, M.C., and Padre Gee.

Appendix 1

———◆ʕʔ◆———

WILLIAM PENN'S DEATH

ON YOUR WAY OLD FRIEND

After the crossing of the River Po I was shaving in our Caravan on April 25th, 1945, and William told me to look out of the window. There in a spot of sunlight were the Alps, far away and snow-covered. They were our first glimpse of our promised land. It was so good to see them, and it was to be some time before they appeared again.

In Summer 1985 William came over to Diss from Christchurch, near Wisbech, to share in our Ruby Wedding celebrations. Soon afterwards he was to develop a cancer, and he was to fight it with courage and dignity for a whole year. He died on November 23rd, 1986. A few days before, Helen and I went to visit him and Julie his wife, in company with David, his local Priest. We all knew that death was imminent, and two Priests were wondering how best to make peace and to prepare for death. In the event it was William who took the first step, and made it so easy for us all. Down the years his great regret had been that he had never been confirmed. So first he affirmed his undying love for his Julia and his splendid family. He made his profession of faith and encouraged Julia to do the same. In a simple act of Communion of Bread and Wine all our continuing love and assurance of immortality came flooding over us.

As at that distant view of the Alps, forty years before, we had glimpsed our promised land, so Bill and Julia, David and Helen and I glimpsed the Glory Land. A few days later he went Home, and we gathered in his village church in deep thanksgiving, to commend him to his Loving Lord.

So my wartime driver and constant friend went Home in faith. We all left with our memories, and our knowledge of his continuing fellowship, in the Communion of Saints.

Perhaps Helen's verse sums it up best:

> Through misty winter sun they carry Bill
> Into the Church — they promised him 'We will'.
> David the Priest, so helpful through his pain,
> Leads on the rose-crowned coffin and its train.
> The Padre stands by him, black scarf war-starred;
> His old friend's fight is won — the battle hard.
> 'This was my mate, whom now I see no more,
> My Driver in six mobile years of war.
> You glimpsed those Alps, and you are first to come
> To see the glories of our Heavenly Home.
> Comrade in crises, down the years my friend,
> A Dieu, in peace, to life that knows no end.
> You soldiered on, keeping topside your pain;
> We gather in your honour, who remain —
> Your lovely family, neighbour and friend,
> To fuller life, in love, their Bill commend.'
> We have saluted you, our Fare Well made;
> For you and yours, and us, we all have prayed.
> Friendship lives on, memories ever green . . .
> Nunc Dimittis/Begin the (quiet) Beguine . . .*
> We look ahead as we all journey home . . .
> Friendship and love will grow in years to come.

---

* Cole Porter's haunting music of *Begin the Beguine* made a fitting background to the words of Nunc Dimittis, as they bore him from the Church. This tune had been their favourite from their courting days.

Appendix 2

RUBY WEDDING – FORTY YEARS ON

When plans were afoot for celebrations during 1985 – forty years after the end of the War – we realised that it would also be the year of our Ruby Wedding. After ministry in Derbyshire parishes we had retired to Ipswich, and it was from there that we came back to call at Diss Rectory. Here the Rector welcomed us to plan a Eucharist in St. Mary's Church, on the anniversary of our Wedding. We sat in the room where we had met, where Bill declared his love and where we had our Wedding Reception. The tentative question was posed – 'Why don't you come home to Diss to live?'.

During the Summer Diss Parish Magazine announced:

> 'In August it really will be two score years since Canon J. A. Appleton (then Rector) married his daughter, Helen, to Bill Cook, Chaplain of the Derbyshire Yeomanry. After Bertie Harrison had chimed them out of church with his handbells, the tower bells rang out, breaking into a rare peal after years of war. Five of the wedding party were on leave – the bridegroom and best man from Carinthia.
>
> There may still be many who recall those days of few goods and great comradeship, with memories of D.Y. armoured cars, the canteen in the (old) Church Hall, and church parades filling St. Mary's with deep singing of 'The D.Y. hymn' ("O my Saviour lifted . . .") – soon to be chanted in varied and contrasting settings in N. African and European theatres of war.'

'Everyone is invited to the service of Thanksgiving for Marriage, here, on August 23rd at 11 a.m. This is primarily a celebration for Bill and Helen Cook who were married here forty years ago, BUT, in addition to their many friends and relations, there is an open invitation to all to share in the service of rejoicing. And for all married couples who attend, there will be an opportunity to reaffirm their own Marriage vows.'

During the summer we moved to Diss, and so it was as members of St. Mary's that we joined sidesmen in welcoming a churchful of neighbours, relations and friends. We remembered the garland of dahlias at the Screen; now there were many beautiful arrangements of flowers. A Mothers' Union member said 'I thought you must have a posy today and this is all there was in our garden'. She handed Helen three tiny roses. Together they tucked the stems under the wooden memorial tablet to Canon J. A. Appleton, and there the crimson roses glowed. To our surprise, on this busy market day . . . the BELLS rang out!

The Service began with the Rector's welcome; then at his invitation, couples all over the Church stood up, holding hands and, looking into each other's eyes, re-affirmed their commitment. So moving did one husband find this, that afterwards, he bought his wife a tiny Cross and chain.

In a great burst of joy 'Praise to the Lord, the Almighty, the King of creation' . . . everyone sang, as the colourful procession filed up the Church. On came the Cross and lighted candles, leading five Priests and a Deaconess (with whose Ordination we had been closely associated); our first ordinand, 19 years ago, David Coulton, the Chaplain of Radley, was at the organ.

Our three daughters, Margaret Gribble, Susan Hall and Rachel Horton, led us in prayer; the Celebrant was Malcolm (Vicar of Bostall Heath), the Epistoler Richard and the Gospeler Trevor, their respective husbands. In intercession we thanked God for giving marriage as a source of blessing to mankind, for all the blessings of marriage and family life, for partners, parents, children, relatives and friends in all generations, and for bringing us together to worship in the fellowship of His Love. We lifted in prayer all who are married, world-wide; we prayed for every parent and child, for young-sters in their growing and their friendships, for families in the distress of broken homes and for babies not yet born. Then we thanked God that, in Jesus, we are in fellowship with family members and friends now home with Him, and, rejoicing in the fellowship of Saint Mary, Saint Joseph and all the Saints, we commended ourselves and all God's people to His unfailing love.

Then out came the seven grandchildren, and all the family helped in sharing the Peace. The eldest son from each family led their grandparents in the Offertory procession. So flowed the Eucharist, the taking, blessing, breaking, giving; and we were honoured to lead over a hundred communicants, all to receive blessing at the sharing of the Bread of Life. So to the Blessing and 'Love Divine . . .' the sounds of 'Blaenwern' swelled . . . 'joy of Heaven to earth come down . . .' but this final hymn to bring us down to earth again, left us 'lost in wonder, love and praise'! And there was the smiling sideslady who had welcomed us all, presenting us with an armful of glowing red carnations 'from all at Saint Mary's'. We were sent out into the sunshine and the future 'to love and serve the Lord . . . In the name of Christ . . . Amen'.

Now came the challenge – to find our cars and extricate them from the milling crowds of market day in Diss! . . . and to re-assemble at Brome Grange, two miles away on the A140, for a family meal. The Banqueting Hall is the adapted Tithe Barn where we used to play badminton, during the war, when Helen's Uncle (Egerton Appleton) lived there.

We were a chatting throng – friends meeting after years . . . and the children being introduced and, to some, their parents too. About twelve of us had been at our wedding, in 1945, including the bell ringer, Mr. Bertie Harrison, and his wife. He had recently passed captaincy of the Tower to his daughter, who had mustered ringers for the morning peal. Mrs. B's daughters and their husbands and grandaughter, William Penn and a former D.Y. Officer, Keith Leslie and his wife were there. Our Bridesmaid, now Cara Ross with teen-age children, reminisced about the long walk up the aisle, and the difficulty they had in finding the way to Diss as there were still no signposts then.

In our midst stood Margaret's cake, crowned with clusters of large roses sculpted in white icing. An armful of red roses arrived from Stibbard.

Three times in our family, when a Priestly father was to marry a daughter, we had appealed to Helen's brother to give the bride away. On these occasions Jay also agreed to propose the toast to the happy couple. We could not do better than to have the pertinent oratory of a Professor with the calculated risk, part of the fun of these occasions, of his acquaintance with this couple's past!

On this occasion Jay reminisced about our worthy Uncle, beneath whose heavily beamed former roof we were assembled. He refrained from telling too many home truths about his sister and her soldier Love, and concluded in verse:

> A Ruby Anniversary
> Prompts this extended family
> To call those happenings to mind
> Which Father Time has left behind.
>
> Four decades of connubial bliss
> Bring bride and bridegroom back to Diss,
> In old surroundings to revive
> Events of nineteen-forty-five.
>
> The pattering of tiny feet
> Which made their happiness complete
> Have been succeeded down the years
> By even tinier patterers.
>
> Now Gribbles, Hortons, Cooks and Halls,
> Gathered today within these walls,
> Collectively proclaim abroad
> The gracious favours of the Lord.
>
> And many a joy we wish them yet
> Back in the place where first they met,
> So raise a glass and toast with me
> Their Ruby Anniversary.

On their way home, some of our guests called to see our new home. When we had waved goodbye to them all we sank into our easy chairs, sipping refreshing tea (from Crown Derby posy cups — gifts from Young Wives and the Playgroup when we retired). We were surrounded by cards and bowls and pots of flowers, tokens of love, prayers and good wishes from an amazing number of friends, through whom we had experienced so many blessings. So, as we thought over the day and the Eucharist, and reminisced about our Wedding, and how we met . . . it came home to US that we had come home.

HELEN'S CONFESSIONS

To the men in my life with love from their wife.

> *I married a Padre,*
> *I married a Priest,*
> *A Rector, a Vicar,*
> *A man called Bill,*
> *A Priest in Charge*
> *And last not least*
> *A canon of Derby;*
> *I love them still*
> *And always will,*
> *Especially my man called Bill.*

———◆———

POSTSCRIPT

The publication of this book coincides with Bill's Golden Jubilee in the Priesthood. Most of this Ministry we have been privileged to share, in growing love; and in a series of Parishes we have proved that life can have an eternal quality; that the hoped-for Kingdom is not only sometime in the future, but also in the here and now. We have been part of the process whereby many, many lives have been changed from being creatures of time to sons and daughters of eternity. We know that one day in His own good time our loving, living Lord will call us home. And then the glimpses of Heaven, the Intimations of Immortality which we have known, early or late, and through all our careers, and in our lives from childhood to old age, will add up to an Eternal Joy.

With St. John we say 'Beloved now are we the Sons of God, and it does not yet appear what we shall be'.

Perhaps a paraphrase might be one of our own personal and favourite affirmations that 'The best is yet to be'.

———◆———

A Selection of Christian Books
from Hodder & Stoughton

YOU ARE MY GOD

David Watson

Converted at Cambridge under John Collins, 'followed up' by David Sheppard, David Watson discovered in his first two curacies a deepening commitment to evangelism and a new experience of the Holy Spirit. Then he found himself in York, with an almost empty church. Prayer and fasting led to conversions and growth, transforming the church into a pioneer renowned worldwide.

The story of David's spiritual pilgrimage, the growth of his marriage, and the transformation of the church makes enthralling reading. But this testimony is never triumphalistic – 'The Christian gospel is not about superstars. It is rather about God's extraordinary grace in spite of very ordinary human faults and failing . . . I have tried to write honestly, in my life, my marriage and the church, about the pains and joys we have experienced. No human frailty need be a hindrance to God's infinite grace.'

I BELIEVE IN THE CHURCH

David Watson

David Watson was known, loved and respected worldwide as a gifted teacher and Christian communicator. His dynamic ministry lives on through his writing and *I Believe in the Church* has become a classic. It draws on the years of leadership and learning at St Michael-le-Belfrey, York, to give a crucial message to the Church of the twentieth century.

'You will be staggered at the revolutionary impact of a Christianity which is radical enough to get back to the New Testament, and courageous enough to apply it in practice.'

Michael Green

I BELIEVE IN EVANGELISM

David Watson

Internationally renowned as an evangelist, David Watson was described as one of Britain's finest preachers. The passionate convictions that motivated his ministry are revealed in this important book which explores what evangelism is and how it can be carried out by both Church and individual.

'It is rooted in experience. It is grounded in a remarkable grasp of the New Testament. It is alive with the freshness and power of the Holy Spirit.'

Michael Green

'Fresh, lively and enjoyable ... solid thinking and practical application.'

Baptist Times

Spire Paperbacks

GOD'S FOOL

Julien Green

The Life and Times of Francis of Assisi

God's Fool is the capstone of the writing career of novelist and diarist Julien Green. An emotionally gripping portrait of St Francis of Assisi, it traces Francis' pampered childhood, his lusty young adulthood, his worldly fancies and desires, his brief but pivotal imprisonment, the jolting stages of his conversion, his growth to maturity as a servant of God, and the establishment of the religious order that took his name.

God's Fool is a warm, vigorous, unsentimental account of the most popular and compelling of the saints. It is crafted with literary elegance and is rich in historical detail.

'Altogether a masterpiece.'

Malcolm Muggeridge

ALL THE DAYS OF MY LIFE

Penelope Flint

Written during her third pregnancy, *All the Days of my Life* is a profound autobiography of originality and charm in which Penelope Flint's own growing spiritual awareness mirrors the growth of the child within. Interspersed with her own startling poetry, this book is a vivid account of the inner and outer life of a woman searching for an authentic spiritual reality. The author's knowledge of philosophical and Christian writings, and her understanding of current affairs, enhance this outstanding book.

'I admire the skill and innate wisdom with which she interweaves the real with the more-than-real. She has managed to give another dimension to the problems that beset our age. God knows we need a perspective such as hers.'

Mary Craig

A JOURNEY OF PRAYER

Rosemary Budd

The world of the person who prays is marked by an 'interconnectedness' that contrasts with much of the meaninglessness of today's world, writes Rosemary Budd. Emphasising that the purpose of prayer is to be increasingly open to the love of God, she explores helps in prayer – the prayer diary, a spiritual counsellor, groups for silence – before considering escapism, growth through tensions, and the felt absence of God.

Affirming the unity of the seen and the unseen, *Journey of Prayer* ends with an attempt to integrate prayer and life as a whole – a process which Rosemary Budd describes as 'an education in gladness.' 'Prayer is a constant surprise', she writes, 'and I am a constant amateur.'

A SEVERE MERCY

Sheldon Vanauken

When Sheldon Vanauken and Jean Davis fell in love, they resolved that possessions should not come between them, nor jealousies, nor secrets. Their friends found their closeness uncanny, feeling Van and Davy had discovered some special quality of existence. 'So perhaps we had: the quality of joy'.

Studying English Literature at Oxford, they met C S Lewis and with his guidance made the momentous step into faith. Their life together was utterly changed. When tragedy struck, Lewis was a guide and comforter of piercing insight and compassion.

'Beautiful and moving.'

A L Rowse

'Haunting . . . a book to return to again and again.'

Catholic Herald